THE BOOK OF
DUOS

The stories behind history's
great partnerships

THE BOOK OF
DUOS

The stories behind history's great partnerships

IAN HARRISON

CASSELL ILLUSTRATED

Project Editors Anna Cheifetz, Victoria Alers-Hankey
Editor Barbara Dixon
Art Editor Thomas Keenes
Jacket Design Thomas Keenes
Picture Research Vickie Walters, Jennifer Veall, with
additional research by Thomas Keanes

First published in Great Britain in 2005
by Cassell Illustrated,
a division of Octopus Publishing Group Limited,
2–4 Heron Quays,
London E14 4JP

A CIP catalogue record for this book is available from the
British Library.

ISBN 1 84403 340 6
EAN 9781844033409
Printed in China

CONTENTS

FOREWORD BY DOLCE & GABBANA

When we started on our career path 20 years ago, we never imagined we would have arrived where we are today. Thinking back over the past, undoubtedly the secret to our success – what has allowed us to realize our dreams – is the fact that we work together as a team. Sometimes we ask ourselves if we would have achieved the same results if we had each worked alone. It would certainly be interesting to know.

But one thing is sure: for us, working as a pair is far better than working separately. We talk, we compare notes and often we argue, but above all we stimulate each other. This is why history is full of great duos characterized by their creativity, originality and uniqueness.

The Book of Duos is proof of this, because it examines different stories linked by a common thread: working and interacting as a couple. We are merely one example of the creativity and productivity of which a duo is capable, and fashion is just one of the many fields in which duos have played a role. There are also significant and unforgettable duos in, for example, art, cinema and entertainment, industry, design and sports.

Not only do opposites attract, but quite often the resulting duo is greater than the sum of its parts, and the power that stems from this union is irrepressible. Being a pair is the starting point for communicating, exchanging information, laughing, being angry and loving. One pair of eyes perceives a certain reality, whereas two pairs can convey depth and true perception of the environment. The same holds true with work. Visions are united, mutually supporting each other, and the union creates a common dream that fuels itself. Together, the virtuous cycle of creation and life is set in motion, and the results are often as unexpected as they are surprising.

We create and we love in order to understand that we are never, ever alone. There are two of us. There are two of us whenever we connect with the reality around us and – amidst thousands of stimuli – manage to find that special energy that not only completes and fulfils us as people, but also our fuses our passions and ideals.

Every one of our creations is the result of mental symbiosis. Our minds are naturally different and they travel on separate yet complementary tracks. This is why the ideas of just one of us would not be enough to give our brand the right kind of energy. We must always combine both our insights, even though they may be opposite and seemingly discordant.

We cannot cite a particular anecdote about our work as a duo, nor can we come up with a motto. Nevertheless, we love to recall our endless discussions, how we start with an idea, develop it into a sketch and tuck it away somewhere, only to take it out again, talk about it and spawn a brand-new and unique idea: the Dolce & Gabbana idea.

We often wonder how other duos work together as partners, but so far we have not figured out the answer. Perhaps this is because we are utterly attached to our method, which is the only one we know. And, so far, it has worked.

We are convinced that the same holds true for all other duos, who in their diversity are able to discover the common trait that binds them and makes them special.

Domenico Dolce & Stefano Gabbana, Milan March 2005

RIGHT *Stefano Gabbana and Domenico Dolce*

BIBLICAL & MYTHICAL

ADAM & EVE

The Bible's first duo

Adam

According to Genesis, the first book of the Holy Bible: 'The Lord God formed man of the dust of the ground, and breathed into his nostrils the breath of life; and man became a living soul.' God then created the Garden of Eden and placed the man there, telling him that he may freely eat of all the trees in the garden except for the fruit of the tree of the knowledge of good and evil. Having thus warned His creation, God decides: 'It is not good that the man should be alone; I will make him an help meet for him.' Genesis does not say that God named the man He had created, but from this point on the King James Version refers to him as Adam, the Hebrew word for 'man'.

Eve

God then calls upon Adam to name all the animals, but Adam does not find 'an help meet' among them, so God puts him into a deep sleep, removes one of his ribs and creates the first woman from the rib. Adam is pleased with his companion and says: 'This is now bone of my bones, and flesh of my flesh: she shall be called Woman because she was taken out of Man.' Later, Adam names his wife Eve, 'the mother of all living'.

The Fall

It should have been the perfect wedding, but Adam and Eve's time in the Garden of Eden was to be limited because the serpent beguiled Eve into eating the forbidden fruit of the tree of the knowledge of good and evil. Eve then offered the fruit to Adam, who also ate, and as a result both were cast out of paradise, an event known as the Fall of Man. Adam blamed Eve for tempting him, but it is clear that Adam was equally at fault: both knew the fruit was forbidden, both were tempted and both were found wanting.

ADAM & EVE FAQS

Do Adam and Eve appear in the holy books of any other religions?
According to the Mohammedans, God sent four angels in turn to fetch seven handfuls of differently coloured earth from which to fashion Adam, which accounts for the skin colours of the various races of mankind. According to Muslim writers, Adam and Eve were separated for 100 years after the Fall, but were reunited at Arafat; they also record that Adam died at the age of 930.

What is Adam's Ale?
Water. The name derives from the fact that water was the only thing that Adam had to drink in the Garden of Eden. In Scotland it is sometimes called Adam's Wine.

Why is the Adam's apple so-called?
The front part of the larynx, which forms the 'Adam's apple' in a person's throat, is so-called from the tradition that part of the apple eaten by Adam and Eve stuck in Adam's throat.

HAVE YOU HEARD?

The anonymous couplet *On the Antiquity of Microbes* is often claimed to be the world's shortest poem:

Adam
Had 'em.

In his poem *The Glory of the Garden*, Rudyard Kipling wrote:

Oh, Adam was a gardener, and God who made him sees
That half a proper gardener's work is done upon his knees.

ABOVE *Detail of Tommaso Masaccio's fresco* Adam and Eve Banished from Paradise *(c. 1427) in the Brancacci Chapel, Santa Maria del Carmine, Florence, Italy* **OPPOSITE** *Manuscript Illumination of Adam and Eve, from* The Activities of Noble Women and Men *(15th century)*

CAIN & ABEL

Ur-sibling rivals

The Biblical story of Cain and Abel illustrates the increasing power of sin over mankind following Adam and Eve's expulsion from the Garden of Eden. The Book of Genesis tells how Eve gave birth to two sons, first Cain and then Abel, and how both became farmers, Cain 'a tiller of the ground' and Abel 'a keeper of sheep'. When the time comes for the brothers to give offerings to God, each makes an appropriate offering: 'Cain brought of the fruit of the ground... And Abel, he also brought of the firstlings of his flock and of the fat thereof.'

God is happy with Abel's offering, but not with that of Cain, who 'was very wroth [angry] and his countenance fell'. God warns Cain: 'If thou doest not well, sin lieth at the door', but instead of heeding God's warning and doing better, Cain becomes murderously jealous of his brother: 'And it came to pass, when they were in the field, that Cain rose up against Abel his brother, and slew him.'

Cain's punishment is that the ground will no longer yield to him when he tills and that he is banished from the presence of the Lord for evermore as 'a fugitive and a vagabond'. His place of banishment has given modern culture both a synonym for going to bed and the title of a John Steinbeck novel that was made into a film starring James Dean: 'And Cain went out from the presence of the Lord, and dwelt in the land of Nod, on the east of Eden.'

CAIN & ABEL FAQS

Weren't Adam and Eve a bit upset by all this?
Yes, but God gave them another son: 'Adam knew his wife again; and she bare a son, and called his name Seth: For God, said she, hath appointed me another seed instead of Abel.'

Who were the Cainites?
A 2nd-century heretical sect who claimed that Cain suffered a miscarriage of justice. The Cainites renounced the New Testament and instead followed their *Gospel of Judas*, which they said justified the actions of Judas and the subsequent Crucifixion of Christ. The Cainites claimed that heaven and earth were created by an evil force and that the descendants of Cain, themselves among them, had been deprived of their rightful inheritance.

And have they been deprived of their inheritance?
Richard Le Gallienne doesn't seem to think so. If his poem *The Cry of the Little Peoples* is anything to go by, he thinks that the descendants of Cain have inherited the earth:

The cry of the Little People goes up to God in vain
For the world is given over to the cruel sons of Cain.

ABOVE *Undated Italian Renaissance painting depicting Eve with Cain and Abel*
RIGHT *Cain killing his brother Abel, from* Cottage Pictures From The Old Testament *(1857)*

HAVE YOU HEARD?
In his song 'Dirt in the Ground', Tom Waits *(see p206)* provides a modern synopsis of the Cain and Abel story:

Now Cain slew Abel
He killed him with a stone
The sky cracked open
And the thunder groaned.

SODOM & GOMORRAH

Biblical cities destroyed by God

The Bible does not give details of the iniquity practised in the cities of Sodom and Gomorrah, but we can infer from the modern word sodomite the kind of behaviour that was considered 'grievous' in the eyes of the Lord. God decides that He will destroy the cities, but first tells the patriarch Abraham, who asks: 'Wilt Thou destroy the righteous with the wicked?' and persuades God to save the cities if there are even 10 righteous people living there.

God sends two angels to Sodom, but the only righteous people they find are Abraham's nephew Lot and Lot's wife and two daughters. The men of Sodom then surround Lot's house and demand that he sends the angels out to them, threatening to break down his door, but the angels afflict the attackers with blindness and warn Lot and his family to leave the city. The men of Sodom try to prevent them from leaving, but again the angels intercede and take Lot and his family out of the city, saying: 'Escape for thy life; look not behind thee, neither stay thou in the plain; escape to the mountain, lest thou be consumed.'

The next day God destroys the iniquitous cities: 'Then the Lord rained upon Sodom and upon Gomorrah brimstone and fire from the Lord out of heaven; And He overthrew those cities, and all the plain, and all the inhabitants of the cities, and that which grew upon the ground.'

Unfortunately, Lot's wife failed to follow the angels' instructions. She looked back at all the destruction behind her and was turned into a pillar of salt.

ABOVE *The destruction of Sodom and Gomorrah, with Lot and his family fleeing (1754)*
RIGHT Burning of Sodom, *by Jules A. Laurens*

HAVE YOU HEARD?

Referring to the apples of Sodom, which were said to bear fruit that appeared healthy but was full of ashes, the playwright John Webster wrote in *The White Devil*:

You see, my lords, what goodly fruit she seems;
Yet like those apples travellers report
To sow where Sodom and Gomorrah stood,
I will but touch her, and straight you will see
She'll fall to soot and ashes.

SODOM & GOMORRAH FAQS

Sounds like it could have been an earthquake?
Yes, modern secular interpretations of this story hold that the catastrophe was a violent earthquake that released gases, ash and lava, smothering the plain where Sodom and Gomorrah stood. Abraham's view of the destruction is certainly consistent with such an earthquake: 'And he looked toward Sodom and Gomorrah, and toward all the land of the plain, and beheld, and, lo, the smoke of the country went up as the smoke of a furnace.'

So what's there now?
It is thought that the plain may later have been flooded by the Dead Sea. There are many salt deposits on the lower slopes of the hills around the Dead Sea, including one 50-foot salt column that has been eroded into the shape of a woman and is known as Lot's wife.

Didn't The Pogues have an album about Sodom?
It was called *Rum, Sodomy And The Lash*, but it wasn't actually about sodomy. The title was taken from a comment by Sir Winston Churchill, who said: 'Don't talk to me about naval tradition. It's nothing but rum, sodomy and the lash.'

And what happened to the righteous Lot after all this was over?
According to the Book of Genesis, he got both his daughters pregnant after they had plied him with wine, and became patriarch of the Moabites through Moab, his son by his elder daughter, and of the Ammonites through Benammi, his son by his younger daughter.

SAMSON DELILAH

The strongman and his treacherous lover

Samson

The Old Testament's Book of Judges tells of the exploits of various Israelite leaders, known as 'judges', in the ongoing fight for the newly settled Promised Land. The most famous of the judges was Samson, who was not only an Israelite, but also a member of a group known as the Nazirites, who took special vows to God, including a vow not to cut their hair. Samson's legendary strength derives from this vow, and his fatal weakness lay in his attraction to women from the enemy race of Philistines.

Samson's first marriage was to a Philistine woman who betrayed him to the men of Timnath by enticing him into revealing the answer to a riddle he had set the men. Never one for half measures, Samson killed 30 of the men and the matter then escalated – Samson burnt the Philistines' crops and the Philistines burnt Samson's wife and father-in-law; Samson ended the dispute by killing 1,000 men with the jawbone of an ass.

Samson and Delilah

Despite the outcome of his first marriage, Samson fell in love with another Philistine woman, Delilah, and the Philistine leaders offered to pay Delilah if she could entice Samson into revealing the secret of his strength. Three times she asked him, three times he gave her a false reason, and three times he awoke in the night to find that Delilah had set the Philistines upon him thinking his strength had gone. Delilah complained that he cannot truly love her if he will not reveal his secret, and Samson, not heeding the fact that she had tried three times to betray him, told her that if his hair was shorn: 'Then my strength shall go from me, and I shall become weak, and be like any other man.'

After the Philistines had shaved Samson's head, they overcame him, put out his eyes and threw him in prison in Gaza. Then, during their pagan festivities, they took Samson into their amphitheatre to taunt him for their amusement, but Samson prayed to God to return his strength and pulled down the pillars supporting the roof, killing himself and some 3,000 Philistines.

RIGHT Samson and Delilah, *by Matthias Stom (1630s)* **INSET FAR RIGHT** Samson and Delilah and the Destruction of the Temple *(19th century)*

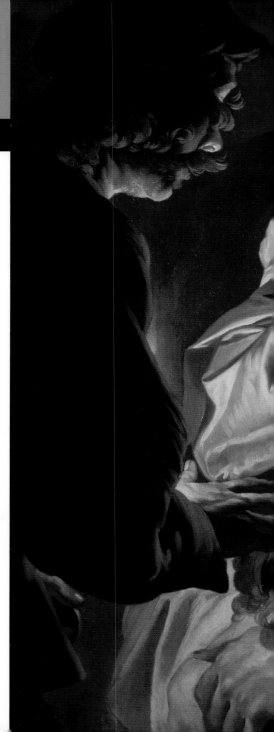

SAMSON & DELILAH FAQS

What was the riddle that Samson set the men of Timnath?

'Out of the eater came forth meat, and out of the strong came forth sweetness.' None of the men could guess the riddle until Samson's wife told them that Samson had recently eaten honey that he had found in the carcase of a lion. An illustration of this story is used as the trademark on tins of Lyle's Golden Syrup, showing the dead lion and the second half of the riddle. *(See Tate & Lyle, p222.)*

Isn't it a bit extreme to kill 30 men because your wife gives away a riddle?

There was more to it than that – or at least, Samson thought so. Thinking that they had seduced his wife into giving away the secret, he said: 'If ye had not plowed with my heifer, ye had not found out my riddle.'

I thought plowing with another man's heifer was against the seventh commandment?

It is, but the Philistines were bad people. That's why God gave Samson the strength to fight them.

DAVID
GOLIATH

Shepherd boy and giant

Goliath

A champion warrior of the Philistines, Goliath would be a giant even by modern standards, standing between eight and nine feet tall – the Bible's First Book of Samuel records that 'his height was six cubits and a span'. Samuel wrote that Goliath 'had an helmet of brass upon his head, and he was armed with a coat of mail; and the weight of the coat was five thousand shekels of brass. And he had greaves of brass upon his legs, and a target of brass between his shoulders. And the staff of his spear was like a weaver's beam; and his spear's head weighed six hundred shekels of iron.'

The Philistines and the Israelites were ready to do battle, facing each other from the high ground at each side of a valley, when the awesome figure of Goliath stepped forward from the Philistine ranks and, for 40 days in a row, challenged the Israelites to 'choose you a man for you and let him come down to me' to decide the battle by single combat.

David

At this time, David (later King of all Israel) was a young shepherd boy sent by his father to take food to his three older brothers, all of whom were serving in King Saul's army. While David was delivering the food he heard Goliath's challenge and, to everyone's disbelief, volunteered to fight him.

The slaying of Goliath

Explaining to Saul that his faith in God would protect him, David refused to wear armour or carry a sword, but went to face Goliath armed only with his staff, his sling and five stones that he picked out of a stream. After exchanging insults, David and Goliath approached each other and David felled Goliath with the first shot from his sling: '[he] smote the Philistine in his forehead, that the stone sunk into his forehead; and he fell upon his face to the earth.' While Goliath lay there, David ran forward and used Goliath's own sword to cut off the giant's head, at which the Philistine army turned and fled, giving victory to the Israelites.

DAVID & GOLIATH FAQS

Presumably King Saul was pretty pleased with David?
At first he was. David married Saul's daughter and befriended his son, but David's growing popularity made Saul jealous, so David had to flee for his life to the Judean hills.

So why didn't he just use his sling on Saul?
He twice had the opportunity to kill Saul, but didn't do so because Saul was his king. Saul eventually killed himself after being defeated by the Philistines in David's absence.

David must have enjoyed a bit of Schadenfreude at that news?
No, he was devastated, and wrote a lament that gave us one of our great Biblical quotations: 'The beauty of Israel is slain upon thy high places: how are the mighty fallen.'

So David was a bit of a poet?
Yes, he also wrote several of the Psalms.

And what else did he do?
After Saul's death, he was made King of Judah and later King of all Israel, extending the Israelites' territory and making Jerusalem the capital. He was succeeded by his son Solomon.

OPPOSITE LEFT David and Goliath, *from a* Book of Hours, *by Jean Colombe (c.1470)* **OPPOSITE RIGHT** David and Goliath, *attributed to Andrea Mantegna*

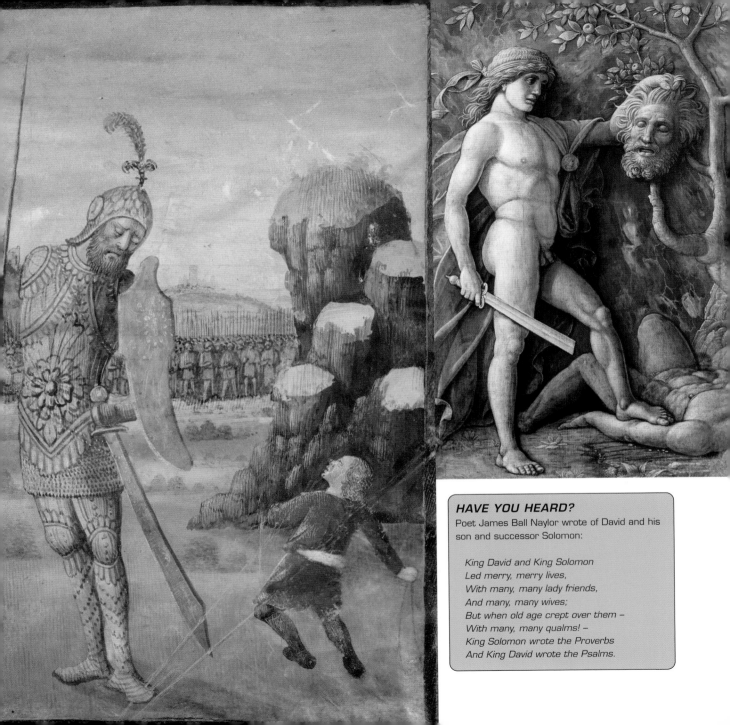

HAVE YOU HEARD?

Poet James Ball Naylor wrote of David and his son and successor Solomon:

King David and King Solomon
Led merry, merry lives,
With many, many lady friends,
And many, many wives;
But when old age crept over them –
With many, many qualms! –
King Solomon wrote the Proverbs
And King David wrote the Psalms.

Ancient Egyptian deities

Osiris

The origins of the ancient Egyptian cult of Osiris are obscure, but it is thought that he was the king of a district centred on Busiris, in the Nile delta, and was later elevated to the status of a local god. His influence increased until he was the chief god of several districts, during which time he assimilated the features of some of the gods he superseded. These included Sokar, through whom Osiris assumed his best-known role as ruler of the kingdom of the dead, and Andjeti, from whom he appropriated his characteristic insignia of the shepherd's crook and the flail.

Isis

The origins of Osiris' wife, the goddess Isis, are even less clear, but it seems that she, too, began as a local goddess in the Nile delta and gradually assumed greater influence. Like many mythological systems, that of the Egyptians has many variations and, according to the hierarchy of gods evolved by the priests of Heliopolis, Isis and Osiris were both born of Geb, the earth-god, and Nut, the sky-goddess, making them brother and sister, although they are better known as husband and wife.

Isis and Osiris

According to Plutarch, Osiris was murdered and his body cast adrift at sea by his jealous brother Seth, the god of darkness. Isis, sister/wife of Osiris, scoured the earth for his body and returned it to Egypt, keeping watch over it while she awaited the birth of their child, the god Horus. However, Seth discovered the body of Osiris, dismembered it and scattered the parts throughout Egypt, after which Isis sought and found all the pieces and buried them where she found them. A more familiar version tells that she reassembled all the parts of Osiris' body, ordered his son Anubis to embalm it and then brought it back to life, a variation that reinforces the connection between the cult of Osiris and the Egyptian practice of mummification. Both variations end with Osiris being avenged by his son Horus, who succeeds to his father's earthly throne and becomes an archetype of filial devotion.

ISIS & OSIRIS FAQS

Weren't there lots of Osirises?
Egyptian kings were thought of as living incarnations of Horus, the son of Osiris. When a king died and his son became the embodiment of Horus, it was a natural progression to think that the king became Osiris. Gradually these ritual privileges were extended to ordinary people until every Egyptian was considered an Osiris after death.

Where was the kingdom of the dead that Osiris ruled over?
Below the western horizon. For this reason Osiris is sometimes associated with the setting sun, although he was not originally part of the Egyptian sun-cult. The kingdom of the dead was known as the Fields of Reeds (pre-empting the Greek Elysian Fields), represented as a group of islands that could be reached only by a supernatural boat.

Isn't Isis often associated with a cow?
Yes – just as Osiris assimilated the features of minor local gods that he superseded, Isis assimilated the influence of the cow-goddess Hathor. The cow became the sacred animal of Isis, the horns of the cow in pictograms also representing the crescent moon with which she was associated.

Why is Oxford University's boat race crew called Isis?
It isn't – the reserve crew is called Isis, and that has nothing to do with the Egyptian deity. It is taken from the alternative name of the stretch of the River Thames that flows through Oxford, which is thought to derive from *Tamesis*, the Latin name of the river.

OPPOSITE *Detail of relief at Abydos, Egypt, showing Osiris and Isis*

SCYLLA & CHARYBDIS

Sea-monster and whirlpool of Greek mythology

Scylla

According to some accounts, Scylla was originally a beautiful nymph whose troubles began when she rejected the love of the sea-god Glaucus. Glaucus went to the enchantress Circe for a potion that would win Scylla's love, but Circe fell in love with Glaucus and, in a fit of jealousy, poisoned the waters where Scylla bathed so that the next time Scylla entered the water she was transformed into a hideous sea-monster.

This part of the story does not appear in Homer's *Odyssey*, in which Circe warns Odysseus what to expect when he encounters Scylla: 'Her voice is no more than a new-born puppy's but she herself is an evil monster ... she has twelve feet, all waving in the air, and six long necks with a frightful head on each, all with three rows of teeth packed close together.'

Charybdis

Charybdis was a mythical whirlpool that sucked in and disgorged the sea three times each day. In Homer's *Odyssey*, Odysseus describes the immense power of the whirlpool: 'Terrible was the way she sucked down the sea's water, and when she spewed it up, the whole sea would boil in turbulence, like a cauldron on a big fire ... but when she sucked down the sea's salt water ... the ground showed dark with sand at the ocean bottom.'

Scylla and Charybdis

According to Greek mythology, Scylla and Charybdis dwelt on opposite sides of a narrow sea passage traditionally thought to be the Straits of Messina, separating Sicily from Italy. As such they posed twin dangers because the strait was so narrow that it was impossible to avoid both, as a result of which they have traditionally been used as a metaphor for equal dangers, in such phrases as 'avoiding Scylla, he fell into Charybdis', and 'caught between Scylla and Charybdis'. Despite Circe's warning, Odysseus decided to sail closer to Scylla and risk losing six members of his crew to her six heads, rather than sail closer to Charybdis and risk losing his ship and all of his crew in the whirlpool.

RIGHT *The perilous trip of the ship of Ulysses between Scylla and Charybdis*

SCYLLA & CHARYBDIS FAQS

Wasn't Scylla the daughter of King Nisus?

That's a different Scylla. The one you're thinking of betrayed her father to King Minos, with whom she was in love and who was waging war against Nisus, but Minos so despised her treachery to her father that he spurned her love. Various accounts say that Minos dragged her behind his ship until she drowned; that he sailed away and she drowned trying to swim after him; and that she threw herself from a rock into the sea and drowned. Different accounts also say that she was turned into a lark and Nisus into a hawk, or she into a sea bird and he into a sea eagle – in either case she was destined to be pursued by him forever for her treachery.

Didn't Odysseus escape from Charybdis?

Yes. The first time he sailed through the strait, Odysseus avoided Charybdis by instead facing Scylla, who took six of his men with her six heads. But later, after Zeus had wrecked his ship and killed his men, Odysseus drifted back into the strait on a raft he had built. The raft was sucked into the whirlpool, but Odysseus saved himself by clinging to an overhanging fig tree and waiting for Charybdis to disgorge the remains of his raft, on which he sailed away.

HERO & LEANDER

Ill-fated lovers who drowned in the Hellespont

Hero and Leander were mythical lovers who lived on opposite sides of the Hellespont, the narrow strait of water, now known as the Dardanelles, which separates Europe from Asia. Hero was a priestess of Aphrodite, the goddess of love (known to the Romans as Venus), and lived in a high tower at Sestos on the northwestern shore of the strait. One summer she fell in love with Leander, who lived at Abydos on the southeastern shore, and every night Leander would swim across the Hellespont to lie with her, guided by a lamp that she would place in the window of the tower.

For the whole summer they made love in this way, with Leander returning to Abydos at dawn. When winter came Leander continued

to brave the Hellespont even as the weather worsened, until one night, during a particularly violent storm, Hero's lamp blew out. With no light to guide him Leander lost his bearings and drowned, and the following morning his body was washed up on the shore beneath Hero's tower. Distraught, Hero threw herself from the tower and fell to her death beside Leander. Some versions of the myth have Leander's body floating beneath the tower and Hero throwing herself into the Hellespont to drown in the same waters as her lover.

ABOVE Hero Holding the Beacon for Leander, *by Evelyn De Morgan (c.1885)* **RIGHT** *Tin-glazed earthenware depicting Hero and Leander, by Francesco Xanto Avelli (16th century)*

HERO & LEANDER FAQS

Didn't Lord Byron swim the Hellespont?
Yes, in May 1810 he decided to emulate
Leander's feat. With Lt Ekenhead, he swam
from Sestos to Abydos in just over an hour.

How far is it?
About four miles. Byron caught a chill and
afterwards likened himself to the ill-fated
Leander:

> 'Twere hard to say who fared the best:
> Sad mortals! thus the Gods still plague you!
> He lost his labour, I my jest;
> For he was drowned and I've the ague.

***Plague you and ague is a pretty
dreadful rhyme.***
Byron had worse rhymes. In *Don Juan*, he
wrote of the eponymous hero:

> A better swimmer you could scarce
> see ever,
> He could, perhaps, have pass'd the
> Hellespont,
> As once (a feat on which ourselves
> we prided)
> Leander, Mr Ekenhead and I did.

HAVE YOU HEARD?

A.E. Housman is among the many poets who
have been inspired by the story of Hero and
Leander:

> By Sestos town, in Hero's tower,
> On Hero's heart Leander lies;
> The signal torch has burned its hour
> And sputters as it dies.
> Beneath him in the nighted firth,
> Between two continents complain
> The seas he swam from earth to earth
> And he must swim again.

DAEDALUS & ICARUS

Father and son who flew with wings of wax

Daedalus

Daedalus was an inventor and craftsman of such repute that his name survives in the English words 'daedal' and 'daedalian', meaning skilful, inventive or intricate. He was exiled from Athens after murdering his nephew and apprentice, Perdix, in a fit of jealousy at Perdix's superior skill, and went instead to the court of King Minos of Crete. There he built a hollow cow for Minos' wife, Pasiphae, so that she could crouch inside it and couple with a white bull sent by Poseidon, as a result of which she gave birth to the minotaur, a man with the head of a bull. Minos then commissioned Daedalus to build the Cretan labyrinth as a prison for the minotaur.

Meanwhile, Daedalus had been doing some coupling of his own with one of the palace slave girls, who gave birth to his son Icarus. But Icarus was not able to enjoy court life for long – when the Athenian hero Theseus came to kill the minotaur, Minos's daughter Ariadne fell in love with Theseus; Daedalus helped the lovers by providing a ball of thread to guide Theseus out of the labyrinth and Minos, outraged by this treachery, imprisoned both father and son in the labyrinth.

Daedalus and Icarus

Imprisoning a man as inventive as Daedalus was never going to work for long, and soon he had made wings for himself and Icarus out of wax and feathers. When the day came for their escape Daedalus gave Icarus strict and clear instructions: do not fly too low, or the spray from the sea will weigh down the feathers; and do not fly too high, or the heat of the sun will melt the wax. Together they took

DAEDALUS & ICARUS FAQS

Isn't Daedalus a character in a James Joyce book?
No, that's Stephen Dedalus, who appears in *A Portrait of the Artist as a Young Man* and *Ulysses*. But the name is a conscious evocation of Daedalus as a symbol for creativity.

How did Daedalus kill Perdix?
By throwing him from the Acropolis – a bit ironic considering his own son was later killed by a fall. It is said that the goddess Athena loved Perdix because of his skills, so she turned him into a partridge (the Latin name of the grey partridge is *Perdix perdix*). The memory of the fall from the Acropolis is said to be the reason that partridges fly low and nest on the ground.

Didn't Daedalus build a temple to Apollo at Cumae?
Yes, according to Virgil, who also wrote that Daedalus attempted to commemorate Icarus in the temple: 'And you, too, Icarus, would have had a great part in this splendid work, but for Daedalus' grief. Twice he tried to shape your fall in gold, and twice his hands, a father's hands, dropped helpless.'

What about the threaded shell?
Oh yes – Minos tried to track down Daedalus by offering a reward to anyone who could pass a thread through a spiral shell, knowing that only Daedalus would be capable of doing so. Daedalus duly succeeded by tying the thread to an ant and getting the ant to walk through the spirals of the shell. When his protector, King Cocalus, showed the shell to Minos, Minos knew that Cocalus must be harbouring Daedalus and demanded he surrender him. Before Cocalus could do so, his daughters scalded Minos to death in his bath in order to save Daedalus.

ABOVE Theseus and the Minotaur, *mosaic in the House of the Labyrinth at Pompeii* OPPOSITE The Fall of Icarus, *by Carlo Saraceni (c.1580–1620)*

off and flew out over the Aegean Sea, but Icarus, overcome with youthful enthusiasm at being able to fly, soared upwards too close to the sun. The wax melted, the wings disintegrated, and Icarus fell into what is now known as the Icarian Sea. The distraught Daedalus recovered the body of Icarus from the water and buried it on the island known ever since as Icaria.

HAVE YOU HEARD?

The Roman poet Ovid put the myth of Daedalus and Icarus in the context of ordinary working people when he wrote:

Perhaps some fisherman wielding his quivering rod, or a shepherd leaning on his crook, or a ploughman resting on his plough handle, caught sight of them and stood stupefied, thinking these must be gods who could fly through the air.

CASTOR & POLLUX

Twin sons of Zeus, or Jupiter

Leda and the Swan

The story of Castor and Pollux involves not one duo but five, the first of which is Leda and the Swan. According to Greek mythology, Zeus, the king of the gods (known in Roman mythology as Jupiter), assumed the form of a swan and seduced the beautiful Leda, as a result of which she produced two eggs. One of the eggs contained Castor and Clytemnestra, while the other contained Polydeuces (better known by his Latin name Pollux) and Helen, later famous as Helen of Troy. According to some versions of the myth Castor and Pollux were only half-brothers, Castor and Clytemnestra being the children of Leda's mortal husband, Tyndareos, and Pollux and Helen the children of Zeus. However, the brothers are also known as the Dioscuri, from the Greek *Dios kouros*, meaning 'sons of Zeus'.

Castor and Pollux

The Dioscuri were accomplished athletes, Castor renowned for his horsemanship and Pollux for his boxing, and they had many adventures together, including sailing with Jason and the Argonauts in pursuit of the Golden Fleece. They had power over the wind and waves, and, as gods, they later became patrons of athletes, sailors and the *equites*, a Roman order of knights. Their earthly partnership ended when they quarrelled with their cousins, Idas and Lynceus – Idas mortally wounded Castor and, in vengeance, Pollux and Zeus killed Idas and Lynceus.

Rather than see Castor die, Pollux begged to share his own gift of immortality (a benefit of being the son of Zeus) with his half-brother. Zeus granted his wish and the brothers spent their existence alternating between Mount Olympus, the home of the gods, and Hades, the land of the dead. Together they were worshipped as gods and Zeus placed them together among the stars in the form of the constellation Gemini, The Twins.

CASTOR & POLLUX FAQS

Weren't Castor and Pollux characters in a play?
The Dioscuri appear as *dei ex machina* (gods lowered onto the stage to resolve problems arising in the course of a play) in two plays by Euripides: the tragedies *Electra* and *Helen*. Castor and Pollux Troy were also the names of criminal brothers played by Nicholas Cage and Alessandro Nivola in the 1997 film *Face/Off*.

What do Castor and Pollux have to do with St Elmo's fire?
St Elmo's fire is the name given to the electrical luminescence that sometimes forms what looks like a ball of fire in the rigging of ships during a storm. As the patron gods of sailors, Castor and Pollux were closely associated with the phenomenon, which Roman sailors referred to as 'Helen' (the sister of Castor and Pollux) if there was one flame and 'Castor and Pollux' if there were two or more. One flame was said to indicate that the storm would get worse, two or more that it would abate due to the protective presence of the Dioscuri.

Isn't Gemini a sign of the Zodiac?
Yes. Gemini (from the Latin for 'twins') is an air sign, symbolized by Castor and Pollux, who were placed among the constellations by Zeus. Traditionally, people born under the sign of Gemini are said to be clever, curious, expressive and witty. However, they are also said to have a two-sided personality, be prone to sudden mood swings and to see both sides of an argument, all of which can make them restless and indecisive. Their special talent is said to be communication.

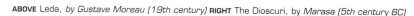

ABOVE Leda, *by Gustave Moreau (19th century)* **RIGHT** The Dioscuri, *by Marasa (5th century BC)*

HAVE YOU HEARD?

In his poem *Leda and the Swan*, W.B. Yeats describes the union from which Castor and Pollux were created:

A sudden blow: the great
wings beating still
Above the staggering girl,
her thighs caressed
By the dark webs, her nape
caught in his bill,
He holds her helpless
breast upon his breast.

HELEN & MENELAUS

Paragon of beauty and her cuckolded husband

Helen of Sparta

Famed as the most beautiful woman who ever lived, Helen was the daughter of Zeus and Leda, born of an egg produced by Leda after Zeus took the form of a swan and seduced her. When Helen was old enough to marry, the most revered leaders and heroes of all Greece presented gifts to her stepfather, Tyndareos, in the hopes of winning her hand. Aware of the risk of choosing one suitor from so many, Tyndareos made them all swear to help the chosen husband recover Helen should she be abducted. Tyndareos then chose Menelaus and abdicated in his favour, making Menelaus King of Sparta.

Helen and Paris

Helen and Menelaus were well suited and had a happy marriage, but trouble was brewing far away on Mount Ida. There, Paris, a prince of Troy, had been asked to judge which of the goddesses Hera, Athene and Aphrodite was the most beautiful. All three offered him bribes and Paris chose Aphrodite, who had bribed him with the love of the most beautiful woman in the world. Paris duly travelled to Sparta, where he was entertained for nine days by Helen and Menelaus. On the tenth day Menelaus was called away to Crete to bury his grandfather, at which point Paris seduced Helen and eloped with her to Troy.

Helen and Menelaus

Bound by their oath to support Menelaus, all the former suitors of Helen joined him as he sailed against Troy with a fleet of 1,000 ships, beginning a war that was to mirror the entertainment of Paris – it lasted nine years, with Troy destroyed in the tenth after the Greeks had entered the city in the Trojan horse. Paris was killed, the city sacked and Helen reunited with Menelaus, whose first reaction was to draw his sword intending to kill her for her infidelity. However, when he saw her beauty again he forgave her and they returned to Sparta to live out their days, according to most versions of the myth, in domestic bliss.

HELEN & MENELAUS FAQS

Wasn't Menelaus already Helen's brother-in-law when she married him?
Not quite, but he was the brother of her brother-in-law. Helen's sister Clytemnestra (or half-sister, depending which version of the myth you're reading) was already married to Menelaus' brother Agamemnon.

Isn't a Trojan horse a computer virus?
It is, but it is named after the original Trojan horse of this myth. Unable to break down the walls of Troy, the Greeks pretended to sail home, leaving a gigantic wheeled wooden horse outside the city gates, which they let it be known was an offering to Athena for a safe journey. Seeing the Greeks leave, the Trojans pulled the wooden horse into the city and began their victory celebrations, but in fact the horse was filled with Greek soldiers, who emerged after dark and sacked the city. Beware of Greeks bearing gifts!

HAVE YOU HEARD?

In his play *Doctor Faustus*, playwright Christopher Marlowe has Faustus ask:

> *Was this the face that launch'd a thousand ships,*
> *And burnt the topless towers of Ilium?*
> *Sweet Helen, make me immortal with a kiss!*

In Jeremy James Taylor's musical *Helen Come Home*, Achilles taunts Agamemnon, suggesting that the older man goes back home to Greece:

AGAMEMNON: 'I don't think my poor boat would get out of the bay, it's so old.'
ACHILLES: 'But it's supposed to be the finest warship in the fleet.'
AGAMEMNON: 'It was. "The launch that faced a thousand ships!"'

ABOVE *Cameo bust of Menelaus, by Vasily Kalugin and Ivan Galkin (1842)* **OPPOSITE** *Detail of* Head of Helen, *by Antonio Canova*

DIDO & AENEAS

Tragic lovers separated by duty

Dido

Dido is the alternative name of Elissa, a princess of Tyre who was driven out of the country after her brother, having succeeded to their father's throne and murdered her husband, Sychaeus, for his wealth. Dido and her followers fled to Libya, where a native king named Iarbas agreed to sell her as much land as could be encompassed by a bull's hide. The cunning Dido cut a hide into thin strips and tied them together so that it encompassed enough land for her to build the city of Carthage, over which she ruled as queen. Fearing the growing power of Carthage, Iarbas proposed marriage to Dido and threatened to attack Carthage if she refused. Dido pretended to accept his proposal, but rather than marry him she burned herself to death on a pyre that had been built to make a sacrifice to bless the wedding.

Dido and Aeneas

The legend of Dido was adapted by Virgil as part of his epic poem *The Aeneid*, describing the life and adventures of the Trojan hero Aeneas. According to Virgil, Aeneas was on his way from Troy to Italy when he was blown off course by a storm and landed at Carthage. His mother, Venus, sent Cupid to inspire Dido to fall in love with Aeneas and, while sheltering from a storm together in a cave while out hunting, they consummated their love: 'The firmament flickered with fire, a witness of wedding.' But it was not to be a happy marriage, as Virgil immediately makes clear: 'That day was the beginning of her death and the beginning of all her sufferings.'

At first Dido and Aeneas thought of nothing but each other until eventually Jupiter sent Mercury to remind Aeneas that he must fulfil his destiny. Knowing that it was his fate, not a matter of choice, Aeneas left for Italy to found the Roman race. Dido was so distraught that she persuaded her sister Anna to help her build a pyre, saying that she wanted to burn everything that reminded her of Aeneas. She then climbed onto the pile of wood and, in an embellishment of the original myth, made it her funeral pyre by killing herself with the sword of Aeneas.

BIBLICAL + MYTHICAL

32 + 33

DIDO & AENEAS FAQS

Sounds like Aeneas made the wrong decision?

There was no decision to make, it was his destiny – Romans reading this story would have admired the fortitude he showed in abandoning love to fulfil his duty. However, for most future romanticists it is Dido who is the real heroine, placing love above even her own life.

Didn't Dido drown herself?

No, she burned herself to death in one version of the story and fell on Aeneas' sword in another. You're confusing the founder of Carthage with 21st-century pop star Dido Armstrong, who sang: 'I will go down with this ship… I'm in love and always will be.'

HAVE YOU HEARD?

The 18th-century classicist Richard Porson boasted that he could rhyme on any subject. When challenged to rhyme the Latin gerunds *-di, -do, -dum*, he wrote the couplet:

When Dido found Aeneas would not come,
She mourned in silence and was Di-do dum(b).

ABOVE Aeneas telling Dido of the Disaster at Troy, *by Baron Pierre-Narcisse Guerin (1815)* **OPPOSITE** The Departure of Aeneas and Dido's Death, *from a French edition of Virgil's* The Aeneid *(1469)*

ROMULUS & REMUS

The twin brothers who founded Rome

Romulus and Remus

The mythical story of the foundation of Rome by Romulus and Remus begins with their grandfather, Numitor. Numitor was ousted as ruler of Alba Longa (the Italian city founded by Aeneas) by his younger brother, Amulius, who, in order to prevent a legitimate claim to his new throne, killed Numitor's sons and forced the erstwhile King's daughter, Rhea Silvia, to become a Vestal Virgin. But Amulius was foiled by the intervention of the gods – Mars seduced Rhea Silvia despite her vow of virginity and she gave birth to the twins, Romulus and Remus.

Rhea Silvia was condemned to death for breaking her vows, and Amulius ordered that the boys be thrown into the River Tiber. They were put in a basket, pushed out into the river and left to die, but floated ashore near a fig tree, where they were suckled by a she-wolf and fed by a woodpecker, two of the creatures sacred to their father, Mars. The twins were brought up by a shepherd named Faustulus and their existence eventually became known to their grandfather, Numitor. Once their true identity was known, the boys led an attack on Amulius and restored Numitor to his throne.

The founding of Rome

Soon after the restoration of Numitor, Romulus and Remus decided to found a great city of their own, but they could not agree on which of them should be king. Because they did not know which was the elder twin they asked the gods for a sign, which came in the form of vultures – first Remus saw six vultures and then Romulus saw twelve. Both of them claimed precedence, Remus because his vultures had appeared first, and Romulus because he had seen more of them. In the end the question was resolved by force, in the course of which Remus was killed, leaving his brother to be king of the new city, which he founded on the Palatine Hill and named Rome, after himself.

There are several other versions of the myth, but in all the variations the end result was the same – Romulus founded the city alone and named it after himself.

ABOVE *The she-wolf suckling Romulus and Remus (c.500–480BC)* **OPPOSITE** Romulus and Remus Nursed by the She-Wolf, *by Domenico Corvi (18th century)*

ROMULUS & REMUS FAQS

We've heard about the death of Remus, but how did Romulus die?
He was inspecting his troops in the Campus Martius (Field of Mars) when a storm blew up and he was enveloped in a thundercloud. When the cloud dispersed, Romulus had vanished and the senators who had been standing near him said that he had been taken up to heaven in the cloud.

Doesn't that sound a bit improbable?
That's what the Roman historian Livy (Titus Livius) thought. In what must be one of the world's earliest conspiracy theories, Livy claims that Romulus may have been murdered by the jealous senators under cover of the storm and then torn to pieces before the cloud dispersed.

HAVE YOU HEARD?

German 'new wave' pop band Dschinghis Khan celebrated Romulus and Remus in the English-language version of their song 'Rome':

Romulus and Remus, the two brothers, raised among the wolves like no others.

ST GEORGE
THE DRAGON

Patron saint and sparring partner

St George

Although he is the patron saint of soldiers, chivalry, the English nation, the Portuguese nation and, popularly, the England soccer team, little is known about the life of Saint George. The few facts have been obscured by subsequent myth and by the fallibility of 18th-century historian Edward Gibbon and others, who confused him with an Arian bishop, George of Cappadocia.

St George of the Eastern Church, who lived earlier than George of Cappadocia, was a real person, but he has taken on the air of a mythical character because of the acts attributed to him, such as the slaying of the dragon. It is thought that he may have died in Lydda, Palestine, c.250AD, or been put to death by the Roman emperor Diocletian in 303AD.

The dragon

Dragons take their name from the Greek *drakon*, meaning serpent, and the concept of dragons dates back at least to the classical myth of the serpent guarding the golden apples in the garden of the Hesperides. In Christian symbolism the dragon represents evil, Christian art taking its lead from references such as the Book of Revelation, which refers to Satan as 'the great dragon', and from Psalm 91, which states 'the dragon shalt thou trample under feet'. From this perspective, the legend of St George and the dragon, rather than being a record of an actual physical struggle, is an allegory of the triumph of a Christian hero over evil.

St George and the dragon

As with many myths and legends, there are various versions of this story, the earliest appearing in the *Legenda Aurea* ('Golden Legends'), a collection of lives of the saints by the 13th-century Italian prelate Jacobus de Voragine. One version of the story states that George was a tribune (a form of magistrate) who was called upon to kill a dragon that lived near Silene, Libya, and fed on the local townspeople. George duly arrived, rescued Princess Sabra from the clutches of the dragon (hence his association with chivalry) and then assured his place in folklore by killing the dragon into the bargain.

ST GEORGE & THE DRAGON FAQS

Who made George patron saint of England?
St George was popular in England from the 11th century because he is said to have assisted the Crusaders at Antioch, after which he became patron saint of Aragon, Portugal and many Norman knights. However, he did not officially become patron saint of England until he was adopted during the 14th century by King Edward III.

What is the George Cross?
Saint George's cross is a red cross on a white background – the flag of England, and one of the three crosses incorporated in the Union Flag (a.k.a. 'Union Jack'). The George Cross is very different – Britain's second highest decoration (after the Victoria Cross), awarded for gallantry. The George Cross is named not after St George but King George VI, during whose reign it was instituted, but, confusingly, at the centre of the cross is a circular medallion depicting St George slaying the dragon.

Wasn't Shakespeare born on St George's Day?
No one is certain when Shakespeare was born. It is known that he was baptized on 26 April 1564, and babies were often baptized three days after their birth, so tradition has it that he was born on 23 April, St George's Day. The tradition has been reinforced by the fact that he died on St George's Day, 23 April 1616.

If the Psalms tell Christians to trample dragons under their feet, how come no other saints killed dragons?
They did, among them St Michael, St Martha, St Margaret, St Silvester, St Samson, St Pol, St Donatus, St Clement of Metz, St Romain of Rouen, St Philip, St Florent, St Cado, St Maudet and St Keyne of Cornwall.

OPPOSITE *Ukrainian icon depicting St. George and the dragon (late 16th century)*

HAVE YOU HEARD?

The most famous St George quotation of all, firmly associating him with the English cause, is in Shakespeare's *Henry V*, at the end of the 'once more unto the breach, dear friends' speech:

> I see you standing like greyhounds in the slips,
> Straining upon the start. The game's afoot:
> Follow your spirit; and, upon this charge
> Cry 'God for Harry, England and St George!'

('Harry' was the popular name for King Henry.) In *Richard III*, Shakespeare acknowledges that the invocation of St George was already an age-old tradition:

> Our ancient word of courage, fair St George,
> Inspire us with the spleen of fiery dragons!

GOG & MAGOG

Giants who guard the City of London

Gog and Magog are the names given to two giants whose statues stand in London's Guildhall, symbolically guarding the City. Their origins are unclear and their names seem to have been arrived at by an amalgamation of earlier myths and legends, the names Gog, Magog and Gogmagog appearing in both pagan and Judeo-Christian cultures.

According to one version of British legend, Gog and Magog were descendants of the Roman emperor Diocletian, who was said to have had his 33 daughters cast adrift in a ship as punishment for murdering their husbands. They were washed ashore in Albion (the ancient name for England) where they bred with a group of demons and gave birth to a race of giants. The giants were eventually slain, with the exception of Gog and Magog who were brought to the City of London and forced to serve as porters at the court buildings that preceded the Guildhall. According to another version, the two giants were originally named Gogmagog and Corineus. Gogmagog was an ancient Briton and Corineus a warrior representing the Trojan invaders who defeated the inhabitants of Albion and founded the ancient city of London as New Troy. In time the name Corineus was forgotten and the giants became popularly known as Gog, the name of the ancient British pagan sun god, and Magog, the name of the Gaulish horse goddess.

In both versions of the legend, the giants became strongly associated with the City of London. Wickerwork effigies of Gog and Magog stood in the Guildhall and were carried in City pageants and processions from at least as

long ago as the 15th century until they were destroyed in the Great Fire of 1666. The original effigies were replaced in 1708 by carved figures 4m/13ft high, which were destroyed during the Blitz and were in turn replaced after the Second World War by limewood carvings of what by then were known as 'London's giants'.

ABOVE *Detail of the church clock of St Dunstan's in the West* (see Have You Heard?) **OPPOSITE** *Limewood carvings of Gog and Magog, sculpted by David Evans, arrive at the Guildhall to replace the figures that were destroyed in 1940 during the Blitz (20 May 1953)*

LANCELOT & GUINEVERE

Adulterous lovers of Arthurian legend

Lancelot of the Lake

According to the Arthurian romance *Lancelot du Lac*, Sir Lancelot (or Launcelot) was born the son of King Ban of Brittany, France, but was stolen in his infancy and brought up by Vivienne, the Lady of the Lake. (The Lady of the Lake is also named in various other romances as Nimue and as Morgen, a.k.a. Morgan le Fay.) When Lancelot reached manhood, Vivienne presented him to King Arthur and he duly became the first of the Knights of the Round Table.

Lancelot and Guinevere

Lancelot is usually presented as the very model of chivalry, and, with Sir Galahad, often overshadows King Arthur himself for his bravery and heroism. However, in the 14th-century poem *Le Morte Arthur* (which precedes Malory's more famous *Le Morte d'Arthur*), Lancelot proves not to be so chivalrous, becoming the adulterous lover of King Arthur's wife, Guinevere, and thus starting the chain of events that leads to Arthur's death. In this version of the story the lovers are betrayed by Arthur's nephew Sir Agravain, who breaks in on the lovers with 12 other knights, all of whom are slain by Lancelot except Arthur's treacherous nephew Mordred.

Lancelot and Guinevere escape to Lancelot's castle in the north of England, but are besieged there by Arthur and Sir Gawain (Agravain's brother) until Lancelot returns Guinevere to Arthur. Arthur and Gawain then pursue Lancelot to Brittany, but while they are there Mordred seizes the kingdom and seduces Guinevere. Arthur returns and, in the ensuing battles for the kingdom, all the knights of the Round Table are slain, including Arthur and Mordred who mortally wound each other. Lancelot belatedly arrives to help Arthur only to discover that Arthur is dead and Guinevere has become a nun; repenting his treachery, he becomes a priest and stands guard over Arthur's grave.

ABOVE *Sir Lancelot depicted in stained glass designed by William Morris (1862)* **RIGHT** *Lancelot and Guinevere, from* Lancelot du Lac *(c.1470)*

LANCELOT & GUINEVERE FAQS

Wasn't it Morgan le Fay, not Agravain, who revealed the lovers' intrigue to Arthur?
In some versions of the story, but not in this one. She is said to have revealed the intrigue out of loyalty because she is Arthur's sister.

But I thought she was the Lady of the Lake?
In some versions of the story she is. And just to add to the confusion, not only does she prove her loyalty to Arthur in some versions by revealing the lovers' tryst, but in other versions she also plots to kill Arthur.

And wasn't Mordred Arthur's son, not his nephew?
In some versions of the story, but not in this one.

How come there are so many different versions of these stories?
Because they have been written and rewritten in various languages from medieval times onwards by writers drawing on history, folklore and mythology, often embellishing the stories from their own imagination as they go.

HAVE YOU HEARD?

In his poem *Sir Launcelot and Queen Guinevere*, Alfred, Lord Tennyson describes the attraction between the lovers:

Then, in the boyhood of the year,
Sir Launcelot and Queen Guinevere
Rode thro' the coverts of the deer
With blissful treble ringing clear.
She seem'd a part of joyous Spring:
A gown of grass-green silk she wore,
Buckled with golden clasps before;
A light-green tuft of plumes she bore
Closed in a golden ring.

FANTASY & FICTION

DON QUIXOTE & SANCHO PANZA

Would-be knight and his faithful squire

Spanish author Cervantes' satirical romance *Don Quixote de la Mancha* has been described as 'the most carelessly written of all great books', perhaps because Cervantes could not have known when he started writing how great his work would be. He set out to write a satire on the chivalric romances that were then losing their popularity, but as the work progressed it metamorphosed into something far greater: the character of Don Quixote deepened and the scope of the book widened to such a degree that it has often been hailed as the precursor of the modern novel.

Don Quixote is a poor, amiable country gentleman from La Mancha, Spain, who becomes crazed by reading too many of the chivalric romances that Cervantes is satirizing. Quixote imagines himself to be one of the great knights, called upon to redress the world's ills, and sets forth in rusty armour, on his old nag, Rosinante, to seek out adventures and to avenge the oppressed. To complete his transformation into a knight errant he needs a squire, whom he finds in the form of Sancho Panza, a local peasant who is shrewd enough to deter Quixote from his worst excesses, but gullible enough to accompany him on the promise that Quixote will make him governor of an island.

Together they have a number of adventures, including one that has survived into the 21st century as a metaphor for someone battling against imaginary enemies: tilting at windmills. Quixote and Panza are riding through the plains of Montiel when Quixote sees 30 or 40 windmills ahead of them, which, he tells Panza, 'are giants, two leagues in length or more'. He rides towards them with his lance (a knightly form of attack known as tilting) and drives valiantly at one of these 'monsters dreadful as Typhoeus', but his lance is caught in the sail of the windmill, lifting Quixote and Rosinante into the air and dumping them unceremoniously on the ground. Typically, Quixote's injuries do not jolt him into a sense of reality and he tells Panza that the magician Freston must have changed the giants into windmills 'out of malice'.

KEY DATES

1547 Saavedra Miguel de Cervantes is born on 29 September in Alcalá de Henares, Spain

1569 Cervantes publishes his first known work, a collection of writings on the death of Philip II's queen

1575 Cervantes is captured by pirates and held prisoner in Algiers for five years

1585 Cervantes publishes his first major work, *La Galatea*

1597 Cervantes is imprisoned for three months for irregularities in his work as a tax collector. Legend has it that he begins writing *Don Quixote de la Mancha* while in prison

1605 The first part of *Don Quixote* is published and proves popular, but Cervantes fails to follow it with a conclusion

1614 A writer using the pseudonym Alonso Fernandez de Avellaneda publishes a spoof conclusion to *Don Quixote*

1615 Spurred by the spoof, Cervantes writes the second part of *Don Quixote*

1616 Cervantes dies on 22 April in Madrid, aged 68

RIGHT *Miguel de Cervantes* **OPPOSITE** Sancho Panza finds Don Quixote after Don Quixote unsuccessfully attacks a windmill, *illustration by French artist Jules David (1835)*

JULES DAVID

PUNCH & JUDY

Puppet wife-beater and his unfortunate spouse

The origins of Punch and Judy are extremely hazy, but it is clear that Punch derives mainly from a 16th-century Italian theatre form known as *Commedia dell'arte* (*Commedia*). This form of theatre was based on stock characters and storylines, with new characters occasionally being introduced by particularly accomplished performers. One such performer was Silvio Fiorillo, who is usually credited with inventing two *Commedia* characters – the braggart Capitano Matamoras and a dim-witted servant called Pulcinella, although there is some dispute about the latter.

Whatever his origins, Pulcinella soon became an established part of the *Commedia* tradition and, during the early 17th century, was one of several *Commedia* characters who also became popular in puppet theatre in Italy and elsewhere in Europe. In France the puppet character of Polichinelle, based on Pulcinella, developed from the simple servant of the *Commedia* into a grotesque and powerful character with a hooked nose, hunched back and bright clothes. In the second half of the 17th century several Italian puppeteers visited England and brought with them a character based on the Pulcinella/Polichinelle puppet, whose name the English found difficult to

KEY DATES

16th century *Commedia dell'arte* develops in Italy

c.1570 Silvio Fiorillo is born in Italy

c.1600 Fiorillo reputedly invents the character Pulcinella

c.1632 Fiorillo dies

early 17th century Many of the masked characters of *Commedia dell'arte* become popular puppet characters

mid-17th century In French puppet theatre, Pulcinella develops into the more grotesque character of Polichinelle

1660s Puppet shows featuring a character based on Pulcinella/Polichinelle are introduced to Britain, where the character becomes known as Mr Punch

early 18th century Punch's 'scolding wife', Joan, begins to

appear with Punch in puppet shows and on puppet playbills

1742 A newspaper in Philadelphia, USA, contains the first known written evidence that Punch has arrived in America – an advertisement for a puppet show that includes 'a merry dialogue between Punch and Joan his wife'

early 19th century Joan's name changes to Judy (perhaps via 'Joaney')

1828 English publisher Septimus Prowett commissions John Payne Collier to write the first 'definitive text' of *Punch and Judy*, illustrated by George Cruikshank; Collier consults an Italian immigrant puppeteer named Piccini, who happens to use the new name of Judy rather than the century-old name of Joan

1841 The humorous magazine *Punch*, named after Mr Punch, is launched on 17 July

ABOVE Punch and Judy, *by Janet and Anne Johnstone (20th century)*

pronounce and was corrupted, via Punchinello, to Punch or Mr Punch. In England Punch was incorporated in a well-established puppet tradition and met a host of new companions, including his unfortunate wife, Judy (known at first as Joan), and the story evolved into its now-traditional form.

The exact plot varies from performer to performer, but the basic outline is that Punch kills his own child in a fit of anger, Judy discovers what he has done and beats him with a stick, and Punch takes the stick from her and bludgeons her to death. His dog, Toby, attacks him, so he kills the dog, a doctor visits him when he is ill, so he kills the doctor, and he is then arrested (after beating the policeman) and sentenced to death. However, Punch tricks the hangman into putting his own head in the noose, hangs the hangman and is finally visited by the devil himself, whom Punch outwits to make his escape. Like many fairy tales, Punch and Judy is a violent tale of dubious morality that has delighted generations of children.

ABOVE The Great Actor, or Mr Punch in All his Glory, *by Robert Cruikshank from* The English Spy, *by Charles Molloy Westmacott (c.1824)*

ROMEO
JULIET

Shakespeare's star-cross'd lovers

It is apt that Shakespeare set his romantic tragedy *Romeo and Juliet* in Italy, not in England, because these most famous of lovers were conceived not by Shakespeare but by an Italian cleric named Matteo Bandello. As a Dominican, Bandello was driven out of Italy by the Spanish in 1525 and settled in France, where he wrote 214 romantic tales, many of which, including the story of Romeo and Juliet, were used by Shakespeare as source material.

Two noble Veronese families, the Montagues and the Capulets, are ancient rivals and, writes Shakespeare: 'From forth the fatal loins of these two foes/ A pair of star-cross'd lovers take their life.' Lord Montague's son Romeo falls in love with Lord Capulet's daughter Juliet and they persuade a friar named Laurence to marry them secretly. Soon afterwards, Romeo is banished to Mantua for killing a Capulet in an armed fight and, coincidentally, Lord Capulet proposes an arranged marriage for Juliet. She seeks the advice of Friar Laurence, who tells her to consent to the marriage but on the eve of the wedding to drink a potion that will temporarily make her appear dead. Meanwhile he will warn Romeo, who will rescue her and take her to Mantua. But Friar Laurence's message fails to reach Romeo. Hearing that Juliet is dead, he visits the vault where her body is laid, gives her one last kiss and then poisons himself. She then awakes and, finding him dead beside her, stabs herself and dies by his side.

Romeo and Juliet are such famous lovers that people often refer to the romance between them while forgetting the tragedy that surrounds it. Lovers often quote the famous line 'Romeo, Romeo, wherefore art thou Romeo?' thinking that it means 'where are you my love?' rather than its actual meaning: 'Why are you Romeo rather than some other person whom I am not forbidden to love?' ('Wherefore' means 'why', not 'where'; and the issue is confused by the fact that after Romeo's death Juliet asks Friar Laurence: 'Where is my Romeo?') With similar optimism, people sometimes refer to lovers as 'star-cross'd' in the belief that the phrase means the stars will bring happiness, while its true sense indicates that the lovers are ill-fated and doomed to be thwarted in their love.

KEY DATES

c.1485 Matteo Bandello is born in Castelnuevo, Italy

1554–73 Bandello writes 214 tales (later collected as *Novelliere*), one of which is the story of Romeo and Juliet

1561 Bandello dies

1564 William Shakespeare is born in Stratford-upon-Avon, England

c.1591 Shakespeare begins work on his first play, *Henry VI part I*

c.1594–95 Shakespeare writes his first tragedy, *Romeo and Juliet*

1616 Shakespeare dies on 23 April in Stratford-upon-Avon, aged 51

1968 The feature film *Romeo and Juliet* is released, directed by Franco Zeffirelli and starring Leonard Whiting and Olivia Hussey

1996 The feature film *William Shakespeare's Romeo and Juliet* is released, directed by Baz Luhrmann and starring Leonardo diCaprio and Claire Danes

HAVE YOU HEARD?

Caspar James refers to Romeo and Juliet in the title, if not the content, of his poem *Star-cross'd Lovers*, which begins:

We walk hand in hand, she and I,
while the wind feels inside our coats.
Ahead of us, a Star blows across the street
and fetches up against the kerb.
I glance at it as we pass – the headline,
crumpled
and greasy now with chip-fat, cannot be read.

OPPOSITE ROMEO: 'Farewell! Farewell! One kiss and I'll descend.' *Postcard of Romeo and Juliet kissing (c.1909)*

ROSENCRANTZ & GUILDENSTERN

Attendant lords to Hamlet, Prince of Denmark

In Tom Stoppard's 1966 comedy *Rosencrantz and Guildenstern Are Dead*, an actor performing a play within the play explains to Rosencrantz and Guildenstern: 'The bad end unhappily, the good unluckily. That's what tragedy means.' The actor's explanation is certainly true of Shakespeare's tragedy *Hamlet, Prince of Denmark*, the play in which the characters of Rosencrantz and Guildenstern first appeared some 366 years before Stoppard's duo.

In *Hamlet*, Rosencrantz and Guildenstern are minor characters – attendant lords charged with escorting Hamlet to England, where Claudius (now King of Denmark, having murdered the previous king, who was his brother and Hamlet's father) has arranged to have Hamlet killed. Hamlet discovers the letter ordering his death and swaps it for one ordering the death of the bearers; the ship is then attacked by pirates who take Hamlet prisoner, but leave Rosencrantz and Guildenstern to sail on towards England, and death. Whereas Shakespeare reports all this shipboard action in a few lines between Hamlet and his friend Horatio, Stoppard makes an entire play out of it, making the attendant lords the stars of the show and Hamlet a minor character with very few lines.

Stoppard's Rosencrantz and Guildenstern, confined for the entire play on the ship, are used to explore comically the kind of existential angst expressed more formally by Shakespeare's Hamlet. For Stoppard's duo, the ship is a metaphor for life: 'Where we went wrong was getting on a boat. We can move, of course, change direction, rattle about, but our movement is contained within a larger one that carries us along as inexorably as the wind and current...' In Stoppard's play Hamlet simply disappears after the attack of the pirates, depriving Rosencrantz and Guildenstern of their *raison d'être*:

> ROS: He's dead then. He's dead as far as we're concerned.
> PLAYER: Or we are as far as he is. Not too bad, is it?

But it is that bad. As Guildenstern points out, close to tears: 'Nothing will be resolved without him...' In trying to act out how they will explain things to Claudius, Guildenstern opens and reads the letter that Hamlet describes

F A N T A S Y + F I C T I O N

50 + 51

KEY DATES

1564 William Shakespeare is born on 23 April in Stratford-upon-Avon, England

c.1600-01 Shakespeare creates the characters of Rosencrantz and Guildenstern in writing the tragedy *Hamlet, Prince of Denmark*

1616 Shakespeare dies on 23 April in Stratford-upon-Avon, aged 51

1937 Tomas Straussler is born on 3 July in Zlin, then Czechoslovakia

1946 Straussler and his mother move to England, where he changes his name to Tom Stoppard and works as a freelance journalist, theatre critic and radio playwright

1966 Stoppard's first stage-play, *Rosencrantz and Guildenstern Are Dead*, premieres at the Edinburgh Festival Fringe, Scotland

1967 *Rosencrantz and Guildenstern Are Dead* is staged at the National Theatre, London, England

1990 The feature film *Rosencrantz and Guildenstern Are Dead* is released, directed by Tom Stoppard and starring Gary Oldman and Tim Roth

1997 Stoppard is knighted

ABOVE *Tom Stoppard* **OPPOSITE** *Adrian Scarborough and Simon Russell Beale in* Rosencrantz and Guildenstern Are Dead, *at Britain's National Theatre (December 1995)*

to Horatio in Shakespeare's play, ordering the deaths of the bearers. It is this fate that elevates the attendant lords from minor characters in a 17th-century tragedy to the lead characters in a 20th-century comedy, as Rosencrantz voices the realization that: 'They had it in for us, didn't they? Right from the beginning. Who'd have thought that we were so important?'

VLADIMIR & ESTRAGON

Tramps who waited for Godot

Samuel Beckett's tragi-comedy *Waiting for Godot* has been described as 'an elegant aural discipline for maintaining a dialogue when there is nothing to say' and, most famously, 'a play in which nothing happens, twice'. The central characters of Vladimir and Estragon, part clown, part everyman, are staged in the guise of tramps, and their interminable wait for Godot reflects Beckett's vision of the human condition – a bleak beginning followed by an existence tormented by a search for meaning and finally an uncertain ending.

Vladimir and Estragon, a.k.a. Didi and Gogo, have no history and no background. They come from nowhere and they go nowhere. There is no indication of how they met or how long they have known each other, but the depth of their reliance on each other is absolute. Estragon continually forgets things and Vladimir continually reminds him; in this way their conversation progresses and together they bolster each other's sense of being:

ESTRAGON: 'We always find something, eh Didi, to give up the impression that we exist?'
VLADIMIR: 'Yes, yes, we're magicians. But let us persevere in what we have resolved, before we forget.'

The bleak beginning is in the setting – 'A country road. A tree. Evening' – and in the opening line, spoken by Estragon: 'Nothing to be done.' The tormented existence is in the hopelessness and boredom of Didi and Gogo's wait for Godot, reflected in their pathological need to pass the time. (When Vladimir celebrates passing a small amount of time Estragon replies: 'It would have passed in any case.' And when Estragon celebrates passing a small amount of time, Vladimir replies: 'Yes, but now we'll have to think of something else.') And their uncertain end lies in their daily dilemma:

VLADIMIR: 'We'll hang ourselves tomorrow. (*Pause.*) Unless Godot comes.'
ESTRAGON: 'And if he comes?'
VLADIMIR: 'We'll be saved.'

HAVE YOU HEARD?

Samuel Beckett's view of the human condition is expressed in one of his most famous lines, spoken by the incidental character of Lucky in *Waiting for Godot*:

'They give birth astride a grave, the light gleams an instant, then it's night once more.'

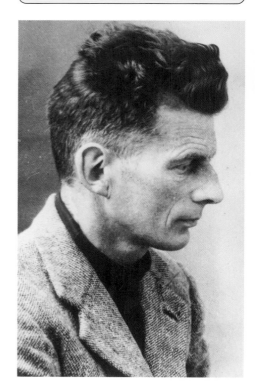

ABOVE *Samuel Beckett (c. 1950)*

Their relationship is a very human one, veering from mutual affection and solidarity in the face of a pointless existence to frustration with each other because of it. They discuss going it alone, but stick together by default. They discuss not waiting for Godot, but continue to wait by default. They decide to move on, but stay put by default, the first act of the play ending:

ESTRAGON: Well, shall we go?
VLADIMIR: Yes, let's go.
They do not move.

And the second act ending:

VLADIMIR: Well? Shall we go?
ESTRAGON: Yes, let's go.
They do not move.

Nothing happens. Twice.

KEY DATES

1906 Samuel Barclay Beckett is born on 13 April in Dublin, Ireland, and later educated at Trinity College, Dublin

1932 Beckett moves to France, where he spends most of his life

1953 Beckett creates the characters of Vladimir and Estragon for his play *En Attendant Godot*, first performed in English in 1955 as *Waiting for Godot* (published in English 1956)

1969 Beckett is awarded the Nobel Prize for Literature

1989 Beckett dies on 22 December in Paris, France, aged 83

2000 The feature film *Waiting for Godot* is released, directed by Michael Lindsay-Hogg and starring Barry McGovern as Vladimir and Johnny Murphy as Estragon

ABOVE *Julian Glover and Alan Doble in* Waiting for Godot *(1998)*

THE OWL & THE PUSSY-CAT

Eponymous lovers of Edward Lear's poem

A hunting bird and a small mammal may not seem the ideal marriage partners, but that mattered little to English artist and humorist Edward Lear, who proudly described his verse as 'nonsense'. In Lear's most famous poem, *The Owl and the Pussy-cat*, the wise Owl knows exactly how to charm the demure Pussy-cat, taking her on a luxury cruise, wooing her with wealth and sweet delicacies and then providing a starlit serenade:

> *The Owl and the Pussy-cat went to sea*
> *In a beautiful pea-green boat,*
> *They took some honey, and plenty of money,*
> *Wrapped up in a five-pound note.*
> *The Owl looked up to the stars above,*
> *And sang to a small guitar;*
> *'O lovely Pussy! O Pussy, my love,*
> *What a beautiful Pussy you are…'*

Bowled over by such chivalry, the Pussy-cat falls head over heels in love and begs the Owl to marry her, but at this stage their budding relationship hits a problem: no wedding ring. However, the young lovers are undeterred and, in the spirit of all great romances, toil for a year and a day to remedy the problem:

> *Pussy said to the Owl, 'You elegant fowl!*
> *How charmingly sweet you sing!*
> *O let us be married! too long we have tarried:*
> *But what shall we do for a ring?'*
> *They sailed away for a year and a day,*
> *To the land where the Bong-tree grows,*
> *And there in a wood a Piggy-wig stood,*

ABOVE The Owl and the Pussy-cat, *illustration by Lynton Lamb from* Other Travellers for the Orion Line *(20th century)*

With a ring in the end of his nose...

'Dear Pig, are you willing to sell for one shilling
Your ring?' Said the Piggy, 'I will.'
So they took it away, and were married next day
By the turkey who lives on the hill.

And, of course, no wedding is complete without a feast and all-night dancing:

They dined on mince, and slices of quince,
Which they ate with a runcible spoon;
And hand in hand, on the edge of the sand,
They danced by the light of the moon,
    The moon,
    The moon,
They danced by the light of the moon.

KEY DATES

1812 Edward Lear is born on 12 May in London, England, the youngest of 20 children, and is later educated at home by his sister Anne

1832 Lear is commissioned by the 13th Earl of Derby to make drawings of the birds and animals in the menagerie of Knowsley Hall, Lancashire (now Merseyside)

1830s–40s Under Derby's patronage, Lear tours Italy and Greece making sketches and paintings of the landscape, later published in *Sketches of Rome* and *Illustrated Excursions in Italy*. He also entertains Derby's grandchildren with his nonsense verse

1846 Much of Lear's verse, illustrated with his own sketches, is published anonymously as *A Book of Nonsense*

1867 Lear writes *The Owl and the Pussy-Cat*

1870 Lear publishes *Nonsense Songs, Stories, Botany and Alphabets*

1871 Lear publishes *More Nonsense Rhymes*

1876 Lear publishes *Laughable Lyrics*

1888 Lear dies on 29 January in San Remo, Italy, aged 75

HAVE YOU HEARD?
Edward Lear wrote of himself:

How pleasant to know Mr Lear!
Who has written such volumes of stuff!
Some think him ill-tempered and queer,
But a few think him pleasant enough.

ABOVE *Edward Lear (1840)*

DR JEKYLL
MR HYDE

The good and evil sides of a single personality

The two most famous characters created by Scottish author Robert Louis Stevenson, and one of the best known duos in fiction, are in fact one person. In Stevenson's allegorical thriller *The Strange Case of Dr Jekyll and Mr Hyde*, Dr Henry Jekyll is a physician who becomes fascinated with the balance between good and evil in people, both in humanity generally and in himself in particular. Jekyll ponders whether it would be advantageous if these two aspects of a person's character could be split into separate personalities (a question that schizophrenics would no doubt answer in the negative) and sets about creating a drug that will effect this.

When he takes this drug Jekyll undergoes a physical transformation into

the repulsive Mr Edward Hyde, who is a distillation of the evil aspects of Jekyll's character and gives rein to Jekyll's suppressed evil impulses. However, once these impulses have been awakened they are hard to ignore and each time Jekyll takes the drug the Hyde character exerts greater and greater control over him, causing him eventually to commit a gruesome murder. Jekyll soon begins to find himself transformed into Hyde against his will, while the drug becomes less and less effective in restoring him to his original form. Eventually, in despair, and just as he is about to be arrested for the murder, Jekyll kills himself.

Stevenson's story is a precursor of the psychological thrillers of the 20th century, and the characters of Jekyll and Hyde survive as a metaphor for anyone who in certain situations appears to undergo a complete change of personality.

KEY DATES

1850 Robert Louis Balfour Stevenson is born on 13 November in Edinburgh, Scotland, the son of Thomas Stevenson, engineer to the Board of Northern Lighthouses

1867 Studies engineering at Edinburgh University and later transfers from engineering to law

1875 Qualifies as an advocate, but never practises

1878 Publishes his first major work, *Inland Voyage*, describing his travels in Belgium and northern France

1883 Publishes *Treasure Island*

1886 Publishes *Kidnapped* and *The Strange Case of Dr Jekyll and Mr Hyde*

1888 Leaves with his family for the South Seas, settling in Samoa in 1889

1894 On 3 December dies in Samoa, aged 44, of a ruptured blood vessel in the brain

1920 The feature film *Dr Jekyll and Mr Hyde* is released, directed by John S. Robinson and starring John Barrymore

1931 The feature film *Dr Jekyll and Mr Hyde* is released, directed by Rouben Mamoulian and starring Fredric March

1941 The feature film *Dr Jekyll and Mr Hyde* is released, directed by Victor Fleming and starring Spencer Tracy

HAVE YOU HEARD?
Robert Louis Stevenson wrote that: 'To travel hopefully is a better thing than to arrive, and the true success is to labour.'

ABOVE *Detail of* Robert Louis Stevenson and His Wife, *by John Singer Sargent (1885)* **OPPOSITE** *Spencer Tracy in the film* Dr Jekyll and Mr Hyde, *directed by Victor Fleming (1941)*

TARZAN
JANE

Husband and wife who met in the jungle

FANTASY + FICTION

58 + 59

With *Tarzan of the Apes*, only the third story that he submitted for publication, American author Edgar Rice Burroughs created a character that was to become so well known that Tarzan now seems as much an element of history as of fiction. When it was first published, readers proclaimed *Tarzan of the Apes* one of the best adventure tales ever written, but it was not just excellent storytelling that created the Tarzan phenomenon. Burroughs also aggressively marketed his creation, selling rights for newspaper comic strips, radio programmes and, of course, films, in which Johnny Weissmuller was the most famous Tarzan of them all. Burroughs also licensed Tarzan merchandise ranging from statuettes to food and clothing – a common enough idea today, but virtually unheard of in 1912.

As well as introducing the hero, the first Tarzan story also introduced the love interest. Tarzan has grown up in the jungle after being stranded there with his parents, English aristocrats Lord and Lady Greystoke, who died when he was an infant. Years later a party of Americans is stranded in the same jungle, among whom Tarzan sees the 19-year-old Jane Porter and, in true pulp style, his feelings are awakened: 'In his savage, untutored breast new emotions were stirring … He knew that she was created to be protected, and that he was created to protect her.' After saving Jane from one of the beasts of the jungle, during which 'the veil of centuries of civilization and culture was swept from the blurred vision of the Baltimore girl', Tarzan 'did what no red-blooded man needs lessons in doing. He took his woman in his arms and smothered her upturned, panting lips with kisses'.

Despite this smothering, panting introduction, *Tarzan of the Apes* ends with Jane having doubts about her feelings for Tarzan and getting engaged instead to his obviously unsuitable cousin: 'In her groundless apprehension that she might make a terrible mistake, she had made a worse one.' It was the hook that made readers clamour for a follow-up and an end to the lovers' anguish. In the second story, *The Return of Tarzan*, they marry and begin an often passionate, always faithful, but occasionally distant marriage that is notable for Jane's thirteen-year absence from the stories when Burroughs was going through his own marital crisis.

KEY DATES

1875 Edgar Rice Burroughs is born on 1 September in Chicago, USA

1903 Johnny Weissmuller, the actor who will later portray Tarzan, is born on 2 June in Freidorf, Romania

1908 The Weissmuller family emigrates to the USA, for which country Johnny wins five Olympic gold medals in swimming

1912 Burroughs introduces Tarzan and Jane to the world in his story *Tarzan of the Apes*, which first appears in the October issue of *The All-Story* magazine

1912–42 Burroughs writes 23 more Tarzan novels (as well as more than 50 not involving Tarzan)

1932–48 Weissmuller plays Tarzan in 19 feature films

1950 Burroughs dies, aged 74, on 19 March, a millionaire from his 70-plus novels and from the radio programmes, comic strips and serial and feature films based on his creation of Tarzan

1984 Weissmuller dies on 20 January, aged 80

ABOVE RIGHT *Edgar Rice Burroughs (c. 1920)* **OPPOSITE** *Johnny Weissmuller and Maureen O'Sullivan in* Tarzan and His Mate, *directed by Cedric Gibbons (1934)*

HAVE YOU HEARD?

In the original *Tarzan of the Apes*, Tarzan cannot speak a human language, but he has taught himself to write English. Having fallen in love at first sight, his first communication with Jane is in the form of a letter:

'I am Tarzan of the Apes. I want you. I am yours. You are mine. We live here together always in my house. I will bring you the best of fruits, the tenderest deer, the finest meats that roam the jungle. I will hunt for you … When you see this you will know that it is for you and that Tarzan of the Apes loves you.'

JEEVES & WOOSTER

Literature's great upstairs-downstairs duo

Jeeves and Wooster are a quintessentially English duo born in the USA. Their creator, English-born author P.G. Wodehouse, was living in America when he wrote the short story *Extricating Young Gussie*, the first of a series of stories that would become known collectively as the 'Wooster–Jeeves cycle'. Wodehouse later wrote that he blushed to think of the understated way in which he had introduced his two greatest characters to the world, with Jeeves announcing to Wooster on the first page: 'Mrs Gregson to see you, sir.'

Bertram Wilberforce Wooster, like Wodehouse, was born into a noble family and was in line of succession to an earldom and a baronetcy. Unlike Wodehouse, he is somewhat dim-witted, and relies on his valet, Jeeves (whose Christian name is never revealed), to extricate him from the various situations into which his dim-wittedness leads him. In a relationship that has informed countless comic duos since, Wooster's awareness of his own shortcomings, and of Jeeves' intelligence, does not alter the hierarchy between them: 'It beats me why a man of his genius is satisfied to hang around pressing my clothes and whatnot. If I had half Jeeves' brain, I should have a stab at being Prime Minister or something.'

Apart from Jeeves' skill at extricating Wooster from trouble, he is also an indispensable valet seemingly possessed of a sixth sense. In one story, Wooster comments: 'He seems to know when I am awake by a sort of telepathy. He always

ABOVE *P.G. Wodehouse (c.1920)* **OPPOSITE** *Stephen Fry (r) as Jeeves and Hugh Laurie as Wooster*

floats in with a cup exactly two minutes after I come to life.' It does not do for a gentleman to reveal his emotions, but in *Stiff Upper Lip, Jeeves*, Wooster comes as close as he ever will to voicing his personal feelings about Jeeves, although he immediately follows this revelation by narrating a more objective view of their relationship. After a period of absence, Wooster says: 'I felt like a child of tender years deprived of its Nannie. If you don't mind me calling you a Nannie?' 'Not at all, sir.' 'Though, as a matter of fact, I was giving myself a slight edge, putting it that way. My Aunt Agatha generally refers to Jeeves as my keeper.'

SHERLOCK HOLMES DR WATSON

The original detective-and-sidekick duo

Today it seems an obvious fictional device to pair a detective with a sidekick who will act as companion, confidante and as a foil for his skills. But it was not such an obvious idea before 1887, the year that Arthur Conan Doyle's novella *A Study in Scarlet* introduced to the world the original detective duo – amateur sleuth Sherlock Holmes and his assistant Dr John Watson. Doyle practised medicine before making his name as a writer and elements of his medical background are to be found in Holmes and Watson, most obviously in the fact that Watson is a doctor. Holmes's medical connections are less obvious: his name is derived partly from American physician, poet and novelist Oliver Wendell Holmes, whose writing was much admired by Doyle, and the character of Holmes was inspired by the unusually acute powers of observation and deduction shown by Dr Joseph Bell, one of Doyle's lecturers in forensic medicine at Edinburgh University.

In *A Study in Scarlet*, Holmes and Watson meet by chance when they agree to share the expenses of a flat at the immortal address of 221b Baker Street. Thereafter, as Holmes's biographer, Watson 'was allowed to cooperate with him and to keep notes of his doings' for 17 of the 23 years that Holmes spends as an amateur private detective, becoming a participant in and narrator of many of Holmes's adventures. The relationship between them is very one-sided, being based on Watson's out-and-out admiration for Holmes as 'the best and wisest man whom ever I have known'. Holmes rarely shows his feelings for the man he describes in one story as his closest friend, but he does occasionally praise Watson, remarking in various tales on his unselfishness, reliability, zeal and intelligence, and telling him in *The Hound of the Baskervilles*: 'It is at the hour of action that I turn to you.'

In one story Watson writes: 'I was a whetstone for his mind. I stimulated him', but despite this glimmer of self-awareness it is always more evident to the reader than to either of the characters that Watson is one half of a duo that would be hugely diminished without him, whether or not the partnership extends to close friendship. Ultimately, Holmes is a loner and no-one will ever be close to him, as Watson observes in *The Illustrious Client*: 'I was nearer to him than anyone else and yet I was always conscious of the gap between.'

HAVE YOU HEARD?

In *The Sign of Four*, Holmes explains to Watson one of his most famous tenets:

'How often have I said to you that when you have eliminated the impossible, whatever remains, *however improbable*, must be the truth?'

ABOVE *Sir Arthur Conan-Doyle (c. 1912)* **OPPOSITE** *Dr Watson (Nigel Bruce) looks on while Sherlock Holmes (Basil Rathbone) kneels over the dead body of Sir Henry Baskerville (Richard Greene) on the moor. Scene from* The Hound of the Baskervilles, *directed by Sidney Lanfield (1939)*

KEY DATES

1837 Joseph Bell, who later becomes the model for Sherlock Holmes, is born on 2 December in Edinburgh, Scotland

1859 Arthur Conan Doyle is born on 22 May in Edinburgh, Scotland, one of seven children of a civil servant

1879 Doyle's first published story appears in *Chambers' Journal*

1887 Sherlock Holmes and Dr Watson make their first appearance, in Doyle's novella *A Study in Scarlet*

1890 The second Holmes mystery, *The Sign of Four*, is published

1891–93 *Strand Magazine* publishes a series of Holmes's tales

1893 Doyle kills off Sherlock Holmes

1902 Due to public demand, Doyle resurrects Holmes, in *The Hound of the Baskervilles*. Doyle is knighted

1903 *Strand* Magazine resumes publication of Holmes's tales

1930 Doyle dies of a heart attack on 7 July in Sussex, England, aged 71

MULDER & SCULLY

FBI partners investigating the X-Files

Cult TV series *The X-Files* was created by sci-fi/suspense addict and ex-surfing writer Chris Carter, inspired by childhood viewing that included *The Twilight Zone*, *Alfred Hitchcock Presents* and Carter's greatest influence *Kolchak: The Night Stalker* – Carter even went so far as to describe *The X-Files* as 'a *Kolchak* for the nineties'. Carter's series revolved around the adventures of two FBI agents investigating a repository of unsolved case-files that have been marked with an X, signifying that officially the FBI does not want them investigated further, all of them having been abandoned because they involve the inexplicable or the paranormal.

In the pilot episode Agent Fox Mulder, played by David Duchovny, is assigned a new partner, Dana Scully, played by Gillian Anderson. Mulder has been working with the FBI's Violent Crimes Unit, but he has discovered the existence of the X-Files and has become obsessed with investigating the truth behind them. (It later transpires that the reason for his obsession with the paranormal is that when he was 12 his sister was abducted by what he believes were extra-terrestrials.) Much to Mulder's annoyance, Scully has been assigned to work with him because their superiors hope that, as a well-qualified scientist, she will debunk Mulder's theories, find logical explanations for the X-Files cases, and so break his obsession. However, Scully finds it impossible to find scientific explanations for the cases they investigate together, and ultimately has to accept that Mulder may be correct.

The dynamic between Mulder and Scully kept viewers hooked for nine seasons, their professional relationship providing a dramatic balance between credulity and scepticism, while their personal relationship developed from distrust to tolerance and then from friendship to romance. At the end of the final season Mulder and Scully go on the run together after Mulder escapes prison, having been falsely convicted of murder. The last episode ends in a hotel room, in an echo of a scene from the pilot episode, with Scully lying on the bed and Mulder sitting on the floor beside the bed. The difference is that this time Mulder climbs onto the bed, and *The X-Files* ends with the formerly frosty colleagues lying together in each other's arms.

INSET RIGHT *Series creator Chris Carter (l), Gillian Anderson and David Duchovny at the Golden Globe Awards (1997)* **RIGHT** *Duchovny and Anderson in the feature film* The X-Files *(1998)*

KEY DATES

1960 David William Duchovny is born on 7 August in New York, USA

1961 According to information disclosed in *The X-Files*, Fox William Mulder (played by Duchovny) is born on 13 October in Chilmark, Massachusetts, USA, and later gains a degree in Psychology from Oxford University, England

1964 According to information disclosed in *The X-Files*, Dana Katherine Scully (played by Anderson, *see 1969*) is born on 23 February in Maryland, USA, and later gains a degree in Physics from the University of Maryland and a degree in Medicine from an undisclosed medical school

1969 Gillian Leigh Anderson is born on 9 August in Chicago, Illinois

1993 *The X-Files* is first broadcast in the USA, starring Duchovny and Anderson as Mulder and Scully

1994 *The X-Files* is first broadcast in Britain. Gillian Anderson marries *X-Files* series designer Clyde Klotz (they divorce in 1997)

1998 The feature film *The X-Files* is released

STARSKY & HUTCH

1970s cop duo

The best fictional duos thrive on the differences between the two partners at least as much as the similarities between them, and Starsky and Hutch were no exception. Detective Dave Starsky, played by 1970s pin-up Paul Michael Glaser, was a wisecracking, street-talking, junk-eating maniac who carried an army-issue .45 automatic and burned rubber in a 1974 Ford Torino adorned with Starsky and Hutch's trademark go-faster flash. Detective Ken Hutchinson, played by another pin-up and later schmaltzy pop singer David Soul, was something of a contrast, and not just as the blond counterpoint to the dark-haired Starsky. He was well educated, practised yoga, ate health food, carried a slightly more subtle .357 Magnum and rode shotgun in the bright red Torino.

Their beat was one of the roughest parts of Los Angeles, which every week brought them into violent conflict with a lot of unsavoury characters – and, off-screen, into conflict with an anti-violence campaign led by the Church and the American Parent–Teacher Association. The violence was duly toned down after the first season, but there was more to Starsky and Hutch than the cases they had to solve and the means they used to solve them. The show was driven by the relationship between the two bachelor cops, who played off each other, bailed each other out of trouble, avenged each other's wrongs and comforted each other when relationships went bad – and they always did go bad, in order to prevent any romantic interest from upsetting the balance between the two central characters.

KEY DATES

1943 Paul Manfred Glaser, a.k.a. Paul Michael Glaser, is born on 25 March in Cambridge, Massachusetts, USA. David Solberg, a.k.a. David Soul, is born on 28 August in Chicago, USA

1975 The characters of Starsky and Hutch are launched in a 90-minute made-for-television movie entitled *Starsky & Hutch*, starring Glaser and Soul as Starsky and Hutch respectively

1975–79 A total of 88 one-hour episodes of *Starsky & Hutch* is made in the USA

1976–81 *Starsky & Hutch* is broadcast in Britain

2004 The feature film *Starsky & Hutch* is released, directed by Todd Phillips and starring Ben Stiller as Starsky and Owen Wilson as Hutch

ABOVE *Paul Michael Glaser (l) and David Soul arrive at the premiere of the feature film* Starsky & Hutch *(February 2004)* OPPOSITE *Paul Michael Glaser and David Soul in* Starsky & Hutch *(c.1977)*

BATMAN
ROBIN

The original dynamic duo

Bob Kane and Bill Finger

The story of Batman and Robin begins with the story of another duo, cartoonist Bob Kane and comic-book scriptwriter Bill Finger. After meeting at a party and discovering a mutual interest in comics they decided to work together, subsequently creating two cartoons, which they sold to titles owned by DC comics. DC's most successful character at the time was Superman and editor Vin Sullivan told Kane that he was looking for something similar for another DC Comics title, *Detective Comics*. The result, which Kane showed to Sullivan a few days later, was to become a 20th-century icon: Batman.

The genesis of Batman, or The Batman as he was at first known, was a visual exercise, not a story-based one. Kane began by using Superman as a blueprint, sketching his basic features of muscular physique, tights and trunks. Then he put a piece of tracing paper over the sketch and began trying out additional features and new elements of costume. He overlaid bird wings, which made him think of Leonardo da Vinci's 15th-century design for a flying machine called an ornithopter, and this in turn reminded him of the 1930 feature film *The Bat Whispers*, which featured a costumed murderer known as the Bat. His other major inspiration was the 1920 feature film *The Mask of Zorro*: 'It left a lasting impression on me. Later, when I created Batman, it gave me the dual identity. You're influenced at one point by another character, but then you embellish and bring your own identity to it.'

Kane then showed his sketches to Finger, who suggested various changes: he pointed out that bats have pointed ears, and Kane altered the Zorro-like mask to a hood incorporating the ears; he thought that the rigid wings looked clumsy, 'so I suggested he make a cape and scallop the edges so it would flow out behind him when he ran and look like bat wings'; and, inspired by newspaper-strip character the Phantom, Finger suggested that it would be more atmospheric if the eyes were blank behind the mask.

So the character that Kane and Finger presented to Sullivan was a genuinely joint effort, inspired by a number of cultural references. Batman instantly won Sullivan's approval and made his debut in May 1939, in issue no.27 of *Detective Comics*. ▶

RIGHT *Burt Ward as Robin and Adam West as Batman (1966)*

Batman and Robin

As the lone Caped Crusader, Batman was such a success that Kane soon had to take on an assistant, saying later: 'I was getting nosebleeds from working on it sixteen hours a day.' Then Kane had the idea of giving Batman a sidekick. In April 1940 issue no.38 of *Detective Comics* introduced: 'The Sensational Character Find of 1940 – Robin, the Boy Wonder.' The Dynamic Duo of Batman and Robin was born, sales of *Detective Comics* doubled, and Kane's workload increased yet further. Indeed, Batman and Robin proved so popular that DC Comics even gave them their own publication, *Batman*, devoted exclusively to their adventures.

Though delighted with the success of Batman and Robin as a duo, Kane sometimes regretted his new creation, and not just because of the increased workload: he also missed the slightly sinister character of the solitary Caped Crusader. Not so Finger, whose influences in writing the early stories included the

KEY DATES

1914 Bill Finger is born on 8 February in Denver, USA. The family soon moves to New York

1915 Bob Kane is born Robert Kahn on 24 October in New York City, USA

1934 Kane joins the Max Fleischer studio as a trainee animator, where he works briefly on *Betty Boop* cartoons among other things

1936 Kane makes his comic-book debut with *Wow*

1938 Kane and Finger sell *Rusty and his Pals* to *Adventure Comics* (a DC Comics title)

1939 Kane and Finger create Batman, who makes his debut in issue no.27 of *Detective Comics*

1940 Batman and Robin (B and R) team up for the first time, in issue no.38 of *Detective Comics*. B and R are given their own publication, *Batman*

1943 Columbia Pictures produces *Batman* as a motion picture serial in weekly instalments of approximately half an hour, shown at local cinemas. Batman is played by Lewis Wilson and Robin by Douglas Croft

1943–46 B and R are syndicated in newspapers across the USA from 25 October. Kane's reaction is: 'That's the big time'

1945 B and R make their first radio appearance, as guests on *The Adventures of Superman*, a show first aired in 1940

1949 Columbia Pictures produces *Batman and Robin* as a motion picture serial starring Robert Lowery as Batman and Douglas Croft as Robin

1950 A 15-minute pilot is recorded for a proposed radio show entitled *The Batman Mystery Club*, but the show is not commissioned

1966–68 Beginning on 12 January 1966, a total of 120 half-hour episodes of *Batman* is broadcast on television in the USA and Britain, starring Adam West as Batman and Burt Ward as Robin

1969 The feature film *Batman* is released, starring Adam West as Batman and Burt Ward as Robin

1974 Finger dies

1980s The 1960s *Batman* television series continues to be broadcast in 106 countries, with a total estimated audience of 400 million

1989 The feature film *Batman* is released, starring Michael Keaton as Batman

1992 The feature film *Batman Returns* is released, starring Michael Keaton as Batman

1995 The feature film *Batman Forever* is released, starring Val Kilmer as Batman and Chris O'Donnell as Robin

1997 The feature film *Batman & Robin* is released, starring George Clooney as Batman and Chris O'Donnell as Robin

1998 Kane dies on 3 November, in Los Angeles, California, aged 83

ABOVE *Batman and Robin take the fast route down to the Batcave (still from 1960s TV series)*

comic strip *Dick Tracy*, the character of D'Artagnan from *The Three Musketeers* and the legendary fictional detective Sherlock Holmes. 'The thing that bothered me was that Batman didn't have anyone to talk to,' Finger said years later – but with the arrival of Robin, he gained his own Dr Watson.

Art assistant Jerry Robinson remembers that Kane introduced Robin because: 'He wanted someone the younger readers could identify with more readily than this masked, mysterious figure.' But Robin was more than just a conduit for younger readers – he fundamentally altered the entire dynamic of the Batman stories. Visually, his red, yellow and green costume brightened the look of the strips and atmospherically his character brightened the mood. Another influence on Finger had been contemporary American pulp fiction, especially *The Phantom Detective* and *The Shadow*, but he said: 'The pulps were grim, lacking in humour.' The arrival of the Boy Wonder allowed Finger to change the style of the *Batman* stories: 'The puns were there; the dialogue easy, fluid and flowing. [Robin] brightened up the strip and added characterization to the main figure of Batman.'

It was the humour brought by the arrival of the Boy Wonder that enabled Batman and Robin to develop into the legendary dynamic duo, a team whose exploits would graduate from the pages of DC Comics into newspapers and onto radio, television and the big screen by the end of the millennium, earning them a joint place in 20th-century folklore.

HAVE YOU HEARD?
Most of Bill Finger's work on Batman was unaccredited, something for which Bob Kane felt guilty in later life:

'I always felt rather badly that I never gave him a by-line. He was the unsung hero.'

William Dozier, Executive Producer of *Batman* for ABC television and the 1969 feature film, said:

'ABC bought the *Batman* concept without the slightest idea what to do with it. Camp solved that problem. What we had on *Batman* was an exaggerated seriousness that became amusing to adults and provided high adventure for the youngsters.'

RIGHT *George Clooney as Batman and Chris O'Donnell as Robin in the film* Batman & Robin *(1997)*

TOM
JERRY

Cartoon cat and mouse

The original Tom and Jerry

The names Tom and Jerry were associated as a famous duo more than a century before animation partners William Hanna and Joseph Barbera *(see p174)* created their famous cartoon cat and mouse duo in 1939. The original Tom and Jerry were created by 19th-century English author Pierce Egan, who made his name in 1820 with a serialization of his *Life in London; or the Day and Night Scenes of Jerry Hawthorn and his elegant friend Corinthian Tom*. Egan's work was illustrated by eminent English caricaturist and illustrator Robert Cruikshank together with his brother George, who later went on to illustrate books by Charles Dickens and William Makepeace Thackeray *(see p75)*.

Life in London was a lively evocation of the life of the 19th-century 'man about town' and is noted for its exposition of the manners and lifestyle of the day, including the introduction to print of a number of slang phrases. The adventures of the eponymous duo proved so popular that the names Tom and Jerry came to be used in various phrases alluding to over-enthusiastic or riotous behaviour, including 'Tom and Jerry shop' for a cheap tavern and 'Tom and Jerry' for a rum and eggnog Christmas cocktail.

Hanna-Barbera's Tom and Jerry

In 1937 cartoon animators William Hanna and Joseph Barbera joined the new MGM animation studio in Hollywood where, quickly establishing a rapport, they determined to make their mark on the department by creating a cartoon with what Hanna calls 'its own distinctive hallmark'. They decided that the action should be driven by an ongoing conflict between two characters and therefore settled on the natural adversaries of cat and mouse. The result was a menacing, villainous cat named Jasper and a 'wide-eyed victim' named Jinx who first appeared in 1940 in a seven-minute cartoon entitled *Puss Gets the Boot*.

At first MGM was sceptical, telling Hanna and Barbera not to make any more Jasper and Jinx cartoons because cat and mouse duos were already old hat, but the studio's attitude changed when a major distributor asked ▶

RIGHT *Tom and Jerry*

whether there would be more of 'those delightful cat and mouse cartoons'. 'Suddenly,' writes Hanna, 'cat and mouse teams gained a new respectability. They were no longer a tired and stale format, but "a tried and true concept given an original new treatment".'

An Academy Award nomination for *Puss Gets the Boot* secured the future of Jasper and Jinx, but in a new incarnation. Hanna and Barbera decided to refine the characters: 'The villainy of the cat was softened by giving him a sleeker form and a less sinister expression. The mouse was also given a makeover and redrawn as a cuter, cuddlier, chubby-cheeked fellow rather than [a] lean little fugitive.' As well as a new image, they also chose new names. Hanna claims not to recall which of them originally suggested the names, but it seems likely to have been Barbera, who in the 1930s had worked on a series of animations about two boys named Tom and Jerry. What Hanna does remember is that 'we had to secure legal consent for them to adopt their new identities from the famous drink', suggesting that both of them may have been unaware of Egan's 19th-century Tom and Jerry.

Hanna-Barbera's Tom and Jerry became immediately and lastingly popular, not just because of their madcap exploits, but also because there was a genuine relationship between the two, something about which Hanna is both mystified and justifiably proud: 'Chemistry can occur in cartoons as surely as it does in live action movies. There is something magical about the way that characters can in their performances develop a spontaneous and often unpredictable charisma that goes beyond any calculated charm assigned to them as mere concepts.'

HAVE YOU HEARD?

Explaining the reasoning behind the choice of names for Tom and Jerry, William Hanna writes:

'We needed something that would sing in the tradition of such famous and phonetically pleasing name combinations as Lewis and Clark, or Gilbert and Sullivan, or, for that matter, Laurel and Hardy. At last we came upon something that suited both of us: Tom and Jerry.'

(See Lewis & Clark, p102; Gilbert & Sullivan, p182; Laurel & Hardy, p166)

ABOVE *William Hanna (l) and Joseph Barbera with their creations, Tom and Jerry (1990)* **RIGHT** *Tom and Jerry at a Coffee Shop near the Olympic Theatre, Strand, Midnight,* by George Cruikshank, published in Life in London (1820)

The ever-thwarted Tom always played stooge to Jerry's wit and cunning, but the chemistry went beyond this comic relationship. The real key to their success was what Hanna calls 'the poignancy beneath the hilarity', deriving from the fact that, ultimately, Tom and Jerry are not adversaries, but a team: 'There was a buddy system to their rivalry… Theirs was a private, joyful conflict. In extreme emergencies when either or both was threatened by a real villain, Tom and Jerry would team up and show a staunch loyalty to each other.'

FRED FLINTSTONE BARNEY RUBBLE

Animated Stone-Age neighbours and friends

'Yabba-dabba-doo!' Fred and Barney are one of the world's most popular cartoon duos and together they scored a number of television firsts: their series *The Flintstones* was the first animated sitcom, the first animated series to run at more than a few minutes per episode and the first animated series to feature human characters. Despite hostile reviews such as 'an inked disaster' (*New Yorker*) when it was first broadcast in 1960, the series proved immensely popular, spawning two spin-off animated series and two live-action feature films.

Fred and Barney were conceived after cartoon-creating duo William Hanna and Joseph Barbera *(see p174)* were commissioned to create a half-hour primetime animated sitcom with 'kidult' appeal. Hanna-Barbera's template for Fred and Barney was the relationship between another television duo, the characters of bus driver Ralph Kramden and his neighbour Ed Norton in the sitcom *The Honeymooners*, and when artist and storyboarder Dan Gordon drew them as Stone-Age characters dressed in animal skins, a legendary duo was born.

The Flintstones fulfilled its 'kidult' brief, combining simple cartoon jokes with the more complex relationships of live-action sitcom. Following the model of *The Honeymooner*s, Fred Flintstone (a dinosaur-powered crane operator instead of a bus driver) was a bit of a know-all, with a penchant for get-rich-quick schemes, who always managed to involve his wife and neighbours in his hair-brained schemes. And as in *The Honeymooners*, the comic foil was Fred's neighbour (Barney Rubble), a likeable character who was daft enough always to follow Fred's lead. This established format was embellished with glorious visual caveman jokes such as a baby elephant whose trunk served as a vacuum cleaner, a buzzard under the kitchen sink as a waste-disposal unit, Barney Rubble playing 'rock' music on a record deck whose needle was a Stone-Age bird with a long beak, and Fred and Wilma Flintstone's Stoneway piano. *The Flintstones* also found space for television industry in-jokes, with characters such as lawyer Perry Masonry, who never lost a case, and the involvement of actor Tony Curtis, who voiced the character of a Stone-Age actor named Stony Curtis.

KEY DATES

1960–66 A total of 166 half-hour episodes of *The Flintstones* is first broadcast in America by ABC television

1961 *The Flintstones* is first broadcast in Britain

1971 The spin-off animated series *Pebbles and Bamm Bamm* is first broadcast

1986–89 The spin-off animated series *The Flintstone Kids* is first broadcast in America by ABC

1994 The feature film *The Flintstones* is released, directed by Brian Levant and starring John Goodman as Fred Flintstone and Rick Moranis as Barney Rubble

2000 The feature film *The Flintstones in Viva Rock Vegas* is released, directed by Brian Levant and starring Mark Addy as Fred Flintstone and Stephen Baldwin as Barney Rubble

HAVE YOU HEARD?

As well as co-writing the series, William Hanna also wrote the lyrics for *The Flintstones'* theme song, which he quotes in his autobiography:

Flint-stones – Meet the Flint-stones
They're a modern Stone-Age fam-i-ly
From the – town of Bed-rock
They're a page right out of his-to-ry
Let's ride – with the family down the street
Through the – cour-te-sy of Fred's two feet
When you're – with the Flint-stones
You'll have a yabba dabba doo time
A dabba doo time
We'll have a gay – old – time!

OPPOSITE *The Flintstones (1969)*

BILL & BEN

The Flowerpot Men

The launch in 2001 of a modern version of classic children's television programme *The Flowerpot Men* sparked off much argument about which was better – the simple innocence of the black-and-white original, with its home-made puppets and visible strings, or the full-colour, high-tech, stop-frame animation of the new series. Part of the charm of the original series was the formulaic storylines: when 'the man who worked in the garden' went for his dinner, Bill and Ben would emerge from their flowerpots and, communicating in a gibberish language of flibbadobs and flobbadobs, would proceed to cause some minor mishap in the garden. Their friend Little Weed would appear, saying 'Weeeeeeeeeeeed' in her high-pitched voice, and the narrator would ask who was responsible for the mishap: 'Was it Bill or was it Ben?' Bill or Ben would own up, the gardener would be heard returning, and the flowerpot men would return to their pots until the next episode.

Like many children's classics, *The Flowerpot Men* was written for and about specific children close to the author – in this case, brothers William and Benjamin Wright (Bill and Ben) and their younger sister Phyllis (Little Weed). Hilda Wright, who loved children and later became a primary school headmistress, wrote the stories for her younger siblings and included aspects of their lives together: when one of the boys had been naughty, their mother would shout, 'Was it Bill or was it Ben?', which became a catchphrase of the show, and their 'flobbadob' language was based on the sound of the brothers breaking wind in the bath.

In 1951 Wright, who was by then married and known as Hilda Brabban, sold her three original Flowerpot Men stories to the BBC for a guinea each, and that year they were broadcast on the radio programme *Listen With Mother*. The following year *The Flowerpot Men* was made into a BBC television series by Freda Lingstrom (later Head of Children's Television), who claimed never to have heard of Brabban's stories. Lingstrom retained copyright on the characters until her death, while Brabban received not a penny in royalties. However, Brabban was not bitter, saying simply: 'My enjoyment was in the writing.'

HAVE YOU HEARD?

When Hilda Brabban heard in 1996 that there was a campaign to erect a statue of Bill and Ben in the town where she was born and where her brothers, William and Benjamin, ran a grocery shop, she said:

'The people of Castleford have a great sense of humour. It's just the sort of thing they would do.'

INSET TOP RIGHT *Grocers William and Benjamin Wright, the original Bill and Ben* **RIGHT** *Bill and Ben puppets created for the children's television series,* The Flowerpot Men *(1952)*

KEY DATES

1914 Hilda Wright is born in Castleford, England, and later educated at Castleford Grammar School and Peterborough Ladies' College

1930s Writes the stories of *Bill and Ben the Flowerpot Men* for her brothers, William and Benjamin

1938 Marries Donald Brabban

1951 Hilda Brabban sells her three original stories to the BBC for a guinea each and they are broadcast on the radio programme *Listen With Mother*. Brabban never receives any royalties

1952 *The Flowerpot Men* is made into a hugely popular television series, with some 120 fifteen-minute episodes made between 1952 and 1954

1954–70s Brabban is headmistress of Eastfield Infant School, Lincolnshire

1971 *The Flowerpot Men* is taken off the screen after a run of 19 years

2001 The BBC begins broadcasting 26 episodes of a modern version of *The Flowerpot Men*

2002 Brabban dies, aged 88

BARBIE
KEN

The story of Barbie and Ken involves three duos, two real and one fictional. The first is Ruth and Elliot Handler, who married in the 1930s and went on to raise another duo, their children Barbara and Ken. Ruth and Elliot also founded what would become a global toy company and created one of the most memorable duos in toyland – Barbie and Ken. In 1945, together with their friend Harold 'Matt' Matson, the Handlers founded a company they called Mattel, from Matt and Elliot. They initially made picture frames, but Elliot soon found a successful sideline making doll's furniture out of the wood offcuts from the frames, and when Matson sold his share of the company the Handlers decided to concentrate on manufacturing toys.

Meanwhile, Ruth had noticed that their daughter, Barbara, would play with two-dimensional paper fashion dolls (representing grown women) just as often as her three-dimensional baby dolls, and became convinced that Barbara was using the adult dolls to act out fantasies about her future. This inspired Ruth's revolutionary idea of creating the first three-dimensional children's doll to have an adult physiognomy. Mattel executives rejected the idea until Ruth created a prototype based loosely on a German novelty doll for adults named Lilli, that she had bought while travelling in Switzerland. Having convinced Mattel to back the idea, Ruth gave the doll her daughter's nickname and it was launched at the 1959 American Toy Fair in New York as 'Barbie, Teenage Fashion Model'.

Parents, critics and industry experts were sceptical that the idea would work, but Barbie proved an instant and lasting success, appearing in more than 80 guises over the next five decades and selling more than 1 billion dolls in 150 countries. Barbie was also provided with a network of friends, the first of whom appeared in 1961 as Ken, her 'handsome steady'. Barbie and Ken remained faithful to each other until 2004 when, after 43 years as Barbie's 'one and only boyfriend', Ken was unceremoniously dumped for an Australian surfer named Blaine. A spokesman for Mattel announced: 'Like other celebrity couples, [Barbie and Ken's] Hollywood romance has come to an end', but assured fans that the duo 'will remain friends'.

HAVE YOU HEARD?
Ruth Handler said that part of her rationale for creating Barbie was that: 'I believed it was important to a little girl's self-esteem to play with a doll that has breasts.' New York's *Village Voice* thought differently and, disapproving of a children's doll with womanly curves, referred to Barbie as 'Boobs in Toyland'.

ABOVE *Ruth and Elliott Handler holding Barbie and Ken on the day the creators received a Lifetime Achievement Award from* Doll Reader *magazine (12 February 1987)* **OPPOSITE** *1980s catalogue photograph of Barbie and Ken (1980s)*

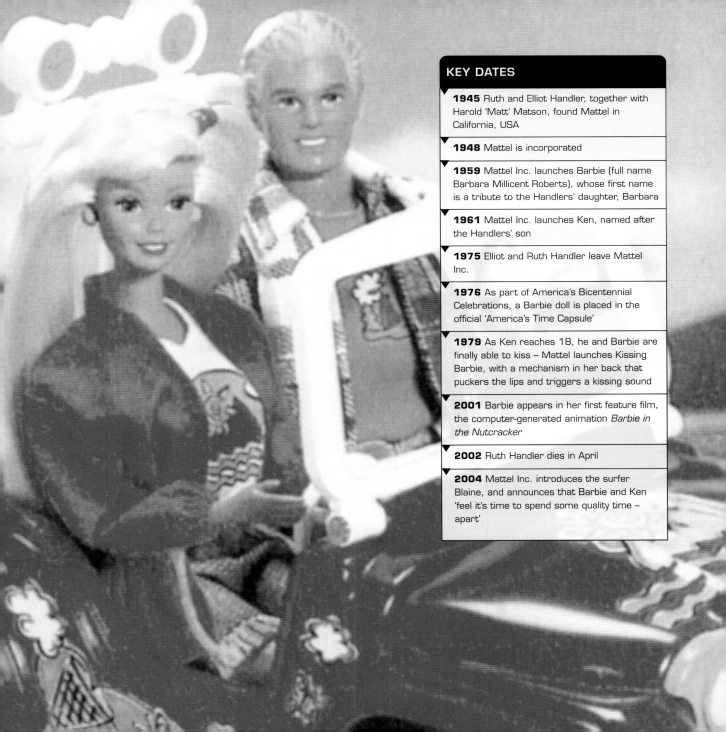

KEY DATES

1945 Ruth and Elliot Handler, together with Harold 'Matt' Matson, found Mattel in California, USA

1948 Mattel is incorporated

1959 Mattel Inc. launches Barbie (full name Barbara Millicent Roberts), whose first name is a tribute to the Handlers' daughter, Barbara

1961 Mattel Inc. launches Ken, named after the Handlers' son

1975 Elliot and Ruth Handler leave Mattel Inc.

1976 As part of America's Bicentennial Celebrations, a Barbie doll is placed in the official 'America's Time Capsule'

1979 As Ken reaches 18, he and Barbie are finally able to kiss – Mattel launches Kissing Barbie, with a mechanism in her back that puckers the lips and triggers a kissing sound

2001 Barbie appears in her first feature film, the computer-generated animation *Barbie in the Nutcracker*

2002 Ruth Handler dies in April

2004 Mattel Inc. introduces the surfer Blaine, and announces that Barbie and Ken 'feel it's time to spend some quality time – apart'

SCOTT
CHARLENE

Australian soap's most famous couple

Scott and Charlene

The characters of Scott Robinson and Charlene Bishop, played respectively by Jason Donovan and Kylie Minogue, were the saving of Australian TV soap opera *Neighbours*. The show initially proved unpopular and was dropped by Australia's Channel 7 after a run of only six months, but series creator Reg Watson managed to sell it to rival broadcaster Channel 10, for whom it became a phenomenal ratings winner. The key to Channel 10's success was a change of style that included the transformation of Scott Robinson from a character originally played by Darius Perkins into the blond surfer-boy played by Jason Donovan, and the introduction of new characters including, in April 1986, tomboy car mechanic Charlene 'Lenny' Bishop. The chemistry between actors Kylie and Jason was projected onto their characters and viewing figures rocketed.

Scott and Charlene's first kiss made front-page news in both Britain and Australia, and the press later described the characters as 'the most popular couple in Australia' and 'Britain's most idolized teenagers, loved by both young and old'. When Charlene's screen mother, Madge Bishop, refused to allow Charlene to live in sin with Scott, he took drastic action – still in his school uniform, he rolled into Charlene's workshop on his skateboard, dragged her out from under the car she was working on and asked her to marry him. The wedding was and still is one of the most popular moments in soap history, and made the cover of the Australian edition of *Time* magazine, which featured Scott and Charlene in a pink heart with the headline: 'Aussie Soaps Capture the World.'

And the reason Kylie and Jason created such successful on-screen chemistry was, of course, that they were having an off-screen romance that *Neighbours* bosses asked them to keep secret.

Kylie and Jason

The relationship between Kylie Minogue and Jason Donovan lasted only three years, but their fame as a couple has lasted much longer because of the hype surrounding their on-screen romance in *Neighbours* and their ▶

HAVE YOU HEARD?

Early in Kylie Minogue's career, one Australian critic described her appeal as her 'blinding ordinariness', while Australian disc jockey Jono Coleman played one of her songs on the radio and said: 'She's a great little actress, but I don't think she'll be giving up the day job any time soon.' Other critics called her a 'singing budgie', a 'little gonk' and a 'prancing dancing antiseptic swab'. These and many others have since had to eat their words.

Of her most recent comeback, Kylie said: 'There were always a lot of Kylie fans in the closet and now they've come out.'

ABOVE *Kylie and Jason singing their duet 'Especially For You' at the Royal Variety Performance (April 1989)* **OPPOSITE** *Jason and Kylie as Scott and Charlene (1988)*

subsequent No.1 single, the duet 'Especially For You'. They first met in 1980, when Kylie appeared as Jason's sister in the Australian television series *Skyways*, but at this stage there was no chemistry and all that Kylie remembers of her screen brother is that he was 'really chubby with a bowl haircut'.

Six years later things were different. By the time Kylie joined the cast of *Neighbours* in 1986 Jason was no longer chubby: he was tanned, muscular and cast as a teenage hearthrob. Kylie was attracted to him, and asked her friend Greg Petherick to find out whether Jason felt the same – he did, and

ABOVE *Kylie performing at the closing ceremony of the Sydney Olympics (2000)*

so began an off-screen romance that moved significantly faster than the on-screen one. The reason *Neighbours* executives asked them to keep it secret was to protect their careers and the show's ratings, which relied on Kylie and Jason's status as the objects of teenage fantasy. The secret was an open one (one record company insider said: 'It was quite bizarre, because everyone knew. They were always holding hands and kissing in the car'), but for some reason the press chose not to publicize it and the romance stayed out of the papers.

After the success of Kylie's first forays into the world of pop music, the next obvious move was a duet between her and Jason. 'Especially For You' went to UK No.1 in January 1989, by which time questions were being asked about their relationship. Kylie skilfully parried one journalist's question of whether or not they were a couple with: 'Everyone believes we are and I suppose it's quite obvious, but no one can be 100% sure, can they? If they knew all about us, where we slept, what we did together, and so on, wouldn't it spoil the mystery?' Sadly, the mystery was revealed later that year – the first confirmation many fans had that there had ever been a relationship was the news that it had broken up. Those who wanted to believe the fairy tale had to re-run their videos of *Neighbours* episode 523.

KEY DATES

1968 Kylie Ann Minogue is born on 28 May in Melbourne, Australia. Jason Sean Donovan is born on 1 June in Malvern, Australia

1980 Kylie and Jason meet for the first time when they appear together in the Australian television series *Skyways*

1985 The TV soap opera *Neighbours* (originally to have been called *One Way Street*) is first broadcast, on Australia's Channel 7. Jason takes over the role of Scott Robinson when *Neighbours* moves to Channel 10

1986 Kylie auditions for *Neighbours* and is given a

13-week contract to play Charlene Mitchell; this is soon extended to 26 weeks due to the chemistry between Charlene and Scott (C and S). Kylie and Jason begin an off-screen romance. *Neighbours* is launched in Britain

1987 Kylie becomes the youngest-ever winner of the Most Popular Actress award at Australia's Logie Awards; Jason wins Most Popular Actor and Best New Talent. Kylie releases her first single, 'The Loco-Motion', which is No.1 in Australia for seven weeks. C and S's marriage in *Neighbours* provides one of world soap's most-watched moments. Kylie begins recording with

producers Stock, Aitken & Waterman (SAW)

1988 Kylie releases her first single outside Australia, 'I Should Be So Lucky', which reaches No.1 in the UK, Australia, Germany, Finland, Hong Kong, Israel and Switzerland. Kylie and Jason film their last scenes for *Neighbours*. Jason begins recording with SAW. Kylie and Jason record the duet 'Especially For You', which reaches UK No.1 in January 1989

1989 Kylie splits with Jason

1991 Jason leaves SAW and takes the lead role in *Joseph and the Amazing Technicolour*

Dreamcoat at the London Palladium, England

1992 Jason signs for Polydor Records. Kylie breaks away from SAW, signing for independent dance label deConstruction in 1993

1998 Kylie leaves deConstruction and signs for Parlophone in 1999

2000 Kylie performs in front of a global audience of 3.7 billion people at the opening of the Sydney Olympics

2003 Kylie is named Woman of the Year at the *Elle* magazine style awards

ABOVE *Jason in the title role of* Joseph and the Amazing Technicolour Dreamcoat *(1993)*

THELMA
LOUISE

Outlaws with a difference

The hugely popular 1991 film *Thelma & Louise* turned the, traditionally male, genre of the road movie on its head – it was the women who found liberation by hitting the road in their Thunderbird convertible while the men waited back home for news of the outcome. The film also sat within another traditionally male genre, the buddy movie, with Thelma and Louise discovering new aspects of their friendship through their adventures on the road. As for the sociopolitical background foisted on the film by many critics, scriptwriter Callie Khouri said: 'This isn't the story of two women who become feminists; it's the story of two women who become outlaws. They aren't martyred wife/girlfriend. They aren't the murder victim, the psycho killer, the prostitute: they are outlaws.'

It all begins when two friends, Thelma and Louise, decide to go off for a weekend together without their husband and boyfriend. The opening sequence establishes Louise as the driving force behind the duo (literally as well as metaphorically: the car is hers) and Thelma as more sheltered, impulsive, almost childish. As they set out on their trip the film seems to be developing along the lines of a light-hearted comedy until, at their first stop, Thelma is attacked and nearly raped outside a bar, and Louise shoots and kills the attacker. The film immediately changes pace and tone. There is no turning back – Thelma and Louise are now outlaws, and instead of being on a weekend jaunt they find themselves on the run to Mexico.

Shortly afterwards the relationship between the protagonists also changes – Louise despairs when her savings (vital to finance their flight to Mexico) are stolen, and Thelma takes control. Actress Geena Davis, who played Thelma, says: 'We were best friends, but in a sense we're just discovering this relationship. Louise has never fallen apart before. It's pretty profound to see this happen. But I realize one of us has to not fall apart, so this is the scene where I start taking control.'

It is Thelma who then gets them back on the road, and it is Thelma who robs a convenience store at gunpoint to replace the stolen money. As they commit more crimes, including blowing up the truck of a leering driver and locking a highway patrolman in the boot of his car, the police move ever ▶

RIGHT *Susan Sarandon (l) as Louise and Geena Davis as Thelma*

KEY DATES

1946 Susan Abigail Tomalin (later Sarandon) is born in New York City, USA

1955 According to the police information disclosed in the script, Louise Elizabeth Sawyer (played by Sarandon) is born on 17 October

1956 According to the police information disclosed in the script, Thelma Yvonne Dickinson (played by Davis, *see 1957*) is born on 27 November

1957 Virginia 'Geena' Elizabeth Davis is born on 21 January in Wareham, Massachusetts, USA

1991 Davis and Sarandon co-star as Thelma and Louise respectively in the film *Thelma & Louise*, directed by Ridley Scott

HAVE YOU HEARD?

Answering critics of the violence in *Thelma & Louise*, scritpwriter Callie Khouri said:

'For [*Thelma & Louise*] to be labelled violent when that same summer *Terminator 2* is being lauded for being so pacifist for shooting all the cops in the knees instead of killing them, it's just mind-boggling.'

And as for being called a male-bashing 'toxic feminist' she said:

'Kiss my a**. Kiss my a**. I was raised in this society. Let them get their ideal worked out about the way women are treated in films before they start hassling me about the way men are treated.'

closer. Finally, a dozen police vehicles pursue Thelma and Louise across the desert towards the Grand Canyon. As they approach the canyon edge Thelma says: 'Let's keep going, go.' They kiss, hold hands and Louise puts her foot to the floor. The car flies out over the edge, a hubcap falling, and the image freezes and fades to white.

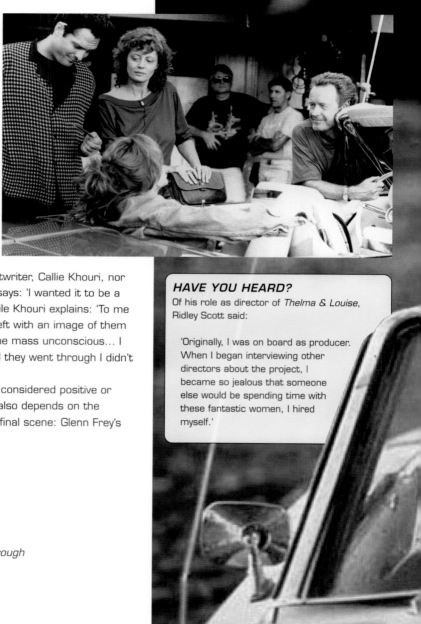

This ending provokes almost as much discussion as the rest of the film put together. The kiss and the handclasp have been interpreted both as lesbian desire and a simple affirmation of friendship, and the freeze-frame is inevitably compared with the ending of *Butch Cassidy and the Sundance Kid*, which is a valid comparison if Thelma and Louise's decision is interpreted as suicide. However, neither the scriptwriter, Callie Khouri, nor the director, Ridley Scott, sees it that way. Scott says: 'I wanted it to be a happy ending ... It's noble ... a touch of class', while Khouri explains: 'To me the ending was symbolic, not literal ... You were left with an image of them flying. They flew away, out of this world and into the mass unconscious... I loved that ending and I loved the imagery. After all they went through I didn't want anybody to be able to touch them.'

The answer to whether the ending should be considered positive or negative, and to the lesbian/friendship question, also depends on the interpretation of the music that accompanies the final scene: Glenn Frey's 'Part of Me, Part of You':

> 'Til we find a bridge across forever
> 'Til this grand illusion brings us home
> You and I will always be together
> From this day on you'll never walk alone
> You're a part of me, I'm a part of you
> Wherever we may travel, whatever we go through
> Whatever time they take away
> It cannot change the way we feel today
> So hold me close and soon you'll feel it too
> You're a part of me and I am part of you.

HAVE YOU HEARD?
Of his role as director of *Thelma & Louise*, Ridley Scott said:

'Originally, I was on board as producer. When I began interviewing other directors about the project, I became so jealous that someone else would be spending time with these fantastic women, I hired myself.'

INSET ABOVE Michael Madsen, Susan Sarandon, Geena Davis and Ridley Scott on set during the filming of Thelma & Louise **ABOVE** Davis (l) and Sarandon as Thelma and Louise

ROYAL & HISTORICAL

ANTONY & CLEOPATRA

Rome united with Egypt in more ways than one

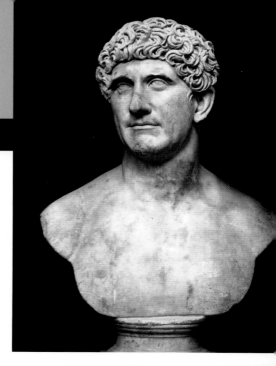

Mark Antony

The story of Antony and Cleopatra is one of history's greatest love stories, immortalized by Plutarch, Shakespeare, Dryden and Hollywood among others. Marcus Antonius, better known as Mark Antony, was a heroic figure, described thus by Plutarch: 'He had a noble presence and showed a countenance of one of a noble house. He had a goodly thick beard, a broad forehead, crook-nosed; and there appeared such a manly look in his countenance as is commonly seen in Hercules' pictures, stamped or graven in metal.'

Antony was appointed Consul to Julius Caesar in 44BC and assumed almost total control of the Roman Empire when Caesar was assassinated later that year. However, his position was challenged by Octavian (later Emperor Augustus), whom Caesar had named as his heir. The result of the ensuing power struggle was that Octavian and a politician named Lepidus ruled jointly as a triumvirate. Antony and Octavian then began consolidating the Empire by force, including the defeat of Cassius and Brutus (who had conspired against Caesar) at the Battle of Philippi. After the battle, Antony summoned Cleopatra to Tarsus to answer charges that she had aided Cassius and Brutus, but when Antony met her face to face the charges were soon forgotten.

Cleopatra

At the age of 18 Cleopatra succeeded to the throne of Egypt jointly with her younger brother, Ptolemy XIII. Three years later she was ousted by Ptolemy's guardians (he was still a minor), but was reinstated by Julius Caesar, who had arrived in Egypt in pursuit of his enemy Pompey. The young Cleopatra then became Caesar's mistress and followed him to Rome, but returned to Egypt after his assassination.

Plutarch says of her: 'Her beauty was not of that incomparable kind which instantly captivates the beholder. But the charm of her presence was irresistible, and there was an attraction in her person and her talk, together with a peculiar force of character which pervaded every word and action, and

TOP Bust of Mark Antony, housed in the Vatican Museum **ABOVE** Fragment of an Egyptian relief believed to be a portrait of Cleopatra (Ptolemaic period)

laid all who associated with her under its spell.' And Plutarch was right: with this charm and force of character she captivated the two most powerful men in the world: Julius Caesar and Mark Antony.

Antony and Cleopatra

Judging from Plutarch's description of Antony and Cleopatra's meeting there is little wonder that Antony's charges against her were so easily forgotten. Cleopatra arrived on her sumptuous royal barge, reclining under a pavilion of the finest gold fabric in an evocation of paintings of the goddess of love – a sight that, writes Plutarch, started 'a rumour in the people's mouths that the goddess Venus was come to play with the god Bacchus for the good of all Asia'.

Antony was 'so ravished with the love of Cleopatra' that he went with her to Egypt, neglecting both his wife, Fulvia, and his duty to defend the Roman Empire from the assembled armies of the Parthians. Plutarch writes that in Alexandria 'they made an order between them which they called *Amimetobin* (as much to say, "no life comparable and matchable with it"), one feasting the other by turns, and in cost exceeding all measure and reason'. After a winter of such indulgence, news from Rome broke the spell and Antony 'began … to rouse himself, as if he had been wakened out of a deep sleep and, as a man may say, coming out of a great drunkenness'.

The news was that Antony's wife, Fulvia, hoping to distract Antony's attention from Cleopatra, had attempted to depose Octavian – and that the Parthians had conquered much of Roman Asia. Antony duly drove the Parthians back and then, Fulvia having died suddenly, he made amends ▶

HAVE YOU HEARD?
In Shakespeare's *Antony and Cleopatra*, Antony's friend Enobarbus says that Antony will never leave Cleopatra because:

Age cannot wither her, nor custom stale
Her infinite variety; other women cloy
The appetites they feed, but she makes
hungry
Where most she satisfies…

ABOVE *Richard Burton as Antony and Elizabeth Taylor as Cleopatra in* Cleopatra *(1963, see p162)*

with Octavian by marrying his sister Octavia. He did not see Cleopatra again until three years later, when continuing disputes with Octavian drove him to leave Rome, abandon Octavia and return to Cleopatra in Egypt.

After six years of uneasy peace between the triumvirs, during which Octavian swung Roman public opinion against Antony's continuing self-indulgence in Egypt, Octavian declared war on Cleopatra. Antony and Cleopatra were defeated at the naval battle of Actium and then, while Cleopatra attempted to negotiate with Octavian, Antony killed himself upon hearing a false report of her death. Devastated by this (and not wanting the ignominy of being paraded through Rome by Octavian), Cleopatra then killed herself with the bite of an asp. To use the title of Dryden's play about them, Antony and Cleopatra had given up virtual control of the civilized world, and their lives, 'all for love'. In Shakespeare's version of the story, Octavian (whom Shakespeare calls Octavius) instructs his men to bury the tragic lovers side by side:

She shall be buried by her Antony.
No grave upon earth shall clip in it
A pair so famous.

94 + 95

HAVE YOU HEARD?

In Shakespeare's *Antony and Cleopatra*, Enobarbus describes how Cleopatra's first impression on Antony 'pursed up his heart':

The barge she sat in, like a burnished throne
Burned on the water: the poop was beaten gold;
Purple the sails, and so perfumèd that
The winds were love-sick with them; the oars were silver,
Which to the tune of flutes kept stroke, and made
The water which they beat to follow faster,
As amorous of their strokes. For her own person,
It beggar'd all description...

KEY DATES

c.83BC Mark Antony (Marcus Antonius) is born into a family related, on his mother's side, to Julius Caesar	**47BC** Caesar reinstates Cleopatra, who reigns jointly with her other brother, Ptolemy XIV	**42BC** Antony summons Cleopatra to Tarsus	**36BC** Cleopatra gives birth to a third child by Antony
69BC Cleopatra is born in Egypt, the daughter of Ptolemy XII Auletes	**46BC** Cleopatra gives birth to a son she claims to be Caesar's, and follows Caesar to Rome	**41BC** Antony goes with Cleopatra to Egypt	**32BC** Octavian declares war on Cleopatra
51BC Cleopatra succeeds to the throne jointly with her brother Ptolemy XIII	**44BC** Antony is appointed Consul to Caesar. Caesar is assassinated. Antony takes power, but is challenged by Caesar's nominated heir, Octavian	**40BC** Cleopatra gives birth to twins by Antony. Antony returns to Rome; his wife Fulvia dies and he heals a political rift with Octavian by marrying Octavian's sister Octavia	**31BC** Antony and Cleopatra are defeated in the naval battle of Actium
48BC Caesar departs to fight Pompey, placing Antony in charge of Italy in his absence. Cleopatra is ousted by Ptolemy. Caesar arrives in Egypt in pursuit of Pompey and falls for Cleopatra	**43BC** After military confrontation, Antony, Octavian and Lepidus, a politician, agree to rule as triumvirs	**37BC** After continuing disputes between Antony and Octavian, Antony returns to Cleopatra in Egypt	**30BC** Antony commits suicide after hearing a false report of Cleopatra's death; Cleopatra commits suicide when she hears the true report of Antony's death

OPPOSITE The Death of Cleopatra, *by Alessandro Turchi (1630s)*

MASON & DIXON

Surveyors of the Mason–Dixon line

Little is known about the early lives of the 18th-century astronomer and surveyor who gave their names to a metaphor for America's north–south divide. Charles Mason was born in England's west country and later served as an assistant astronomer at the Royal Observatory in Greenwich. Jeremiah Dixon was born in the northeast of England and surveyed much of Durham and Northumberland before being appointed by The Royal Society, with Mason, to observe the transit of Venus in 1761, which they did from South Africa.

Two years later Mason and Dixon were again sent abroad together, this time to America to settle a boundary dispute between the colonies of Maryland and Pennsylvania. Lord Baltimore and William Penn, the governors of the two colonies, agreed to abide by the findings of Mason and Dixon, who established and marked out the exact location of the eastern boundary of Maryland, separating it from Delaware, and the southern boundary of Pennsylvania, separating it from Maryland and part of West Virginia. By November 1767 Mason and Dixon had charted the southern boundary of Pennsylvania to a point 244 miles west of the Delaware River when Native American objections halted their survey just 36 miles short of completion. The boundary survey was later completed by others, but the line retained the names of the original surveyors.

The Mason–Dixon line took on a political significance prior to the American Civil War when it, together with the Ohio River and the Missouri–Arkansas boundary farther west, marked the dividing line between the free states of the north and the slave states of the south. The line is still used as a symbolic term for the cultural differences between north and south in much the same way as the metaphoric Watford Gap in England.

Dixon's name is also sometimes given as the possible origin of the terms 'Dixie' and 'Dixieland' for the southern states, although they are more often said to derive from southern banknotes that were printed in French as well as English. Thus 10-dollar bills were denoted *dix* as well as ten, and became known as 'dixes'. In 1860 songwriter Dan Emmett wrote: 'I wish I was in the land of the dixes', which became corrupted to 'the land of Dixie'.

HAVE YOU HEARD?
On the title track of Mark Knopfler's album *Sailing to Philadelphia*, James Taylor sings Knopfler's words:

> *He calls me Charlie Mason*
> *A stargazer am I*
> *It seems that I was born*
> *To chart the evening sky*
> *They'd cut me out for baking bread*
> *But I had other dreams instead*
> *The baker's boy from the west country*
> *Would join The Royal Society.*

KEY DATES

1730 Charles Mason is born in the southwest of England, the son of a baker

1733 Jeremiah Dixon is born on 27 July in Bishop Auckland, County Durham, England, the fifth of seven children

1756–60 Mason serves as an assistant astronomer at the Royal Observatory, Greenwich, London

1761 Mason and Dixon (M and D) are appointed by the Royal Observatory to observe the transit of Venus

1763–67 M and D are engaged to survey the boundary between the British colonies of Maryland and Pennsylvania

1768 M and D are admitted as corresponding members of the American Society for Promoting Useful Knowledge. M and D sail for England from New York on 9 September

1769–1780s Mason makes various observations on behalf of The Royal Society and the Board of Longitude (established to discover a means of determining longitude at sea)

1779 Dixon dies, aged 45, on 22 January in Cockfield, County Durham, England. (He should not be confused with Jeremiah Dixon FRS, 1726–82, of Leeds, England)

1780s Disappointed at the remuneration for his work for the Board of Longitude, Mason returns to America

1787 Mason dies in Philadelphia, USA

ABOVE *Map of the USA, showing the dates on which the southern states seceded from the Union prior to the US Civil War* **TOP** *The modern incarnation of the Mason–Dixon Line*

JOSEPH MONTGOLFIER
ÉTIENNE MONTGOLFIER

Pioneering aeronautical brothers

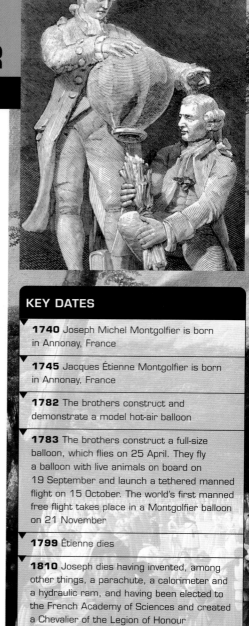

The Montgolfier brothers had the perfect combination of inquisitiveness, opportunity and ability to invent a machine that would enable mankind to leave the surface of the earth for the first time in history. Joseph and Étienne were born five years apart in Annonay, France, the sons of a wealthy paper manufacturer. From an early age, Joseph was interested in science, while his younger brother became a successful architect, the two disciplines giving them a good balance of technical understanding and design skills when they came to work together. In addition, the wealth of the family business gave them the money they needed to develop their ideas, while the nature of the business provided them with the technology to carry them out.

Inspired by watching particles of dust and ash floating upwards from the family's kitchen fire, the brothers began to investigate how heat provided lift, by placing paper bags above the fire and watching them rise even higher than the ash. They then applied their knowledge of design and paper-making to create a model hot-air balloon made from cloth-lined paper, with a cauldron of burning paper beneath the bag. They demonstrated their model in 1782 and, spurred by their success, built a full-size model, which rose to an altitude of 299m/980ft on 25 April 1783. It was a historic moment, but the brothers did not rest there; they were determined to be the first to put a human being in the air.

They repeated their demonstration in the main square of Annonay on 4 June and then on 19 September they sent a sheep, a cockerel and a duck aloft at the Palace of Versailles. The balloon rose to a height of 518m/1,700ft and flew for eight minutes, coming down nearly two miles away with the animals unharmed – a demonstration witnessed by American statesman Benjamin Franklin, who was then US Minister to Paris. Meanwhile, the Montgolfiers' rival, Jacques Charles, had been experimenting with hydrogen balloons, so the Montgolfiers wasted no time in sending a man aloft. On 15 October Françoise Pilâtre de Rozier made a tethered flight in a Montgolfier balloon to become the world's first aeronaut, and on 21 November de Rozier and the Marquis d'Arlandes made a 25-minute flight from the Château la Muette to the Butte-aux-Cailles, the first humans to make a journey by air.

INSET RIGHT *Statue of Joseph and Étienne Montgolfier (c.1883)* **RIGHT** *The Ascent of the Montgolfier Balloon at Aranjuez, by Antonio Carnicero (c.1780s)*

KEY DATES

1740 Joseph Michel Montgolfier is born in Annonay, France

1745 Jacques Étienne Montgolfier is born in Annonay, France

1782 The brothers construct and demonstrate a model hot-air balloon

1783 The brothers construct a full-size balloon, which flies on 25 April. They fly a balloon with live animals on board on 19 September and launch a tethered manned flight on 15 October. The world's first manned free flight takes place in a Montgolfier balloon on 21 November

1799 Étienne dies

1810 Joseph dies having invented, among other things, a parachute, a calorimeter and a hydraulic ram, and having been elected to the French Academy of Sciences and created a Chevalier of the Legion of Honour

LOUIS XVI & MARIE ANTOINETTE

Royal duo deposed by the French Revolution

The marriage of King Louis XVI of France and Marie Antoinette was brought about for political reasons and ended for political reasons of a different nature. In 1770, when Louis was still Dauphin (heir to the French throne), he married Marie Antoinette, the youngest daughter of the Habsburg Empress, in order to strengthen the alliance between Austria and France. When he succeeded to the French throne four years later, relations with Austria were less of a concern than the financial situation he had inherited: the treasury was empty, the state was in debt, and taxation, particularly on those who could least afford it, was at an excessive level.

Although Louis was king, much of the public outrage that eventually boiled over into revolution was aimed at Marie Antoinette, who was strongly criticized for her blatant frivolity and extravagance at a time when the people were suffering such poverty. She was also criticized for her opposition to the efforts of Anne Robert Turgot and Jacques Necker to relieve the nation's financial distress at the expense of the rich, rather than the poor – and it was her influence over Louis in such matters that was to prove their undoing. The national debt tripled between 1774 and 1787, later leading to the extreme measure of assembling the Estates-General (representing the nobility, the clergy and the bourgeoisie), which had not convened for more than 150 years, to resolve the crisis.

This assembly marked the start of the Revolution and for the next two years Louis and Marie Antoinette, hostages in their own palace, alternated between making apparent concessions to the revolutionaries and trying to escape the inevitable. Their best hope was the Comte de Mirabeau, a powerful revolutionary politician who advocated a constitutional monarchy rather than a republic, but when Mirabeau died in April 1791 that hope evaporated. Two months later, Louis and Marie Antoinette tried to escape to her native Austria, but they were caught at Varennes, their flight marking them out as traitors to the Revolution. Louis was found guilty of treason and guillotined on 21 January 1793 and, after several unsuccessful rescue attempts by her supporters, Marie Antoinette met the same fate nine months later.

RIGHT *Louis XVI and Marie Antoinette With Their Children at Versailles, 6 October 1789, by Gyula Benczur (1872)* INSET FAR RIGHT *The beheading of Marie Antoinette (c.1793)*

KEY DATES

1754 Louis is born at the Palace of Versailles, France

1755 Josèphe Jeanne Marie Antoinette is born in Vienna, Austria

1770 Louis and Marie Antoinette (L and MA) marry to strengthen the Franco–Austrian alliance

1774 Louis succeeds to the throne

1789 The Estates-General are summoned to solve a national financial crisis. The Third Estate (the bourgeoisie) declares itself the National Assembly. Louis militarily intimidates the assembly, sparking the storming of the Bastille. L and MA are taken to Paris as hostages of the revolution

1791 L and MA are arrested while trying to escape from Paris

1792 The monarchy is formally abolished and France is declared a republic. Louis faces trial for treason against the new republic

1793 Louis is guillotined on 21 January. Marie Antoinette is guillotined on 16 October

HAVE YOU HEARD?

Marie Antoinette's failure to understand the miseries of the poor are summed up by the words often attributed to her, supposedly on being told that the people had no bread: 'Let them eat cake.' However, if she did utter the words, which is disputed, she did not invent the sentiment: in a publication of 1740 (15 years before Marie Antoinette was born) Rousseau refers to a similar phrase being a well-known saying. Rousseau may have been referring to the words attributed to Marie-Thérèse (d. 1683), wife of Louis XIV, who supposedly asked: 'Why don't they eat pastry?'

LEWIS & CLARK

Explorers who led the first overland trek across America

HAVE YOU HEARD?

The *American National Biography* drily summarizes Lewis' career by saying:

'Lewis had one great triumph in what was generally an undistinguished career, but that triumph has given him a permanent place in American history.'

Lewis and Clark

The combined skills and personalities of Meriwether Lewis and William Clark, born four years apart in 18th-century Virginia, made them two of America's greatest explorers. Clark joined the army in 1789 at the age of 19 and Lewis joined five years later, serving for a time in a rifle company under Clark's command. In 1801 Lewis was appointed personal secretary to US President Thomas Jefferson, who, in 1803, commissioned him to lead an expedition to explore the wilderness of the northwestern USA – territory that had been made accessible that same year by the purchase of Louisiana from France.

Lewis recruited his friend and former superior Clark, who re-enlisted in the army in order to join the expedition. Although Jefferson had placed Lewis in charge, Lewis and Clark agreed that they would lead the expedition jointly, combining Clark's map-making skills with Lewis' expertise as a navigator and naturalist. Clark, officially a lieutenant, was addressed throughout the expedition as captain, putting him on an equal footing with Lewis.

The Lewis and Clark expedition

The so-called 'Corps of Discovery' that had been selected by Lewis and Clark departed St Louis (now in Missouri) on 14 May 1804 and travelled northwestwards up the Missouri River by flat-bottomed keelboat to winter near what is now Bismarck, North Dakota. On 7 April 1805 they continued westwards through what is now Montana and Idaho, crossing the Rockies with the help of Shoshone tribesmen and then continuing northwards along the Clearwater, Snake and Columbia Rivers to reach the Pacific coast on 18 November that year. After building Fort Clatsop and wintering there, they began the return journey on 23 March 1806, returning triumphantly to St Louis on 23 September after a journey of some 8,000 miles.

As well as the wealth of information that Lewis and Clark brought back about the flora, fauna, topography and people of the northwest, the expedition proved politically important in strengthening US claims over those of Britain to the Oregon Territory, leading in turn to the mass settlement of the Pacific northwest.

KEY DATES

1770 William Clark is born on 1 August in Caroline County, Virginia, USA

1774 Meriwether Lewis is born on 18 August near Charlottesville, Virginia, USA

1789 Clark joins the local militia and, in 1791, the army, where he is noted for his skills in intelligence and diplomacy

1794 Lewis joins the army and later serves under Clark

1796 Clerk resigns from the army

1800 Lewis is promoted Captain

1801 Lewis becomes personal secretary to US President Thomas Jefferson

1803 Jefferson secures funds from Congress to explore the northwest and puts Lewis in charge of the expedition. Lewis invites Clark to be joint leader of the expedition

1804–06 Lewis and Clark lead the first overland journey by caucasians across North America to the Pacific

1807 Lewis is appointed Governor of the territory of Upper Louisiana

1809 Lewis dies of gunshot wounds, aged 35, on the night of 10–11 October at Grinder's Stand, Tennessee, in an assumed suicide

1813 Clark is appointed Governor of Missouri Territory

1822 Clark is appointed Superintendent of Indian Affairs for St Louis after a decade encouraging the fair treatment of Native Americans and advocating assimilation rather than subjugation

1838 Clark dies on 1 September, aged 68

OPPOSITE *Montana's official state memorial to Lewis, Clark and the Shoshone guide Sacajawea who was instrumental in their success: from* Explorers by the River, *by Bob Scriver (1976)* **ABOVE** *Illustration of the Lewis and Clark Expedition, from* Journal of Voyages *by Peter Grass (1811)*

BURKE HARE

Notorious murderers in 19th-century Scotland

Robbing graves to supply corpses for medical research was not uncommon in the 19th century, but William Burke and William Hare went a step further – they actually murdered people in order to supply bodies to the anatomist Dr Robert Knox. In 1818 Burke and Hare travelled to Scotland from their native Ireland in order to work as labourers on the Union Canal, the excavation of which had begun the previous year. The canal was completed in 1822, but it was not long before Burke and Hare found an alternative means of employment.

Hare worked as a pedlar and eventually became the keeper of Log's lodging house in Tanner's Close, Edinburgh. There is no record of what Burke did immediately after completion of the canal, but it is known that he arrived at Log's lodging house in the autumn of 1827. On 29 November that year one of the lodgers, a pensioner known only as Donald, died on the premises and instead of reporting the death Burke and Hare sold the body to Knox for 7 pounds and 10 shillings.

Such a huge price led Hare to suggest enticing unknown wayfarers into the lodging house, getting them drunk and then smothering them (a method of killing that left no obvious marks). Burke and Hare subsequently killed 15 people in this way, selling the bodies to Knox for between 8 and 14 pounds. They were caught on 31 October 1828 when, instead of their usual prey, they killed a local woman named Margery Campbell (a.k.a. Margery Docherty), whose body was found on Knox's premises.

In 1828 Burke, Hare, Burke's girlfriend and Hare's wife were arrested and charged with the murders. There was not enough evidence to convict, so the Lord Advocate, Sir William Rae, offered freedom to whichever of them

KEY DATES

1790 William Hare is born in Londonderry, Ulster, Ireland, where he is said to have been 'a vagabond from birth'

1792 William Burke is born on 28 January in Orrery, County Cork, Ireland

1818 Burke and Hare (B and H) move to Scotland to work on the Union Canal

1827–28 B and H sell one body and then commit 15 murders in order to supply subjects for dissection to Dr Robert Knox. Burke is tried on 24 December on evidence supplied by Hare

1829 Burke is hanged for his crimes on 28 January. He is 37. Hare is given his freedom on 5 February

1832 The Anatomy Act, regulating the supply of bodies to medical establishments, is passed to prevent anything similar happening again

c.1860 Hare is thought to die a beggar in London, England

1930 James Bridie completes *The Anatomist*, a play based on the case of Burke, Hare and the anatomist Knox

ABOVE *William Burke (c.1850)* **TOP** *William Hare (c.1850)* **OPPOSITE** *Illustration of 'bodysnatchers' robbing graves to provide corpses for anatomy students – a widespread crime in the 18th and 19th centuries*

turned King's Evidence against the other. Hare did so, and Burke was hanged for the murders on 28 January 1829. The cases against the women were found not proven and Hare was given his freedom a few days later, after which he fled to England, where he is thought to have died in penury some 30 years later.

PAT GARRETT
BILLY THE KID

Sheriff and outlaw

Pat Garrett

Pat Garrett was born in Alabama and raised in Louisiana before working as a cowboy and buffalo hunter in Texas, where he killed fellow buffalo hunter Joe Briscoe in 1876 during an argument. He then moved to Fort Sumner, New Mexico, where, according to various versions of the story, he either made a passing acquaintance with, or became close friends with, the man he was destined to hunt down and kill: Billy the Kid.

Billy the Kid

In 1873 14-year-old Henry McCarty, later known as 'Billy the Kid', moved with his mother from New York City to New Mexico. His mother died the following year and Billy soon succumbed to the wild life of the frontier, killing a man near Fort Grant in 1877 and then going on the run. He settled in Lincoln County, New Mexico, under the alias William H. Bonney and became involved in a long-running dispute known as the Lincoln County cattle war, assembling a gang around himself and gaining notoriety as a cattle rustler and a killer.

KEY DATES

1850 Patrick Floyd Jarvis Garrett is born on 5 June in Chambers County, Alabama, USA, the son of a farmer

1859 'Billy the Kid' is born Henry McCarty, probably in New York City, USA, probably on 15 September (all his early details remain uncertain)

1873 Billy's mother marries William H. Antrim and moves to New Mexico; Billy uses his stepfather's name as an alias, as Henry Antrim and Kid Antrim

1876 Garrett kills Joe Briscoe in an argument, but is not prosecuted

1877 Billy commits a series of crimes including his first confirmed killing

1878 Billy assembles a gang and begins rustling cattle

1880 Garrett is elected sheriff of Lincoln County in November and captures Billy on 19 December

1881 Billy is convicted on

9 April and escapes on 28 April, killing two deputies. Garrett tracks down Billy for a second time and shoots him dead on 14 July

1882 Garrett's book *The Life of Billy the Kid* is published

1883–84 In the Texas Panhandle Garrett leads a law enforcement posse known as the Pat Garrett Rangers

1901 US President Roosevelt appoints Garrett Collector of Customs in El Paso, Texas

1908 On 29 February Garrett is shot in the back of the head by New Mexican rancher Wayne Brazel over a land dispute. He dies, aged 57. Brazel pleads self-defence and is acquitted of murder

1973 Release of Sam Peckinpah's film *Pat Garrett & Billy the Kid* and Bob Dylan's soundtrack album of the same name

ABOVE *Pat Garrett (c. 1890)* **OPPOSITE** *Sheriff Pat Garrett bringing Billy the Kid and his gang to jail (undated, unattributed)*

Lincoln County Road or Armageddon

In 1880 Pat Garrett campaigned to be elected sheriff of Lincoln County, saying that he would stabilize crime by capturing or killing the outlaws who had been running wild since the cattle war. On 19 December, less than a month after being elected, Garrett captured Billy the Kid. Billy was convicted and sentenced to hang, but escaped in April 1881 before the sentence could be carried out, shooting two deputies in the process. According to legend, this brought Billy's killings to 21 men, one for every year of his life, but in fact he is only confirmed as killing five men and being involved in six other gunfight killings in which it is uncertain who fired the fatal shot.

Pat Garrett went after Billy again and finally tracked him down to Fort Sumner where, on the night of 14 July, Garrett went into the bedroom of a mutual acquaintance, Pete Maxwell, to quiz him about Billy's whereabouts. Shortly afterwards Billy entered the room and asked Maxwell who was with him, whereupon Garrett, recognizing Billy's voice in the dark, shot him dead. This killing had the strange effect of reversing both men's reputations. Popular imagination remembers Billy the Kid as a Robin Hood-like folk hero rather than an unprincipled killer, while Garrett's reputation as an efficient lawman was replaced by that of treacherous former friend.

BUTCH CASSIDY
THE SUNDANCE KID

Western outlaws portrayed on film by Newman & Redford

George Roy Hill, the director of the film *Butch Cassidy and the Sundance Kid*, called his film a character study and described Butch Cassidy as 'an affable man who chose to be an outlaw the way others decided to be lawyers or dentists'. But in fact, conforming to a familiar criminal pattern, Cassidy became an outlaw not as a career choice but after an escalation from petty to serious crime.

Born Robert LeRoy Parker, the man later known as Butch Cassidy was the eldest of 13 children. He was raised in Utah where he hero-worshipped a cowhand named Mike Cassidy, who taught him a number of skills including riding, shooting, roping cattle – and rustling cattle. Cassidy and Parker left Utah in 1884 under suspicion of cattle-rustling and Parker subsequently joined a gang in Colorado led by Tom McCarty, with whom he took part in a bank robbery in 1889. Now a fully fledged outlaw, Parker adopted the alias George Cassidy, after his boyhood hero, and moved to Wyoming where he worked in a butcher's shop, thereby acquiring the nickname Butch Cassidy.

In Wyoming he formed a gang known as the Wild Bunch, a.k.a. the Hole-in-the-Wall Gang, and for a decade they carried out bank and train robberies before Cassidy escaped to South America with gang member Harry Longabaugh, a.k.a. the Sundance Kid. They bought a cattle ranch in Patagonia and initially stayed on the right side of the law, but soon returned to robbing banks and once again found themselves pursued by the authorities. Their eventual demise is not documented, but one persistent myth, recreated in Hill's film, is that they were tracked down and killed at San Vicente by a large troop of Bolivian cavalrymen. One of cinema's most memorable scenes is the finale of the film, when the action freezes on Butch and Sundance, hopelessly outnumbered by the cavalry, emerging from their hideout firing two guns each.

KEY DATES

1866 Butch Cassidy is born Robert LeRoy Parker on 13 April in Beaver, Utah, USA

1870 The Sundance Kid is born Harry Longabaugh in Phoenixville, Pennsylvania, USA

1870–84 Parker grows up idolizing cowhand Mike Cassidy

1884 Cassidy and Parker leave Utah

1885 Longabaugh leaves home, later taking his nickname from the town of Sundance

1889 Parker adopts the alias George Cassidy (after his mentor) and moves to Wyoming

1890s Cassidy forms a gang known as the Wild Bunch, a.k.a. the Hole-in-the-Wall Gang, whose crimes escalate from cattle-rustling to bank and train robberies. The Sundance Kid joins Cassidy's gang

1901 Butch Cassidy and the Sundance Kid go to South America to evade the lawmen

c.1908–11 Various reports say that Cassidy and Sundance are killed in a shoot-out with Bolivian cavalrymen, although the dates vary and there are also rumours that Cassidy survives until 1937

1969 Paul Newman and Robert Redford star as the eponymous heroes in the feature film *Butch Cassidy and the Sundance Kid*, directed by George Roy Hill

ABOVE *Newman and Redford in* Butch Cassidy and the Sundance Kid *(1969)* **OPPOSITE** *A portrait of the Wild Bunch: (seated l–r) Harry Longabaugh, a.k.a. the Sundance Kid; Ben Kilpatrick, a.k.a. Tall Texan; Robert LeRoy Parker, a.k.a. Butch Cassidy; (standing l–r) Bill Carver, and Harvey Logan, a.k.a. Kid Curry*

MARIE CURIE
PIERRE CURIE

Husband-and-wife Nobel prizewinners

Marie and Pierre Curie were a remarkable couple, both for the accomplishment of their work and for the devotion they showed to each other. Eight years Pierre's junior, Marie was born in Warsaw and brought up in impoverished circumstances after her father lost money on a bad investment and for political reasons was prevented from working. From the age of 15 she worked as a governess to earn the money to send her sister Bronia to study in Paris and then, in 1891, she followed Bronia to the Sorbonne. There she was one of just 210 women among some 9,000 students and, in an age when women were shown little respect, she shocked them all by graduating top of her class.

In spring 1894, the year after graduating, she met Pierre Curie, who was already a renowned physicist and well on the way to an important doctorate that

KEY DATES

1859 Pierre Curie is born on 15 May in Paris, France

1867 Marie is born Maria (sometimes given as Manya) Sklodowska on 7 November in Warsaw, Poland

1880 With his brother Jacques, Pierre discovers piezoelectricity

1891–93 Marie studies physics at the Sorbonne and is awarded the Polish Alexandrovich Scholarship to study mathematics

1894 Marie and Pierre (M and P) meet

1895 M and P marry. Pierre

gains a doctorate for his studies in magnetism, which include the formulation of Curie's Law and the discovery that ferromagnetic material loses its magnetism at a certain temperature, named after him as the 'Curie point'

1896 Marie discovers that radioactivity is an atomic property of uranium, and coins the term 'radioactivity'

1897 Marie gives birth to their first daughter, Irène, who will win a Nobel Prize for Chemistry in 1935

1898 M and P isolate two radioactive elements, which she names polonium and radium

1903 Marie gains her doctorate. M and P are awarded the Davy Medal of The Royal Society. Marie, Pierre and Antoine Henri Becquerel are jointly awarded the Nobel Prize for Physics. Pierre is admitted to the Académie des Sciences, but Marie is excluded because of her gender

1904 Pierre is appointed to a new chair in physics at the Sorbonne, France. Marie gives birth to their second daughter, Eve, who will become a writer and musician

1906 Pierre is killed, aged 46, on 19 April after being run

down by a horse-drawn carriage in Paris. Marie succeeds him as Professor of Physics at the Sorbonne, becoming the first woman to teach there

1910 Marie isolates pure radium

1911 Marie is awarded the Nobel Prize for Chemistry, becoming the first person to win two Nobel prizes

1934 Marie dies of leukaemia on 4 July near Sallanches, France, aged 67

ABOVE *Marie Curie and her husband Pierre hold hands with their daughter Irène in the garden of their home near Paris, France (c.1899)*

would see his name preserved for posterity in Curie's Law, relating magnetism to temperature. They were brought together by a mutual passion for science, but soon developed a mutual passion for each other, marrying just over a year later on 25 July 1895. Marie later wrote: 'I have the best husband one could dream of. I could never have imagined finding one like him...'

Pierre inspired Marie to investigate the findings of physicist Henri Becquerel, who had discovered that uranium emitted unexplained rays that he called Becquerel rays. Marie discovered that the rays were being emitted by the atoms of the uranium and that in emitting these rays the atoms changed, revolutionizing the accepted thinking that atoms were indivisible. Marie named the phenomenon radioactivity, and in 1898 she and Pierre went on to isolate two more radioactive elements that she named polonium, after her country of birth, and radium, from the Latin for 'ray'. In 1903, in recognition of these discoveries, Pierre Curie and Henri Becquerel were offered the Nobel Prize for Physics – at Pierre's insistence, Marie was belatedly included in the award.

Sadly, the partnership of Pierre and Marie was brought to an end in April 1906 when Pierre was killed in a road accident. Marie continued her work on radioactivity, winning a second Nobel Prize in 1911 for isolating pure radium, and then, during the First World War, developing X-radiology. Ultimately, the cost of her life's work was life itself: she contracted leukaemia, almost certainly from her long-term exposure to radiation, and died on 4 July 1934.

RIGHT Madame Curie and Husband, *unknown artist (c.1910)*

WILBUR WRIGHT
ORVILLE WRIGHT

Pioneers of powered flight

Growing up

Wilbur and Orville Wright were the third and fourth sons of Milton and Susan Wright, both of whom nurtured their children's natural curiosity – something that Orville later acknowledged as one of the reasons for the brothers' success, saying: 'We were lucky enough to grow up in a home environment where there was always much encouragement to children to pursue intellectual interests; to investigate whatever aroused curiosity. In a different kind of environment our curiosity might have been nipped long before it could have borne fruit.'

The two brothers made several early forays into mechanics and flight. In June 1878, when Wilbur was eleven and Orville seven, their father bought them a wind-up toy helicopter powered by rubber bands, which inspired Wilbur to experiment with building his own model helicopters. Three years later Orville began building and flying kites with such expertise that he was able to supplement his pocket money by selling kites to his school friends. Wilbur invented a treadle-operated paper-folding machine to simplify his job of folding the ▶

KEY DATES

1867 Wilbur Wright is born on 16 April in Millville, Indiana, USA, the third son of the Rev. Milton Wright, a bishop of the United Brethren Church

1871 Orville Wright is born on 19 August in Dayton, Ohio, USA

1878 Milton buys the brothers a toy helicopter that sparks their interest in flight

1881 Orville begins designing, making and flying kites

1888–89 The brothers build a printing press and Orville begins publishing *West Side News*

1892 The brothers open a bicycle repair shop

1897 The brothers begin researching flight

1900 The brothers successfully test a glider at Kill Devil Hill, Kitty Hawk, North Carolina

1903 The brothers file a patent for their flying machine

on 23 March (granted 1906). Orville successfully flies the *Wright Flyer* at Kill Devil Hill on 17 December; Wilbur flies the machine later the same day

1909 The brothers found an aircraft production company known appropriately as the Wright Company

1912 Wilbur dies of typhoid fever on 30 May, aged 45

1928 Orville lends the *Wright Flyer* to the Science Museum, London, England

1942 Orville asks the Science Museum to return the *Wright Flyer* to the USA after the war

1948 Orville dies on 30 January, aged 76. The *Wright Flyer* is deposited at the Smithsonian Institution on 17 December

ABOVE *The bike shop that Orville and Wilbur Wright used as a laboratory of flight* **OPPOSITE** Wilbur Wright in Flight at Camp d'Auvours, *by Georges Scott (1908)*

weekly issue of his father's church newspaper and in the mid-1880s the brothers worked together on their first large project: building an 2.5m/8ft lathe that they even fitted with primitive bearings made from marbles.

Their next joint project was even more ambitious – a printing press capable of turning out 1,500 copies an hour, with which Orville published a four-page weekly news-sheet called *West Side News*. The first issue was distributed as a free sample on 1 March 1889 and proved such a profitable exercise that, with Wilbur soon involved as editor, in April 1890 they decided to publish it as a daily called *The Evening Item*. This, however, was a step too far – profits decreased and four months later they suspended operations.

From bicycles to aeroplanes

Early in the new century the Wright brothers would be making news rather than publishing it, but in the meantime they went into business together, opening a bicycle repair shop in Dayton, Ohio, in December 1892. Within three years they were using machines they had designed and built themselves to manufacture bicycles with names such as the Wright Special and the Van Cleve, which they named after their Dutch ancestors.

Then, in 1897, they returned to one of their childhood interests and began to study aerodynamics and flying machines. In 1900 they built a glider and tested it at Kill Devil Hill, North Carolina, where their success in nearly 1,000 glides convinced them that powered flight was an achievable goal. They built a wind tunnel in the bicycle shop and began testing wing designs, as well as developing an aerial propeller and, realizing that conventional engines were too heavy, building their own lightweight four-cylinder engine.

On 17 December 1903 they mounted their engine on the lower wing of their best glider and Orville made the historic flight of some 36.6m/120ft in 12 seconds, since accepted as the first manned, powered, sustained and controlled flight by a heavier-than-air craft. Later the same day Wilbur flew a more convincing 260m/852ft, remaining airborne for 59 seconds. At first, reports of their achievement were met with disbelief and it wasn't until two years later, when a report was published in *Scientific American*, that it was taken seriously. By the end of the decade the Wright brothers had popularized flight around the world, making demonstration flights in numerous countries. Both survived air crashes and in the end this most dynamic of duos was split up when Wilbur died of typhoid fever in 1912. Orville continued as president of their aircraft business, the Wright Company, until 1915, when he sold his interest for more than half a million dollars in order to devote himself to research. He died on 30 January 1948.

HAVE YOU HEARD?

In 1897 Orville suggested to Wilbur that they should perhaps consider expanding the scope of the Wright Cycle Company into car manufacture. Wilbur's response was to scorn the idea:

'To try to build [a car] that would be any practical use, you'd be tackling the impossible. Why, it would be easier to build a flying machine.'

In 1917, the year that the USA joined the First World War, Orville Wright reportedly said:

'When my brother and I built and flew the first man-carrying flying machine, we thought we were introducing into the world an invention which would make further wars practically impossible – what a dream it was; what a nightmare it has become.'

ABOVE *Wilbur and Orville Wright (c. 1903–1912)*

ABOVE RIGHT *F-15 fighters fly over the Wright Brothers National Memorial at Kill Devil Hill, North Carolina (15 December 2003)*

ALCOCK & BROWN

The first men to fly nonstop across the Atlantic

On 15 June 1919 pioneer aviators John Alcock and Arthur Whitten Brown crash-landed in a peat bog in County Galway, Ireland, at the end of a journey that earned them knighthoods, a £10,000 prize from the *Daily Mail* newspaper and a place in the history books for completing the world's first nonstop transatlantic flight. Alcock, the pilot, had gained his aviator's certificate just seven years earlier and had then worked as a racing pilot for the Sunbeam car company before joining the Royal Naval Air Service (later part of the Royal Air Force) at the outbreak of the First World War. In March

ABOVE *Alcock and Brown leave Newfoundland on their unprecedented nonstop transatlantic flight (14 June 1919)*

1919 he left the RAF with the specific aim of trying to fly across the Atlantic and approached Vickers aircraft manufacturers who agreed to back his attempt. Alcock invited Brown, a former lieutenant in the Royal Flying Corps, to be his navigator.

On 14 June 1919 the duo left Newfoundland, Canada, in a converted Vickers-Vimy bomber so heavily laden with fuel that it was barely able to take off. The biplane was specially fitted with long-range fuel tanks for the journey, but there were no luxuries for the aviators, who flew in an open cockpit for 16 hours and 27 minutes through sleet and fog, sustained only by supplies more suitable for a country picnic than a pioneering flight: coffee, beer, sandwiches and chocolate. The airspeed indicator was out of action (probably frozen) and Brown had to navigate by dead reckoning, but despite this difficulty they successfully reached Clifden, Ireland, and attempted to land in what looked like a suitable field, but which turned out to be a peat bog. The plane nearly overturned in the soft ground, damaging the nose and one wing, but both men escaped unhurt to claim the prize and their place in history. Sadly, Alcock did not live long to bask in his glory – he was killed when he sustained a fractured skull in a similarly rough landing in Normandy, France, just six months later.

HAVE YOU HEARD?
John Alcock was very phlegmatic about his and Brown's historic achievement, describing the 16-hour flight through appalling weather as 'a terrible journey'.

KEY DATES

1886 Arthur Whitten Brown is born on 23 July in Glasgow, Scotland, of American parents. He is later apprenticed to the British Westinghouse Electric and Manufacturing Co. in Manchester, England

1892 John William Alcock is born on 6 November in Manchester, England

1909 Alcock is apprenticed to the Empress motor works, Manchester

1910 Alcock moves to Brooklands to act as mechanic to French pilot Michel Ducrocq

1912 Alcock gains his aviator's certificate and becomes a racing pilot

1914 Alcock joins the Royal Naval Air Service (RNAS). Brown joins the University and Public Schools Battalion, later transferring to the Manchester Regiment and then to the Royal Flying Corps (RFC). (The RNAS and RFC amalgamate in 1918 to form the Royal Air Force)

1915 During the First World War Brown is shot down over Germany in November, permanently damaging his leg, and is taken prisoner

1917 Alcock earns the Distinguished Service Cross on 30 September for engaging three enemy planes and downing two of them. Later that day he is captured by the Turks after ditching in the sea when an engine fails during an abortive bombing raid on Istanbul. Brown is repatriated, having spent two years as a POW

1918 Brown leaves the RAF and gains his private pilot's licence

1919 Alcock leaves the RAF in March. Alcock and Brown make the first nonstop transatlantic flight on 14–15 June. Alcock is killed, aged 27, in a plane crash at Côte d'Evrard, near Rouen, France, on 18 December

1939–45 Brown rejoins the RAF for the duration of the Second World War and trains pilots in navigation and engineering

1948 Brown dies, aged 62, on 4 October in Swansea, Wales, after an accidental overdose of barbiturates

ABOVE *Alcock (l) and Brown having breakfast after their historic flight (June 1919)*

BONNIE & CLYDE

American outlaws of the Great Depression

Clyde Barrow

As one of eight children of a tenant farmer during the Depression, Clyde Barrow grew up in extreme poverty. He left school at 16 and immediately followed his brother 'Buck' into petty crime, being arrested for the first time less than a year later for stealing turkeys. Clyde and Buck then began stealing cars and robbing filling stations and cafés, and Clyde received a suspended sentence in 1929. The following year he met the woman with whom he would secure his place in American folklore – Bonnie Parker.

Bonnie Parker

Like Clyde, Bonnie had suffered a deprived upbringing (her father died when she was four), but by contrast she had been a diligent and successful student, winning prizes for essay-writing and spelling. However, the disillusionment brought on by an unsuitable marriage to Roy Thornton when she was 16 was summed up in a diary entry that recorded that she was 'bored crapless'. Both the disillusionment and boredom were to find their outlet in Clyde Barrow and killing.

KEY DATES

1909 Clyde Chestnut Barrow is born on 24 March in Teleco, Texas, USA

1910 Bonnie Parker is born on 1 October in Rowena, Texas

1921 The Barrow family moves to Dallas

1926 Clyde is arrested with his brother 'Buck' for stealing turkeys. Bonnie marries Roy Thornton

1929 Clyde receives a suspended sentence for car theft. Bonnie separates from Thornton when he receives a five-year prison sentence for robbery

1930 In January Bonnie and Clyde (B and C) meet for the first time. In March Clyde is imprisoned for robbery. Bonnie helps him escape, but he is later recaptured

1932 Clyde is paroled, but crashes a car in a police chase just a month later. He escapes, but Bonnie is caught and spends two months in jail during which time Clyde kills three people. B and C and their gang begin a crime and killing spree

1933 B and C kill two policemen during a raid on their apartment

1934 B and C are shot dead at a police roadblock on 23 May. She is 23, he is 25

1967 The film *Bonnie and Clyde* is released, starring Warren Beatty and Faye Dunaway

ABOVE *Bullet holes riddle the car in which Bonnie and Clyde were shot near Arcadia, Louisiana, by six police officers*

Bonnie and Clyde

Bonnie and Clyde met in January 1930. Two months later Clyde was jailed for robbery, but escaped using a pistol smuggled into the prison by Bonnie. He was soon recaptured and, after being released on bail two years later, he made a prophetic vow: 'I'll die before I ever go back into a place like that.' He did not mean that he was going to give up crime, just that he didn't intend being caught, and immediately began a series of armed robberies during which he killed three men including a sheriff and his deputy. After serving a two-month prison sentence of her own, Bonnie joined Clyde in his crimes and together they led a gang in a series of kidnappings, armed robberies and killings.

On 13 April 1933, acting on a tip-off, police raided Bonnie and Clyde's hideout, but the gang escaped after shooting two officers. As the crimes continued so did the attempts to stop the gang, and in July 1933 they were trapped in a deserted amusement park by a force of some 100 police officers, National Guardsmen and vigilantes. Buck was killed, but somehow Bonnie, Clyde and several other gang members managed to escape yet again.

Bonnie and Clyde eventually met their nemesis in Texas Ranger Frank Hamer. On 23 May 1934, acting on information from a gang member hoping to escape prosecution, Hamer set up a roadblock in Louisiana. When Bonnie and Clyde arrived, Hamer asked no questions – he and his men fired 167 rounds into their stolen car, killing them instantly and fulfilling the predictions expressed in Bonnie's poem *The Story of Suicide Sal*.

HAVE YOU HEARD?
In Bonnie's poem *The Story of Suicide Sal*, found during a police raid on their apartment, she wrote:

You have heard the story of Jesse James,
Of how he lived and died.
If you are still in need of something to read,
Here's the story of Bonnie and Clyde...

Some day they will go down together,
And they will bury them side by side.
To a few it means grief,
To the law it's relief,
But it's death to Bonnie and Clyde.

ABOVE *Bonnie, Clyde and shotgun (1932)*

EDWARD & MRS SIMPSON

Adulterous lovers of Arthurian legend

Edward

As Prince of Wales, Edward proved himself popular with ordinary people both in Britain and across the Empire, in contrast with his father, the austere George V, who reportedly once said: 'I don't like abroad, I've been there.' However, Edward proved unpopular with parliament because of his penchant for married women and because of several overtly political interventions in public affairs, and it was the combination of these two character traits that would cost him his throne. Edward's most infamous political intervention was the donation of £10 to a miners' relief fund set up during the General Strike of 1926, with a covering letter stating that he had made the donation because 'it would be an unsatisfactory end to any dispute that one side should have to give in on account of the sufferings of their dependants'. This and similarly outspoken comments about unemployment and poor housing demonstrated a sense of social fairness well ahead of his time, but they were seen as attacks on Conservative economic policy, alienating Edward from the very politicians whose support he would need during the Abdication Crisis.

Mrs Simpson

Wallis Simpson was born in Pennsylvania, USA, two years after Edward. In 1916, at the age of 20, she married a US Navy pilot named Earl Winfield Spencer, but it was not a happy marriage and Spencer's behaviour led to intermittent separation from 1920 and then divorce in 1927. Early the following year Wallis met Ernest Simpson, an English businessman living in Baltimore, who was himself going through a divorce. Just months later they moved to London and married on 21 July 1928 at the Chelsea Registry Office. However, London did not prove the best recipe for a happy marriage, for it was there that Wallis met Prince Edward, the heir to the British throne.

Edward and Mrs Simpson

On 10 January 1931 Thelma, Lady Furness, held a party to which she invited her lover, Prince Edward, and her friend, Wallis Simpson. Edward and Wallis did not meet again until six months later when, at the suggestion of ▶

HAVE YOU HEARD?
Edward had an affinity with America and even spoke with a slight American accent. He once said: 'The thing that impresses me most about America is the way the parents obey their children.'

RIGHT *The Duke and Duchess of Windsor surrounded by press photographers at their temporary home in Sussex (13 September 1939)*

Lady Furness, the Simpsons were presented at the court of George V and Queen Mary. After this second meeting a strong bond quickly developed, with the Simpsons frequently visiting Edward's home near Windsor, and Edward visiting their flat in London. In March 1933 Wallis visited Edward without her husband for the first time, and three months later Edward hosted a birthday party for her at Quaglino's restaurant. Early the following year Lady Furness went to America, telling Wallis to 'look after' the Prince – and look after him she did, with the result that Edward and Mrs Simpson were soon inseparable.

The Abdication Crisis

The love affair caused consternation in the government, particularly when George V died in January 1936 and Edward acceded to the throne as King Edward VIII. When Edward announced his intention to marry Wallis, their affair became a constitutional matter. Ernest Simpson acquiesced, agreeing to a divorce, but Prime Minister Stanley Baldwin was not so easily won over.

> **HAVE YOU HEARD?**
>
> In Edward's abdication broadcast he said:
>
> 'At long last I am able to say a few words of my own… I want you to understand that in making up my mind I did not forget the country and the Empire, which, as Prince of Wales and lately as King, I have tried for 25 years to serve. But you must believe me when I tell you that I have found it impossible to carry the heavy burden of responsibility and to discharge my duties as King as I would wish to do without the help and support of the woman I love… God bless you all. God save the King.'

ABOVE *The Duke and Duchess of Windsor dancing at the Waldorf Astoria, Park Avenue, New York (1953)*

Edward suggested a 'morganatic' marriage (which meant that he would remain king, but Wallis would not become queen and any children would have no right of succession), but parliament ruled this out as unconstitutional. Both Church and parliament were worried about the morality as well as the constitutional implications of the King marrying a divorcee, and ultimately Baldwin told Edward that he must choose between his love and his crown.

A new life in France

Edward chose love, signing the Instrument of Abdication on 10 December, to take effect the following day, after which he set sail for France and a life in exile with his beloved Wallis. On 3 June 1937 they were married at Château de Cande, near Tours, France, in a dual ceremony, one conducted by a Church of England vicar and the other, in compliance with French civil law, by the Mayor of Monts, who welcomed them to a nation 'which has always been sensitive to the charm of chivalrous unselfishness and bold gestures prompted by the dictates of the heart'.

The lovers' faith in each other was well placed, and they enjoyed 35 years of marriage before Edward died in 1972. They are buried side by side in the royal mausoleum at Frogmore, close to Windsor Castle.

KEY DATES

1894 Edward is born on 23 June at White Lodge, Richmond, Surrey, England, the eldest son of King George V and Queen Mary

1896 Bessie Wallis Warfield is born on 19 June in Blue Ridge Summit, Pennsylvania, USA

1901 Wallis's father dies when she is five years old

1911 Edward is invested as Prince of Wales

1916 Wallis marries US Navy pilot Earl Winfield Spencer

1927 Wallis and Spencer divorce on 10 December

1928 Wallis marries English businessman Ernest Simpson

1931 Wallis and Edward (W and E) meet for the first time

1936 Edward accedes to the throne on 20 January. Wallis and Ernest are granted a decree nisi on 27 October. Edward abdicates on 11 December

1937 Edward is created Duke of Windsor and lives the rest of his life outside Britain. W and E marry on 3 June near Tours, France. On 22 October W and E create fresh controversy by having a cordial meeting with Hitler

1940–45 Edward serves as Governor of the Bahamas

1972 Edward dies on 28 May in Paris, aged 77

1986 Wallis dies on 24 April in Paris, aged 91

ABOVE *The Duke and Duchess of Windsor sitting in the drawing room of their home in Paris (c.1964)*

CRICK & WATSON

Co-discoverers of the structure of DNA

Francis Crick and James Watson were born 12 years apart on opposite sides of the Atlantic. Their common interest in genetics brought them together and, soon after their paths crossed in 1951, they made one of the most profound scientific discoveries of the 20th century. Crick was born near Northampton, England, and in 1949 joined a research team at the Laboratory of Molecular Biology, Cambridge, where he began investigating the structure of proteins. Watson was born in Chicago, USA, and, after gaining a PhD from Indiana University, began working at the Cavendish Laboratory, Cambridge, where he met Crick.

From 1951 to 1953 Crick and Watson collaborated in trying to explain the puzzling discoveries that scientists had made regarding the nature of deoxyribonucleic acid (DNA). It was already known that the genetic information to create any living organism must be passed from one cell to another as a physical entity, and there was evidence that DNA was almost certainly that entity. However, the components of DNA seemed too simple to store and pass on such a vast amount of information. British scientists Rosalind Franklin and Maurice Wilkins were already working on DNA, and they produced X-ray photographs of DNA crystals suggesting that the molecules could be helix-shaped, which would explain how something made of such simple components could perform so complex a task. Wilkins showed the photographs to Watson, who became certain that this hypothesis was correct.

Crick and Watson then began to work intensively on the idea that DNA was a helix, and on 7 March 1953 they published their model, showing that idea to be half right – DNA was in fact a double helix, with two intertwined strands of genetic code. The way in which information was passed from cell to cell was surprisingly simple: the two strands of the helix would peel apart and act as templates to build exact copies of themselves, thus creating new DNA with the same genetic information. In 1962 Crick, Watson and Wilkins were jointly awarded the Nobel Prize for Physiology or Medicine in recognition of the importance of a discovery that gave humanity the potential to conquer hereditary diseases; sadly, Franklin had died in 1958 and her vital contribution was not officially recognized.

HAVE YOU HEARD?
On hearing the news of Crick's death, Watson said:

'I will always remember Francis for his extraordinarily focussed intelligence ... He treated me as though I were a member of his family. Being with him for two years in a small room in Cambridge was truly a privilege. I always looked forward to being with him and speaking to him, up until the moment of his death. He will be sorely missed.'

INSET RIGHT *A double helix, echoing the structure of DNA* **RIGHT** *Crick (l) and Watson at a Molecular Biology Symposium (September 1983)*

KEY DATES

1916 Francis Harry Compton Crick is born on 8 June near Northampton, England, and later studies at University College London, and Cambridge University

1928 James Dewey Watson is born on 6 April in Chicago, USA, and later studies at Chicago University and Indiana University

1949 Crick joins the Medical Research Council team at the Laboratory of Molecular Biology, Cambridge

1951–53 Watson works at the Cavendish Laboratory, Cambridge. Crick and Watson (C and W) collaborate on discovering the structure of DNA

1953 C and W publish their model of a double-helical DNA molecule

1959 Crick is elected a Fellow of The Royal Society

1961 Watson is appointed Professor of Biology at Harvard

University, where he has taught since 1956

1962 Crick, Watson and Maurice Wilkins are jointly awarded the Nobel Prize for Physiology or Medicine

1977 Crick is appointed Kieckhefer Professor at the Salk Institute, California, USA

1989–92 Watson serves as director of America's National Center for Human Genome Research

1991 Crick is awarded the Order of Merit

1994 Crick is appointed President of the Salk Institute. Watson is appointed President of the Cold Spring Harbor Laboratory in New York, where he has been a director since 1968

2004 Crick dies on 28 July in San Diego, USA, at the age of 88

HILLARY & TENZING

The first men known to have climbed Mount Everest

Tenzing Norgay

By the time of the famous 1953 expedition, Tenzing (or Tensing) Norgay, nicknamed 'Tiger' Tenzing, was an experienced veteran of Everest climbs. Born into a caste of mountain people living high in the Himalayas, he made his first climb as a sherpa (porter) at the age of 21, on the British Everest Expedition of 1935. Three years later he reached 7,000m/23,000ft with another British expedition, and in 1952 he reached 8,600m/28,215ft, less than 300m/1,000ft from the summit, with a Swiss expedition.

Edmund Hillary

New Zealander Edmund Hillary was an apiarist (beekeeper) by profession as well as a keen climber, learning his hobby in the Southern Alps of New Zealand. In 1951 he was climbing in the Himalayas with fellow New Zealander George Lowe when they so impressed the British Expedition that two years later they were both invited to join eight English climbers for the British Expedition of 1953.

The conquest of Everest

Expedition leader Colonel John Hunt decided to launch two assaults on the summit, one with lightweight oxygen equipment and, if necessary, a second with heavier, but longer-lasting, equipment. Lack of oxygen drove back Tom Bourdillon and Charles Evans in the first attempt and, at dawn on 29 May, Hillary and Norgay set out on the second. Hours later, at 11:30, they became the first men to stand on top of the world's highest peak. Together they spent 15 minutes on the roof of the world, each leaving a token of thanks reflecting their differing backgrounds: Norgay buried sweets and biscuits as an offering to the gods of the mountain, while Hillary left a crucifix given to him by Hunt.

British newspaper *The Evening News* reported on 2 June that Hillary's mother was overjoyed when she was told the news: "'How wonderful,' she said. 'To think of our Edward up there.' Then she shouted up the stairs to her husband: 'Edward is up the top.'" [sic]

KEY DATES

1914 Tenzing Norgay is born on 15 May, probably in Tshechu, Tibet. (There is much controversy as to whether he was born in Tibet, Nepal or India)

1919 Edmund Percival Hillary is born on 20 July in Auckland, New Zealand

1924 George Mallory and Andrew Irvine climb above 8,500m/28,000ft on Everest, but fail to return. Their fate is a mystery, raising the possibility that they may have been the first to conquer Everest and died on the descent

1953 Hillary and Norgay meet as co-members of the British Everest Expedition. They reach the summit of Everest together on 29 May. Hillary is knighted and Norgay is awarded the George Medal

1954 Norgay is appointed head of the Institute of Mountaineering in Darjeeling, India, and president of the Sherpa Association

1957–58 Hillary reaches the South Pole as deputy leader of the British Commonwealth Antarctic Expedition

1985 Hillary and his son Peter are members of an expedition to the North Pole

1985–89 Hillary serves as New Zealand High Commissioner to India, raising funds in NZ to build hospitals and schools in the Himalayas

1986 Norgay dies on 9 May, aged 71

ABOVE *Aerial view of Mount Everest* **OPPOSITE** *Hillary and Norgay enjoying a snack on their return from the summit*

GRACE KELLY
PRINCE RAINIER OF MONACO

Crown Prince marries Hollywood star

Prince Rainier

Rainier Grimaldi was born to be the 26th ruling prince of the House of Grimaldi, a noble Genoese house whose first sons have been lords of the tiny principality of Monaco since 1297. Monaco is smaller than many cities, and is ruled by a constitutional monarchy under the protection of France. In 1918 it was agreed that, if a ruling prince dies without a male heir, Monaco will be incorporated as part of France. Rainier may have felt under pressure to find a suitable bride and produce an heir, but when he did marry it was not for political expediency – he had fallen in love with Hollywood's most glamorous star.

Grace Kelly

Grace Kelly was born into the family of an Irish–American self-made millionaire and went to a convent school before disappointing her family's wishes by pursuing an acting career. She studied at the American Academy of Dramatic Arts and made several stage appearances in New York before making her Hollywood debut in the 1951 film *Fourteen Hours*. Her first visit to Monaco was in 1954 to film Alfred Hitchcock's *To Catch A Thief*, which included a car chase through the principality.

Rainier and Kelly

Prince Rainier and Grace Kelly met in 1955 while she was promoting *To Catch A Thief* at the Cannes Film Festival. They were immediately captivated by each other, announcing their engagement less than a year later, on 5 January 1956, and marrying on 19 April in a televised ceremony that was attended by more than 1,200 guests, including dignitaries from 25 nations.

Becoming Her Serene Highness Princess Grace meant, at Rainier's insistence, that Kelly had to give up her

> **HAVE YOU HEARD?**
>
> When Princess Grace met Lady Diana Spencer, soon to be Princess of Wales, on Diana's first official royal engagement, Diana confided that the Prince of Wales had upset her by saying that her dress was unsuitable for a member of the royal family. Princess Grace replied from experience:
>
> 'Don't worry, it will get a lot worse.'

ABOVE *Grace Kelly and Prince Rainier at the Monte Carlo Ball (1956)*

Hollywood crown and she duly announced her retirement from the film industry shortly after the wedding. However, her film career tragically came back to haunt her in 1982 when, driving along the same stretch of road where she had filmed the car chase in *To Catch a Thief*, she suffered a stroke and lost control of her car, dying the following evening and bringing to an end the 26-year fairytale marriage to her prince.

ABOVE *Princess Grace and Prince Rainier wave from the palace window after their wedding (19 April 1956)*

CARL BERNSTEIN & BOB WOODWARD

Journalists who exposed the Watergate scandal

Carl Bernstein and Bob Woodward's book *All the President's Men* begins: 'June 17, 1972. Nine o'clock Saturday morning. Early for the telephone. Woodward fumbled for the receiver and snapped awake. The city editor of the *Washington Post* was on the line. Five men had been arrested earlier that morning in a burglary at Democratic headquarters, carrying photographic equipment and electronic gear. Could he come in?' Bored at the prospect of yet another break-in story, Woodward nonetheless went in. He had been working for the *Washington Post* for just nine months and was keen to make an impression. The story on which he was about to embark would make an impression not only on his editor but also on the entire world, for this was the start of the Watergate scandal that toppled Richard Nixon's presidency.

Carl Bernstein, a year younger but a more experienced journalist, was assigned to cover the story with Woodward. Together they managed to link the burglary to the White House, specifically to the Committee to Re-elect the President, but most agencies dropped their story in the absence of any evidence to prove the direct involvement of Nixon or his aides in either the burglary or the subsequent cover-up. Nixon was re-elected with a landslide victory, but Bernstein and Woodward did not let go. Pressure from the White House for the *Washington Post* to drop the story only increased their determination, and they painstakingly uncovered enough evidence of corruption, dishonesty, abuse of power and attempts to obstruct justice to ensure that Nixon would almost certainly be convicted if impeached. Rather than let this happen, Nixon agreed in August 1974 to resign in exchange for a pardon for any offences committed while in office.

The Watergate story was a triumph of investigative journalism that won every major journalistic award for Bernstein and Woodward, a Pulitzer Prize for the *Washington Post* and demonstrated the power of the press to root out corruption. A quarter of a century later, lamenting the fact that instead of writing 'the real stories begging to be written', too many modern journalists take the easy option, Bernstein said: 'The media are more powerful than our government institutions, but we are squandering that power.'

HAVE YOU HEARD?

In their book *All the President's Men*, Bernstein and Woodward summarize their first impressions of each other before they began working together:

'Bernstein looked like one of those counterculture journalists that Woodward despised. Bernstein thought that Woodward's rapid rise at the *Post* had less to do with his ability than his Establishment credentials.

They had never worked on a story together. Bernstein was 28, Woodward 29.'

INSET RIGHT *Dustin Hoffman and Robert Redford as Bernstein and Woodward in* All The President's Men *(1976)* **RIGHT** *Woodward (l) and Bernstein at the* Washington Post *(29 April 1973)*

KEY DATES

1943 Robert Woodward is born on 26 March in Geneva, Illinois, USA

1944 Carl Bernstein is born on 14 February in Washington, DC, USA

1950 Bernstein drops out of school and then becomes a copy boy at the *Washington Star*

1960s Woodward graduates from Yale and then serves in the US Navy

1966–77 Bernstein works at the *Washington Post*

1971 Woodward begins working full-time for the *Washington Post*

1972 Bernstein and Woodward (B and W) expose the Watergate cover-up

1973 The *Washington Post* wins the Pulitzer Prize for public service as a result of B and W's work, while B and W themselves win nearly every major award for journalism

1974 As a result of B and W's investigation of the Watergate scandal, President Nixon resigns. B and W write the bestseller *All The President's Men*, which is based on their investigation

1976 The feature film *All The President's Men* is released, directed by Alan J. Pakula and starring Dustin Hoffman as Bernstein and Robert Redford as Woodward. B and W publish *The Final Days*, an account of Nixon's last days in office

1976–present Bernstein works as a senior correspondent for ABC-TV and *Time* magazine and as a freelance writer, consultant, lecturer/speaker and gossip-column habitué. Woodward publishes several bestselling books exposing the workings of American institutions, and continues to work for the *Washington Post*

CHARLES & DIANA

The fairy-tale romance with an unhappy ending

It has often been said that Lady Diana Spencer had more royal blood in her veins than her husband, Charles, Prince of Wales. Charles' royal lineage can be traced back to the Hanoverian king George I, but the Spencer family's royal connections go back 60 years further, to the reign of the Stuart king Charles II. Three Spencer women were mistresses of Charles II, another was a mistress of James II and a fifth was a mistress of George IV, four of these liaisons resulting in illegitimate Stuart–Spencer children. Thus, as Lady Colin Campbell points out in her biography of Diana, Charles and Diana's children were the first royals to unite the bloodlines of the houses of Stuart and Hanover, 'the old and new Royal Families'.

Diana's elder sisters had played with Prince Charles and his sister Princess Anne as children, when Diana was still a baby, but the first time Diana and Charles met as adults was in November 1977. Lady Sarah Spencer, Diana's sister, was having a lukewarm romance with Charles and invited him to the family estate at Althorp for a shooting party. One morning, while they were all standing in Nobottle Field preparing for the day's shoot, Sarah introduced her royal boyfriend to the 16-year-old Diana and, according to one of Sarah's friends: 'Sarah [later] said that they clicked in that ploughed field, that Mr Right had met his Miss Right.' Sarah Spencer's recollection of Charles and Diana's first meeting obviously fitted the fairy-tale requirement of love at first sight, but her unnamed friend went on to say: 'With hindsight, one could stretch a point and make it so, but that's not the way it was.'

In 1979, two years after this highly significant or totally inconsequential meeting, Diana stayed with the Royal Family at Sandringham and Balmoral, but this was because of her family connections rather than because of any romantic attachment on Charles' part. Friends and acquaintances report that Charles took little notice of Diana, $12\frac{1}{2}$ years his junior, preferring the company of 'witty and sophisticated women of the world'. Diana, however, made no secret of her ambitions when she described her career plans to a friend saying: 'It would be nice if I could be a dancer – or The Princess of Wales.'

In the summer of 1980 Diana took a step closer to realizing her ambition. Charles had just ended a romance with Anna Wallace ▶

HAVE YOU HEARD?

At the press conference held immediately after the announcement of their engagement, Charles and Diana were asked whether they were in love. Diana blushingly replied: 'Of course.' Charles added: 'Whatever love means.'

When their marriage was going well, Charles wrote to a friend:

'We've had such a lovely Christmas, the two of us. It has been extraordinarily happy and cosy being able to share it together. Next year will be even nicer with a small one to join us as well.'

Later, his sentiments changed:

'How awful incompatibility is, and how dreadfully destructive it can be for the players in this extraordinary drama. It has all the ingredients of a Greek tragedy. I never thought it would end up like this. How could I have got it all so wrong?'

ABOVE *The fairy-tale kiss on the balcony of Buckingham Palace after the wedding ceremony (29 July 1981)* **OPPOSITE** *The fairy-tale turns sour: Diana and Charles display a distinct lack of interest in each other during a visit to Cameroon (22 March 1990)*

– significantly, the death knell for that relationship had been a ball at which Charles had ignored Anna to spend much of the evening dancing with Camilla Parker Bowles. Weeks later Diana was invited to accompany her sister Jane to Balmoral where, according to one unnamed courtier, Diana 'played Charles like Nigel Kennedy plays the violin'. Finally, on another visit to Balmoral that September, Diana succeeded in attracting the romantic attention of Charles; remembering that development, one member of Charles' household recalls: 'The first time he kissed her his fate was sealed.' So was Diana's.

The Sun newspaper broke the news of Charles' latest romance on 8 September 1980, after which the couple's courtship, engagement, wedding, marriage and divorce were played out in the public gaze. On 6 February 1981 Charles proposed to Diana, at 11:00 on 24 February the Palace officially announced the engagement, and on 29 July the 'wedding of the century' took place at St Paul's Cathedral. Scores of international royalty and dignitaries assembled in St Paul's, some half a million people packed themselves into Hyde Park, and millions more watched on television around the globe. Author and journalist Robert Lacey asserted that the wedding had an uplifting effect on the entire nation ('people seemed to feel that the marriage of this young couple was somehow hopeful, positive, regenerating'), while the Archbishop of Canterbury described it as 'the stuff of which fairy tales are made'.

Sadly, the fairy tale was not to have a happy ending. After the births of Princes William and Harry the cracks began to show in what, despite the hope and romance of the wedding, had proved to be an unsuitable match. The marriage was doomed by mutual incompatibility, media scrutiny and the well-documented infidelities of Diana's affairs and Charles' continued love for

Camilla Parker Bowles (whom he was destined to marry in 2005), all of which led to divorce in 1996. Then, on 31 August the following year, Diana was killed in a car crash in Paris, France, in circumstances that fuelled conspiracy theories to match those surrounding the deaths of Marilyn Monroe (see p158) and John F. Kennedy.

KEY DATES

1948 Prince Charles Philip Arthur George is born on 14 November in London, England, the eldest son of Queen Elizabeth II and Prince Philip, Duke of Edinburgh

1961 Lady Diana Frances Spencer is born on 1 July in Sandringham, Norfolk, England

1971 Charles and Camilla Parker Bowles meet at a polo match near Windsor Castle

1977 Charles and Diana (C and D) meet at the Spencer family estate, Althorp

1979 Diana visits Sandringham and Balmoral. Both trips will later be cited as the start of the romance despite the fact that at Balmoral Charles is photographed cavorting with Anna Wallace

1980 C and D begin their romance at Balmoral in September

1981 C and D marry at St Paul's Cathedral, London, on 29 July

1982 Diana gives birth to Prince William Arthur Philip Louis

1984 Diana gives birth to Prince Henry Charles Albert David (Harry)

1992 On 9 December C and D officially announce that they are to separate

1996 In February C and D announce that they are to divorce, the terms being made public on 12 July

1997 Diana begins a romance with Dodi Fayed. Both are killed in a car crash in Paris, France on 31 August. Diana is 36

2005 Charles and his long-term mistress, Camilla Parker Bowles, marry on 9 April in a civil ceremony at Windsor Guildhall

ABOVE Charles and his then lover, now wife, Camilla (then Mrs Parker Bowles) **OPPOSITE** Welsh Guards carry Diana's coffin into Westminster Abbey, followed by (l–r) Prince Charles, Prince Harry, Diana's brother Earl Spencer, Prince William and the Duke of Edinburgh

ARTS & ENTERTAINMENT

CHRISTO
JEANNE-CLAUDE

Husband and wife avant-garde art duo

Christo is world-famous for his monumental artworks such as curtained valleys, wrapped buildings, and islands surrounded in fabric, but until recently his wife Jeanne-Claude's role in these artworks was less well known. Judged by their backgrounds, Christo and Jeanne-Claude make an unlikely partnership: he, the impoverished artist who defected from behind the Iron Curtain; she, the General's daughter brought up in affluence and comfort in French North Africa. Romantics might consider the fact that they were both born on the same evening, 13 June 1935, as a sign that together they would make their mark on the world, but their joint destiny, as co-creators of some of the late 20th- and early 21st-centuries' most stunning artworks, was far from obvious at their first meeting.

In October 1958 Christo went to meet a new client, Précilda de Guillebon, who received him at her house and introduced him to her daughter, Jeanne-Claude. Christo remembers that Jeanne-Claude was 'very French and very beautiful in a blue dress', but he also recalls that his social status meant that she took little notice of him: 'It was very strange because I felt so nonexistent.' For her part, Jeanne-Claude later said: 'my life began when I met Christo', but evidently the attraction was not immediate. On the day they met she told a friend, 'The man is obviously a homosexual', and joked to her adoptive father: 'Look Papa, Mama has brought home a dog without a leash.'

But as Christo began to visit the house regularly to make portraits of the family, Jeanne-Claude soon began to see him in a different light. They had an affair, but in 1959 she married someone else – then, just a year later, left her husband for Christo while pregnant with Christo's child. In 1962 they married, after pressure from Jeanne-Claude, who later said: 'I very much wanted to be married. He kept saying that an artist must be committed to his art and nothing else. But art competed with our lives, like another woman, only more so.' The solution was for her to become his partner not just in marriage but also in his art. Their marriage and their working relationship were both extremely close, prompting friend and fellow-artist Carole Weiswelier to describe them as a single entity, saying: 'They are an extraordinary couple, like an eagle with two heads.' Biographer Burt Chernow went even further, ▶

RIGHT *Christo and Jeanne-Claude's* Surrounded Islands *in Biscayne Bay, Florida (May 1983)*

HAVE YOU HEARD?

Wolfgang Volz, who was Christo and Jeanne-Claude's right-hand man on several projects, wrote of *Surrounded Islands*:

'The project had one curious outcome: nine months after it was completed, a number of babies were born to workers, monitors and collaborators. Perhaps more than any other project, *Surrounded Islands* required intensive human interaction. Bathing suits were the workers' most common attire.'

writing: 'As if invisibly coupled, they seemed to sense each other, communicating through the smallest gesture. With the passing of time, it became increasingly difficult to picture them separately, or to imagine a project not driven by their dual force. Among the famous couples in art history, it is rare to find one who so completely shared identical goals.'

Despite such observations from those close to them, the art world in general saw Christo as the artist and Jeanne-Claude merely as his wife and art dealer. It was a misinterpretation of roles that persisted even after they made a public announcement in 1994 clarifying their 'longstanding artistic interdependence', acknowledging 'past and present coauthorship of the projects', and declaring that henceforth they were both to be given equal credit for their joint artworks. Jeanne-Claude explained that they had not clarified their position earlier because: 'In the beginning it was hard enough trying to explain that each project was a work of art. Trying to explain that it was a work of art by two artists would have been out of the question.'

Asked about the dynamics of the collaboration that has produced some of the world's most spectacular artworks, Jeanne-Claude said: 'We scream a lot.' Christo's answer was that the details of the partnership are irrelevant, it is the artistic results that count: 'Everybody knows that we have worked together for over thirty years. There's no point arguing about who does what. The work is all that matters.'

HAVE YOU HEARD?

Asked what *The Gates* was for, Jeanne-Claude said:

'It doesn't have any purpose at all. It's a work of art! The projects come out of our two hearts and our two heads. *The Gates* has taken a quarter of a century of effort; this project was not a matter of patience but of passion. New York is our city.'

KEY DATES

1935 Christo Vladimirov Javachef is born on 13 June in Gabrovo, Bulgaria. Jeanne-Claude de Guillebon is born on 13 June in Casablanca, Morocco, of French parents

1951–56 Christo studies at the Fine Arts Academy in Sofia, Bulgaria and then moves to Czechoslovakia

1952 Jean-Claude graduates with a baccalaureate in Latin and Philosophy from the University of Tunis, Tunisia

1957 Christo defects from Czechoslovakia and studies at the Vienna Fine Arts Academy, Austria

1958 Christo moves to Paris, France, where he meets Jeanne-Claude and creates his first packages and wrapped objects

1960 Jeanne-Claude leaves her husband for Christo and gives birth to their son, Cyril

1961 Christo creates photomontages showing his concept for wrapping buildings

1962 Christo and Jeanne-Claude (C and J-C) marry

1964 C and J-C move permanently to New York, USA

1968 Christo wraps a building for the first time, the Kunsthalle in Bern, Switzerland

1983 C and J-C complete their biggest work to date, *Surrounded Islands*

1985 After a decade, C and J-C complete the wrapping of the Pont Neuf bridge in Paris, France

1991 C and J-C complete *The Umbrellas* – 1,340 blue umbrellas in Ibaraki, Japan, and 1,760 yellow umbrellas in California, USA, each more than 6m/20ft tall and nearly 10m/33ft in diameter

1995 C and J-C complete *Wrapped Reichstag, Berlin 1971–95*, in Germany

2005 In February C and J-C unveil *The Gates* (conceived 1979), turning 23 miles of footpaths in Central Park, New York, into a 'golden river' by suspending saffron yellow fabric from 7,500 steel gates

RIGHT *Christo and Jeanne-Claude describing their work* The Gates *at a press conference in New York (22 November 2004)*

DIEGO RIVERA
FRIDA KAHLO

Husband and wife, two of Mexico's greatest artists

Diego Rivera

Metaphorically and physically, Diego Rivera was a huge figure – tall, overweight and imposing, he was also a colossus of Mexican art in three respects: the aesthetics, the scale and the historical importance of his work. But he was not always a gigantic physical figure and he almost did not survive childhood to become a gigantic cultural one. After his twin brother died at the age of 18 months, the weak and sickly Diego was put in the care of an Indian wet nurse, who turned him into a large, healthy three-year-old who then developed quickly: he could read by the age of four, excelled academically at school, and began attending evening art classes at the age of ten.

From the age of 20, Rivera travelled widely in Europe for 15 years, meeting artists, studying European painting and experimenting to find his own style. On his return to Mexico in 1921 he seemed suddenly to find himself, and his painting matured so abruptly that he later said: 'My style was born like a child, in an instant, with the difference that this birth took place after 35 agonizing years of pregnancy.'

The following year Rivera began the first of many epic murals depicting the life and history of the Mexican people, this one at the Escuela Nacional Preparatoria (National Preparatory School). There he was harassed by a group of students who called themselves *Los Cachuchas*, among whom was a 15-year-old girl who hid in the courtyard where he was painting and taunted him verbally. Rivera recalled: 'A year later I heard it was she who had hidden behind the columns and called out and that her name was Frida Kahlo. Yet I could never have dreamt then that she would be my wife.'

Frida Kahlo

Kahlo, on the other hand, was dreaming exactly that, telling her schoolfriends that one day she would have Rivera's child. Her dream came true, but not in the way she had hoped. On 17 December 1925 the bus in which she was travelling through Mexico City collided with a tram – the impact broke 15 of her bones, dislocated two joints, crushed her foot and severely injured her spine, pelvis and hip. She never fully recovered from the accident, living ▶

ABOVE *Diego Rivera and Frida Kahlo at work in their studio (c.1945)*

ABOVE *Frida Kahlo's* Self-portrait with Velvet Dress *(1926)*

the rest of her life in constant pain, but the fact that she survived at all was against all expectation. During Kahlo's two-year convalescence her mother encouraged her to paint, and when she was once again mobile she took her paintings to show Rivera. He remembers that he was working on a mural at the Ministry of Education, and that she demanded he give his opinion of them, saying: 'If you find them interesting, tell me; if not, tell me anyway because then I'll find something else to support my family.'

Rivera and Kahlo

Both of them remember Rivera saying that one self-portrait showed potential, but their memories then differ as to whether Kahlo invited Rivera to visit her home, ostensibly to look at more of her paintings, or whether Rivera told her to paint something else and invited himself to her home, ostensibly to look at the new work. Either way, his visits developed into a courtship that was supported by Kahlo's family despite the 21-year age gap between them. They were married on 21 August 1929, marking the beginning of a stormy but creative union that involved emotional and physical betrayals on both sides, but remained constant in one important respect: an unwavering support for each other's art.

With Rivera already a well-established, internationally famous artist, Kahlo's contribution to his work was inevitably more supportive than influential. Rivera, on the other hand, both supported and influenced Kahlo, taking

KEY DATES

1886 Diego María Rivera is born on 8 December in Guanajuato, Mexico

1896 Rivera attends evening art classes at the Academia de San Carlos

1906 Rivera wins a travel scholarship to study art in Madrid, Spain, and Paris, France

1907 Magdalena Carmen Frida Kahlo is born on 6 July in Coyoacán, Mexico City, the daughter of a Mexican Catholic mother and a German-Jewish immigrant photographer of Hungarian extraction. (She later claims to have been born in 1910 during the Mexican Revolution)

1909–19 Rivera travels to France, Belgium, the Netherlands and England. In Belgium he meets the Russian painter Angelina Beloff, marries her, and lives with her for 10 years in Paris, France

1921 Rivera returns to Mexico

1922 Rivera marries Guadaloupe Marín. Rivera begins the first of many murals, at the school attended by Kahlo

1925 Kahlo is seriously injured in a road accident, curtailing her ambition to be a doctor

1928 Rivera and Kahlo (R and K) begin their romance

1929 R and K marry

1930–34 Rivera is commissioned to paint a number of frescoes in the USA

1939 R and K divorce

1940 Kahlo participates in the International Exhibition of Surrealism in Mexico City. R and K remarry

1954 Kahlo dies on the night of 12/13 July, aged 47

1957 Rivera dies on 24 November, aged 70

1958 The Frida Kahlo Museum opens at Kahlo's former home in Coyoacán

2002 The feature film *Frida* is released, starring Salma Hayek as Kahlo and Alfred Molina as Rivera

ABOVE *Diego Rivera stands on a wooden platform in front of his mural in progress entitled* The Great City of Tenochtitlan, *at the National Palace, Mexico City (c.1954)*

care not to overwhelm her developing style and encouraging her to find her own way rather than adopting the styles of others, his own included. During her lifetime Kahlo's talent remained largely overshadowed by Rivera's fame, but since her death her work has gained ever-increasing respect, partly because Rivera continued to champion her art by donating her childhood home to the City of Mexico, where it now houses a museum of her work. Rivera called the day of Kahlo's death 'the most tragic day of my life', but for the artist herself it was a relief from a lifetime of physical pain. Despite this pain, it was a life that she had lived to the full, and the title of her last painting, a still life with watermelons, is a fitting epitaph: *Viva la Vida* – 'Long Live Life'.

ABOVE *Frida Kahlo's last painting,* Viva La Vida *(1954)*

GILBERT & GEORGE

Partners and avant-garde art duo

In 1967 the artists Gilbert and George met at St Martin's School of Art in London, England, and began a personal and creative partnership that continues nearly 40 years later. Sometimes classified as performance artists, and recently showing a strong affiliation to pop art, Gilbert and George prefer to describe themselves as sculptors – although, in order to force people to think differently about art forms, they stretch the definition of sculpture to include 'singing sculpture, interview sculpture, dancing sculpture, meal sculpture, walking sculpture, nerve sculpture, café sculpture and philosophy sculpture'.

Certainly their first 'singing sculpture', in 1969, was performance art by another name. The piece consisted of Gilbert and George standing on a table, their faces painted gold, performing mechanical movements in six-minute cycles to the Flanagan and Allen song 'Underneath the Arches' – they named the sculpture after the song, with the sub-title 'The most intelligent fascinating serious and beautiful art piece you have ever seen'. For *The Meal*, created that same year, 30 guests joined Gilbert and George in consuming an elaborate meal, and the later *Drinking Sculpture* involved the artists drinking in a number of London East End pubs. All three pieces illustrate what Gilbert and George later came to describe as 'living sculpture', an all-encompassing art form in which they deliberately blur the line between their art and the day-to-day business of living.

As well as through their physical presence in their performance pieces, Gilbert and George have also presented themselves as art in a variety of other media, including canvas and 'photopieces', usually with humour and often with deliberate bad taste. Their public persona is that of a single person, talking and thinking as one and seldom dropping the act that has taken over their lives to such a degree that they write: 'We don't enjoy life, no. We already gave our life away for our art. We're the dead rabbit on the plate. We want to spill our blood, our brains and our seed for art.'

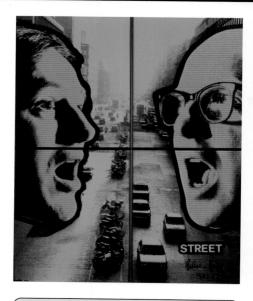

HAVE YOU HEARD?

In 1986 Gilbert and George answered a question that many people had been asking since the 1960s, in a statement entitled 'What Our Art Means':

'We want Our Art to speak across barriers of knowledge directly to People about their Life and not about their knowledge of art. The twentieth century has been cursed with an art that cannot be understood... We say that puzzling, obscure and form-obsessed art is decadent and a cruel denial of the Life of People.'

ABOVE Street *(c.1983)* **OPPOSITE** *Gilbert and George (1990)*

KEY DATES

1942 George Passmore is born on 8 January in Plymouth, England, and later studies at Dartington Hall College of Art and the Oxford School of Art, both in England

1943 Gilbert Proesch is born on 11 September in the Dolomites, Italy, and later studies at the Wolkenstein School of Art, the Hallein School of Art and the Munich Academy of Art, all in Germany

1967–69 Gilbert and George (G and G) both attend St Martin's School of Art, London, England, where they meet in 1967 and, in 1969, create their first 'living sculpture'

1970s G and G are twice chosen to exhibit at the prestigious Venice Biennale, Italy

1986 G and G are awarded the Turner Prize

1990–93 G and G create *The Cosmological Pictures*, which tours 10 European museums from 1991 to 1993

1992 G and G create *New Democratic Pictures*, their largest ever production, which is exhibited at the Aarhus Kunstmuseum, Aarhus, Denmark

PAUL VERLAINE
ARTHUR RIMBAUD

Poets and troubled lovers

The affair between the French poets Paul Verlaine and Arthur Rimbaud lasted less than two years, but had a profound effect on both of them, irrevocably changing Verlaine's life and inspiring Rimbaud to some of his best work, later published as *Les Illuminations*. Almost a century later their relationship was the subject of Christopher Hampton's play *Total Eclipse (see Key Dates 1968)*, a review of which provides an insight into the poets as well as the play: 'Straight away we sense the attractive raffishness and youthful arrogance of the charismatic provincial genius as well as the constricting, bourgeois atmosphere from which he will release the weak, uxorious Verlaine.'

As an aspiring poet Verlaine made a bad choice in becoming a civil servant, and as a homosexual he made a bad choice in marrying Mathilde Mauté. Meanwhile, Rimbaud, 10 years his junior, was making his name with a revolutionary style of poetry that would later be seen as the precursor of symbolism. In 1871 Verlaine invited Rimbaud to Paris and they began their affair, creating a private world for themselves that was completely detached from everyday reality. But the intensity of their passion (and their drinking) could not last, and in July 1873, when Rimbaud tried to end the affair, Verlaine shot him, injuring Rimbaud's wrist. Verlaine was sentenced to two years' hard labour, during which time Rimbaud left him, Mathilde left him, and he converted to Catholicism.

While Verlaine was in prison Rimbaud published another volume of poetry, *Une Saison en Enfer* (A Season in Hell), but was so disappointed at the critical response that he abandoned poetry altogether and instead travelled widely, working as a mercenary, a trader, an explorer and a gun-runner. In 1876 Verlaine published *Les Illuminations*, a collection of the poems that Rimbaud had written during their relationship, crediting them to 'the late Arthur Rimbaud', but Rimbaud reacted with indifference both to Verlaine's audacity and to the critical acclaim for the poems. Verlaine continued to compose poetry almost until his death, but Rimbaud did not write anything further, having reached the conclusion, to quote Christopher Hampton's Rimbaud, that: 'Anything that can be put into words is not worth putting into words.'

RIGHT *Detail of* A Corner of the Table *(1872), by Ignace Henri Fantin-Latour (1836–1904), with Verlaine (l) and Rimbaud (r)*

HAVE YOU HEARD?

In his song 'You're Gonna Make Me Lonesome When You Go', Bob Dylan writes:

Situations have ended sad,
Relationships have all been bad.
Mine've been like Verlaine's and Rimbaud.
But there's no way I can compare
All those scenes to this affair;
Yer gonna make me lonesome when you go.

TED HUGHES & SYLVIA PLATH

Poetry's celebrity marriage

Had Ted Hughes and Sylvia Plath married after they made their names, rather than before, it would have been considered a literary wedding to rival the highly publicized celebrity weddings of the film world. As it was, they married in secret and afterwards few people beyond their own circle of friends registered this union of two great poetic minds: Hughes, who would become the elder statesman of English letters, and Plath, the tragic American poetess.

Hughes won a scholarship to read English Literature at Pembroke College, Cambridge University, but after two years switched courses to archaeology and anthropology: subjects that, along with his native Yorkshire, were profoundly to influence his poems. In addition to his background and education, a third great influence would irrevocably alter his life and his poetry – Sylvia Plath. Born in Boston, Massachusetts, Plath was educated at Smith College, Massachusetts, where she suffered from depression that drove her to attempt suicide. Despite her depression, she managed to win a Fulbright Scholarship to Newnham College, Cambridge University, where she met Hughes at a party thrown by him and a group of his friends to celebrate the launch of their literary magazine *St Botolph's Review*.

Hughes arrived at the party with a girlfriend, but noticed Plath immediately – more than 40 years later in the poem 'St Botolph's' (part of his collection *Birthday Letters*) he describes her gesturing with 'balletic, monkey-elegant fingers' and laughing with eyes bright like 'a crush of diamonds'. For her part, Plath recorded in her journal that she asked someone the name of 'that big, dark, hunky boy, the only one there huge enough for me'. The party was loud and drunken. Hughes approached Plath and she records having to shout at one another 'as if in a high wind': 'I started yelling again about his poems [published in *St Botolph's Review*] and quoting: "most dear unscratchable diamond" and he yelled back, colossal, in a voice that should have come from a Pole, "You like?" and asking if I wanted brandy, and me yelling "yes" and backing into the next room.'

In the next room, according to Plath's journal, Hughes kissed her 'bang smash on the mouth' and ripped off her hairband and silver earrings. She ▶

ABOVE *Ariel*, by Sylvia Plath and *Birthday Letters*, by Ted Hughes **OPPOSITE** *Sylvia Plath (undated photograph)*

in turn bit him on the cheek hard enough to draw blood, something that, as Hughes wrote in 'St Botolph's', marked his soul as well as his body:

...the swelling ring of tooth-marks
That was to brand my face for the next month.
The me beneath it for good.

Both were smitten by this violent, passionate encounter and they married secretly just four months later. But it was not simply a sexual attraction: their effect on each other extended beyond their physical and even their emotional relationship to the very core of their art. Hughes later told an interviewer: 'Once I got to know her and read her poems, I saw straight off that she was a genius of some kind. Quite suddenly we were completely committed to each other and to each other's writing ... I see now that when we met, my writing, like hers, left its old path and started to circle and search.'

Each inspiring the other, Hughes published his first collection of poems, *The Hawk in the Rain*, the following year and in 1960 Plath published her first two volumes of poetry, *A Winter Ship* (anonymously) and *The Colossus*. An obituary of Hughes noted that during this time: 'Their inner worlds, to a large degree, converged', but what had begun as a meeting of body, mind and spirit sadly did not last, and in 1962 they separated after Hughes began an affair. The following year Plath committed suicide, something for which many of her fans have never forgiven Hughes, although it was clear from *Birthday Letters* just how much he had loved her and how difficult the symptoms of her depression had made their lives together.

Plath once wrote: 'For me, poetry is an evasion of the real job of writing prose.' But her poetry has proved more lasting and influential than her novel *The Bell Jar*, although her true poetic talent was not recognized until after her death, with the publication of three collections in 1965, 1971 and 1972, the first being her masterpiece *Ariel*. Hughes went on to establish himself as one of the greatest English poets of the 20th century, being honoured in 1984 with the post of Poet Laureate and, shortly before he died in 1998, with the Order of Merit. Tragically, one question will never be answered: given that Hughes went on to achieve so much, what might Plath have achieved?

ARTS + ENTERTAINMENT

152 + 153

HAVE YOU HEARD?

In *Lady Lazarus*, written the year before her death, Sylvia Plath wrote of suicide:

I have done it again.
One year in every ten
I manage it –
... And I a smiling woman.
I am only thirty.
And like the cat I have nine times to die.
... Dying
Is an art, like everything else.
I do it exceptionally well.

RIGHT *Sylvia Plath's grave, St Thomas' Churchyard, Heptonstall, West Yorkshire, England*
OPPOSITE *Ted Hughes (1986)*

DOMINIQUE LAPIERRE
LARRY COLLINS

Co-authors of blockbuster novels

Lapierre and Collins

Writing novels is usually a solitary experience, but Dominique Lapierre and Larry Collins turned it into a joint exercise, together developing what critic Hugo Young described as 'a uniquely accessible line in documentary reporting with a strong human interest'. Born two years apart, Collins in America and Lapierre in France, they first met in 1954 when both were on military service. They struck up a lasting friendship and, years later, pooled their research and writing skills to write *Is Paris Burning?*, a novel, based on interviews with no less than 1,200 witnesses, that recreated the wartime liberation of Paris. They went on to write four more novels together on a similarly grand scale, and with similarly grand sales, reaching millions of readers in more than 30 languages. Then Lapierre decided to go it alone and proved himself equally successful as a solo writer – and, with his wife, as a humanitarian.

Lapierre and Lapierre

In 1966, after the success of *Is Paris Burning?*, Lapierre and Collins took on a researcher named Dominique Conchon, who worked with them on their next four books and, in 1980, married Lapierre – to avoid confusion, she became Dominique Conchon-Lapierre while he remained Dominique Lapierre. While researching Lapierre and Collins' fourth book, *Freedom at Midnight* (the story of the countdown to Indian independence), the Lapierres were made painfully aware of the extreme poverty in Calcutta, in particular the plight of the city's lepers. Mother Teresa told them that the lepers should be their first target for help if they had any money to spare, and in 1981 the Lapierres made a far greater commitment than simply sparing some money – they set up a charity, City of Joy Aid, specifically to rescue lepers from the slums of Calcutta. Over the next two years Lapierre used the experience to write another bestseller, *City of Joy*, and assigned half his royalties from this and all his earlier work to the charity. He now works tirelessly to ensure that the money reaches the people who need it, while his wife Dominique, as well as working directly with women in India, coordinates the charity's activities in India, France, America, Italy, Spain and Britain.

INSET RIGHT *Dominique Lapierre (l) and Larry Collins in France (12 July 1993)* **RIGHT** *The Lapierres visit Belari Medical Centre, about 55 miles outside Calcutta (1 November 1998)*

KEY DATES

1929 Larry Collins is born on 14 September in West Hartford, Connecticut, USA, and later studies at Yale University

1931 Dominique Lapierre is born in France, the son of a diplomat, and later studies at La Fayette University, USA

1940 Dominique Conchon is born on 4 August in Farges, France

1954 Collins is conscripted into the US Army and serves at Supreme Allied Headquarters in Europe, where he meets Lapierre, who is also on military service

1956 Collins joins the Paris bureau of United Press International (UPI) as a journalist, later becoming News Editor for UPI in Rome, Italy, and then Middle East correspondent in Beirut

1961 Collins returns from the Middle East to France, where he becomes head of the Paris office of *Newsweek* magazine and resumes his friendship with Lapierre

1965 Lapierre and Collins (L and C) write *Is Paris Burning?*

1966 Conchon joins the literary partnership of Dominique Lapierre and Larry Collins as chief assistant and researcher

1968 L and C write *Or I'll Dress You in Mourning*

1971 L and C write *O Jerusalem*

1975 L and C write *Freedom at Midnight*

1980 L and C write *The Fifth Horseman*. Conchon and Lapierre marry

1981 Lapierre founds the charity City of Joy Aid, to rescue children suffering from leprosy from the slums of Calcutta

MILLS & BOON

World-famous publisher of romance fiction

Born within four months of each other in 1877, Gerald Mills and Charles Boon grew up in very different circumstances. Mills had a comfortable childhood and a Cambridge University education before joining publishers Methuen & Co. in 1903 as Educational Manager. Meanwhile, Boon was born into a poor London family and worked at various odd jobs from the age of 12 before joining Methuen in 1893 as an office boy and rising to Sales Manager by the time Mills arrived there a decade later. Feeling that they were not receiving due recognition or reward for their part in Methuen's rapid expansion, Mills and Boon left in 1908 and set up their own publishing house, Mills & Boon Ltd. Now world-famous for romance fiction, Mills & Boon began as an educational and general fiction house, although the company's very first title was, aptly, a romance.

Mills' great satisfaction came from educational books, but after he died suddenly in 1928 Boon steered the company towards romance fiction. During the worldwide Depression of the 1930s Boon noticed a growing trend for escapist fiction as a distraction from the difficulties of life, and realized

KEY DATES

1877 Gerald Rusgrove Mills is born on 3 January in Stourbridge, England, and later studies at Caius College, Cambridge University. Charles Boon is born on 9 May in London, England

1889–93 After the death of his father, Boon leaves school and takes on a series of odd jobs, including working in a bookshop

1893 Boon joins Methuen & Co. as an office boy and warehouse clerk

1893–1903 Boon gains promotion and eventually becomes Sales Manager and General Manager at Methuen

1903 Mills joins Methuen & Co. as Educational Manager, where he meets Boon

1908 Mills and Boon join forces to found the publishing house of Mills & Boon Ltd. Mills puts up most of the capital, so the company is known as Mills & Boon rather than Boon & Mills

1928 Mills dies suddenly on 23 September in London, aged 51

1930s Boon decides to focus purely on romance fiction

1943 Boon dies on 2 December in London, aged 66, leaving Mills & Boon in the hands of his two sons

1949 Canadian Richard Bonnycastle founds Harlequin Books

1957 Harlequin Books begins buying the rights to reprint Mills & Boon titles

1971 Harlequin Books buys Mills & Boon Ltd

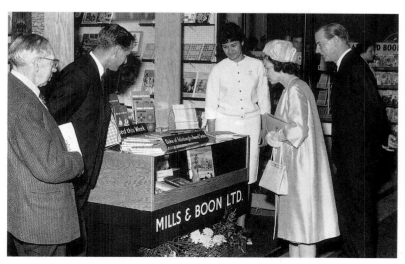

ABOVE *Queen Elizabeth II visits the Mills & Boon display at the London Book Fair (1964)* **INSET ABOVE** *The modern face of Mills & Boon: The Greek Tycoon's Convenient Mistress, by Lynne Graham (2004), and Possessed by the Sheikh, by Penny Jordan (2005)*

that if he produced books cheaply he could sell them to a wider readership. He therefore decided to concentrate on publishing low-cost romances, which were initially sold, through weekly two-penny libraries, in distinctive brown bindings that led Mills & Boon titles to become known affectionately as 'the books in brown'. Two decades later, after Boon's death, executives at Mills & Boon detected another trend in book-buying habits and once again moved quickly to maintain the company's position as the leading romance publisher. Lending libraries were in decline and so Mills & Boon changed its sales pattern and began selling romances through newsagents' shops. As in the 1930s, this forward-thinking proved successful and today Mills & Boon, now a subsidiary of Harlequin Books, remains one of the world's leading publishers of romance fiction.

ABOVE *Detail from the cover of the Mills & Boon romance* Satan's Island, *by Sally Wentworth (undated)*

MARILYN MONROE ARTHUR MILLER

Hollywood duo of film star and writer

Marilyn Monroe

The woman the world knew as Marilyn Monroe had a difficult upbringing, having been raised in an orphanage and in foster homes because her mentally ill mother, Gladys, could not cope. Gladys, née Monroe, had married twice: the first time, aged 14, to her mother's landlord, Jap Baker, by whom she was pregnant, and the second time to meterman Martin Edward Mortenson, a marriage that lasted just four months. Within a year of leaving Mortenson Gladys was pregnant again, probably by another man, but because they had not divorced, Mortenson was legally the father of the child, Norma Jean. Despite this legal technicality, Norma Jean, later known as Marilyn Monroe, was given Gladys' previous surname of Baker.

Like her mother, Norma Jean Baker married young, her wedding to merchant seaman Jimmy Dougherty taking place in June 1942 just after her 16th birthday. The marriage did not last, and Monroe later referred to it as 'a sort of friendship with sexual privileges'. By 1946 her beauty was flowering and she became a photographer's model. This led to several small film roles and then, in 1953, she achieved international fame when she starred with Jane Russell in *Gentlemen Prefer Blondes* and with Betty Grable and Lauren Bacall in *How to Marry a Millionaire*. The following year she married baseball legend Joe DiMaggio, but unfortunately he proved to be a jealous husband. His jealousy combined with her regular flirtations was not a good mix, and the marriage ended in divorce just nine months later.

Having made her name in light comedies, Monroe studied at the Actors' Studio in New York, hoping to gain more serious roles. Her quest to be taken seriously coincided with the flowering of a simmering relationship with America's greatest playwright, Arthur Miller, who, she said: '...attracted me because he was brilliant. His mind is better than that of any man I've known. And he understands and approves my wanting to improve myself.'

Monroe and Miller

When they first met in January 1951 Monroe was still an unknown actress and Arthur Miller, 10 years her senior and married with two children, was ▶

ABOVE *Marilyn Monroe in a publicity still from* Gentlemen Prefer Blondes *(13 March 1953)* **OPPOSITE** *Monroe and Miller at Miller's home in Roxbury, Connecticut, USA (1957)*

already 'America's hottest playwright', having won a Pulitzer Prize for *Death of a Salesman* two years earlier. Miller remembers that first meeting, on the set of the film *As Young As You Feel*, in which Monroe, struggling to cope with the death of a friend, had a bit part:

> 'I saw her in profile against a white light, with her hair coiled atop her head; she was weeping under a veil of black lace that she lifted now and then to dab her eyes. When we shook hands the shock of her body's motion sped through me, a sensation at odds with her sadness amid all this glamour and technology and the busy confusion of a new shot being set up.'

For her part, Marilyn later told a friend that meeting Miller 'was like running into a tree. You know, like a cool drink when you've got a fever'. Both acknowledged the attraction, but Miller left Hollywood a few days later and they did not see each other again until April 1955, at a party in New York. In the meantime, they wrote to each other and in one letter Miller, who was struggling with his conscience about his family, told Monroe that he was not the man to make her happy. But by the time they met again in 1955 Miller's marriage had failed and the attraction between them had not diminished – this time they indulged their passion for each other and married just over a year later, on 29 June 1956.

Despite the differences in their ages and backgrounds it seemed like the perfect match and for a while they were blissfully happy, but before long the relationship became strained. Miller wrote the part of Roslyn Taber for Monroe in his screenplay *The Misfits*, but her performance was marred by the fact that she and Miller argued constantly on set, a symptom of a marital

breakdown that ultimately led to their separation and divorce. *The Misfits* was to be Monroe's last film. She was fired from her next film, *Something's Got To Give*, and in the early hours of 5 August 1962 she was found dead in her bedroom after apparently committing suicide, although conspiracy theories have persisted ever since that she was murdered.

ABOVE *Arthur Miller at home in New York (21 March 2001)* **RIGHT** *Monroe and Miller in New York City, USA (autumn 1956)*

HAVE YOU HEARD?

Photographer Sam Shaw said of Marilyn that 'she represented freedom as few other women have', but he also said:

> 'Any time a woman behaves as freely as Marilyn, one part of us loves it, the other hates and fears it.'

Before they were married, Miller wrote to Monroe:

> 'Bewitch them with this image they ask for, but I hope and almost pray that you won't be hurt in this game, nor ever change.'

KEY DATES

1915 Arthur Miller is born on 17 October in New York City, USA

1926 Norma Jean Baker, later known as Marilyn Monroe, is born on 1 June in Los Angeles, USA

1938 Miller graduates from the University of Michigan

1942 Baker marries for the first time, at the age of 16

1946 Baker becomes a photographer's model

1947 Miller premieres his first successful play, *All My Sons*

1948 As Marilyn Monroe, Baker plays her first sizeable film role, in *Ladies of the Chorus*

1949 Miller premieres his Pulitzer Prize-winning play, *Death of a Salesman*

1951 Miller and Monroe M and M) first meet, on the set of *As Young As You Feel*, in which Monroe has a bit part

1953 Monroe plays her first two leading film roles, in *Gentlemen Prefer Blondes* and *How To Marry a Millionaire*. Miller premieres what will be his most lasting work, *The Crucible*

1955 M and M begin a romance. Monroe stars in *The Seven-Year Itch*. Miller premieres his play *A View From the Bridge*

1956 M and M marry. Monroe stars in *Bus Stop*

1959 Monroe stars in *Some Like It Hot*

1960 Monroe stars in her last film, *The Misfits*, written for her by Miller. M and M separate

1961 M and M divorce

1962 Monroe sings *Happy Birthday Mr President* to John F. Kennedy on 19 May. Monroe dies in controversial circumstances in the early hours of 5 August, aged 36

1964 Miller premieres his play *After the Fall*, which creates a scandal with its harsh portrayal of Monroe

2005 Miller dies of heart failure on 11 February, aged 89

RICHARD BURTON
ELIZABETH TAYLOR

Turbulent Hollywood duo, on screen and off

Richard Burton

Richard Burton had the potential to be one of the world's greatest actors, but instead he became the most famous. His fame was based as much on his spectacular and turbulent private life as on his acting skills, and when he died obituarists were unanimous in describing his talent as unfulfilled – one newspaper even went so far as to say: 'He threw away greatness like it was a soiled sock.'

But, for all that, Burton had made a remarkable journey from the valleys of south Wales, where his father was a coal miner, to the bright lights of Hollywood and the company of stars. It was a dizzying rise to fame, summed up neatly by biographer Penny Junor: 'By 17 he was appearing on the stage in the West End of London. By 27 he was in Hollywood, by 37 embroiled with the most sought-after film star in the world.' That film star was, of course, Elizabeth Taylor.

Elizabeth Taylor

Elizabeth Taylor grew up in very different circumstances to Richard Burton. Born in London of American parents, she spent her first years in England where, despite the worldwide Depression, she was attended by servants, showered with toys and treated to holidays both by the sea and in America. When she was seven her family moved back to America and settled in Los Angeles, where the young Elizabeth soon found herself involved in the city's world-famous film industry. Pushed by her ambitious mother, Sara (Taylor later said: 'I never wanted a career – it was forced on me'), Elizabeth made her screen debut at the age of 10 in *There's One Born Every Minute*. She was miscast and made little impression, but an appearance in *Lassie Come Home* the following year assured her of the career she had never wanted.

Despite her reluctance, she and Hollywood seemed made for each other, and by the time she met Richard Burton in 1962 – to become the most famous showbiz duo of their time – she had won one Academy Award, three nominations and was halfway through her fourth marriage. ▶

HAVE YOU HEARD?

In 1957 the 25-year-old Elizabeth Taylor announced her retirement from the screen, saying:

'I don't want to be a movie star any more. I just want to be a wife and mother ... I've been an actress for 15 years: now I want to be a woman ... I never liked acting that much. It's really been more or less a hobby with me.'

ABOVE *Burton and Taylor talking to director Joseph Mankiewicz on the set of* Cleopatra *(1963)* **OPPOSITE** *Portrait of Burton and Taylor by Douglas Kirkland (c.1964)*

Burton and Taylor

In his book *Meeting Mrs Jenkins*, Burton described his first glimpse of Elizabeth Taylor, at a Hollywood party that he attended in 1953:

'A girl sitting on the other side of the pool lowered her book, took off her sunglasses and looked at me. She was so extraordinarily beautiful that I nearly laughed out loud …

She sipped some beer and went back to her book. I affected to become social with the others but out of the corner of my mind … I had her under close observation …

She was unquestionably gorgeous. I can think of no other word to describe a combination of plenitude, frugality, abundance, tightness. She was lavish. She was a dark, unyielding largesse. She was, in short, too bloody much, and not only that, she was totally ignoring me.'

Nearly a decade later Burton was cast as Mark Antony in the blockbuster *Cleopatra*, with Taylor in the title role. Before they had shot any scenes together Burton watched Taylor shoot a nude scene and, according to friends, 'came back like a man possessed, raving about her beauty'. This

KEY DATES

1925 Richard Walter Jenkins is born on 10 November in Pontrhydyfen, Wales and is later adopted by his English teacher, Philip H. Burton	actress Sybil Williams, who becomes his first wife in 1949	and begin an off-screen romance	**1975** B and T remarry
			1976 B and T divorce again and Burton marries his third wife, Susan Hunt
	1950 Taylor marries her first husband, Nick Hilton, heir to the Hilton hotel chain. Burton makes his Hollywood debut	**1963** B and T co-star in *The VIPs*	
1932 Elizabeth Rosemond Taylor is born on 27 February in London, England		**1964** B and T marry	**1978** Taylor marries her sixth husband, US Senator John Warner
	1952 Taylor marries her second husband, actor Michael Wilding	**1965** B and T co-star in *The Sandpiper*	
1939 The Taylor family moves to Los Angeles, USA		**1966** B and T co-star in *Who's Afraid of Virginia Woolf?*	**1983** Burton marries his fourth wife, Sally Hay
1942 Taylor makes her screen debut at the age of 10	**1957** Taylor marries her third husband, producer Mike Todd	**1967** B and T co-star in *The Comedians*	**1984** Burton dies of a stroke on 5 August in Geneva, Switzerland, aged 58
	1959 Taylor marries her fourth husband, singer Eddie Fisher	**1968** B and T co-star in *Boom*	
1943 Burton makes his professional stage debut			**1991** Taylor marries her seventh husband, construction worker Larry Fortenski
1948 Burton makes his film debut, in *The Last Days of Dolwyn*. During filming he meets	**1962** Burton and Taylor (B and T) co-star as Antony and Cleopatra [see p92] in *Cleopatra* (released in 1963)	**1971** B and T co-star in *Under Milk Wood*	
		1974 B and T divorce	**1996** Taylor divorces Fortenski

ABOVE *Burton and Taylor on their first wedding day (15 March 1964)*

time she didn't ignore him, and soon afterwards the paparazzi revealed
to the world that the stars were sleeping together. Not wanting to be
considered promiscuous, Taylor had a 'strict code of personal morality' by
which she married the men she slept with and so, two years after beginning
their affair, Taylor's fourth and Burton's first marriages were over and they
were married to each other.

Cleopatra marked the beginning of a personal and professional
partnership that would last, on and off, for 14 years, through seven feature
films and two marriages. Their first marriage, described by Junor as 'the
most public, most publicized, most tempestuous and romantic marriage in
the world', lasted 10 years before Burton and Taylor divorced in April 1974
citing 'irreconcilable differences'. Fourteen months later their differences had
seemingly been reconciled, or at least ignored, and they remarried in October
1975. Less than a year later they divorced for a second time. This time
there was to be no remarriage, but the bond between them was never
broken – after Burton's early death eight years later, Taylor visited his family
in Wales, where she stood between his brothers and sisters and said simply:
'I feel as if I am home.'

HAVE YOU HEARD?

Burton once said that he wanted to be 'the
richest, the most famous and the best actor in
the world'. He achieved fame and fortune, but
squandered his chance of greatness because,
as he told the *Daily Star* in a phrase the
newspaper later used as Burton's epitaph:
'I smoked too much, drank too much and made
love too much.'

ABOVE *Taylor and Burton in* Who's Afraid of Virginia Woolf? *(1966)*

LAUREL & HARDY

Cinema's best-loved comedy duo

ARTS + ENTERTAINMENT 166 + 167

Stan Laurel

Born Arthur Stanley Jefferson, the 'thin and wistful half of Laurel and Hardy' was always known simply as Stan and did not adopt the name Laurel until 1918. As a teenager Stan toured with a vaudeville company run by English impresario Fred Karno, where one of his jobs was to understudy another legendary English-born comedian, Charlie Chaplin. He later followed Chaplin's lead in emigrating to the USA, where Chaplin persuaded him to try screen acting as an alternative to vaudeville.

Stan later stated that his first film was the 1917 silent short *Nuts in May*, but Laurel and Hardy experts can find no evidence of this film and consider his debut more likely to have been *Just Nuts*, released in 1918 (*Nuts in May* may have been a working title). Either way, his performance impressed financier Adolph Ramish enough for Ramish to tell him: 'It's my personal opinion that you're funnier than Chaplin', and to give him a contract – his first success in a new career that, some two years later, would bring him into contact with Oliver Hardy.

Oliver Hardy

Like Laurel, Oliver Hardy was determined from a young age to be a performer, running away from home at the age of eight to join a travelling minstrel show. He soon returned home, but did not lose his yen for performing and in 1913 he embarked on a film career, making his debut in the silent short *Outwitting Dad*. Whereas Laurel was always a comic star, Hardy began his career as a character actor, villain and straight man, working for several studios before taking a long-term contract with Hal Roach Studios, probably in 1926 – as with Laurel's memory of his debut, Hardy remembers one date (1924), but documentary evidence suggests another. It was at the Hal Roach Studios, with Roach as producer, that Laurel and Hardy embarked on their prolific, long-lasting and world-famous partnership, beginning in 1926 with the film *Forty-Five Minutes From Hollywood*. ▶

RIGHT *Laurel and Hardy during the filming of the silent short* The Finishing Touch *(1928)*

HAVE YOU HEARD?

Ollie's most famous quotation was first uttered in the 1930 short *The Laurel–Hardy Murder Case*: 'Here's another nice mess you've gotten me into.' The phrase is often misquoted as 'Here's another fine mess you've gotten me into', partly because the next short they released, later the same year, was entitled *Another Fine Mess*.

Laurel and Hardy

There is no doubt that Laurel and Hardy's great partnership began at the Hal
Roach Studios, but there is a preface to the story. About six years earlier,
c. 1920 (not 1917 as sometimes documented), Laurel and Hardy appeared
on screen together for the first time when Hardy played an armed robber in
the Stan Laurel comedy *Lucky Dog*. Laurel played a Keaton-esque character
in blazer and straw boater, Hardy played the comic villain in rollneck and cap,
and the suits and bowler hats were nowhere to be seen. It was a chance
encounter between two otherwise unconnected performers who would not
appear together again until 1926, when they both found themselves working
for Hal Roach.

Forty-Five Minutes From Hollywood was a mediocre debut for the
partnership, and could even be considered a false start. It gave no indication
that its stars were set to become Hollywood's best-loved comic duo, and in
one sense they do not even appear together, their roles being intercut as
characters on opposite sides of a door. It was the only film they would make
together in 1926, but the following year their partnership began in earnest
with the short film *Duck Soup*, which was followed by no less than 13 more
shorts by the end of 1927. In *Duck Soup* the fundamental relationship
between the Stan and Ollie personas is already established, as summarized
by Laurel and Hardy expert Glenn Mitchell: 'Ollie gives the orders, Stan
reluctantly takes them, and neither has any brains.' Their appearance was
yet to be refined, Hardy appearing in top hat and monocle rather
than bowler hat, but the basic ingredients were there.

Over the next 24 years Laurel and Hardy went on
to make more than 100 films together, including
11 feature films. Almost all of them were based
around the slapstick personas first sketched
out in *Duck Soup*, characterized by an
exasperated Ollie fiddling with his tie and
looking to the camera, and a confused Stan
scratching his head and bursting into tears.
The last film they made together was *Atoll K*
(a.k.a. *Utopia*), in which Laurel is clearly
seriously ill. He later recovered, but six years
later Hardy died of a stroke, ending a 30-year
partnership that Laurel, deeply saddened by
the news, summed up by saying simply:
'He was like a brother to me.'

ABOVE *Laurel and Hardy out of costume but still in character (13 February 1947)* **RIGHT** *Laurel and Hardy make it to the top (c.1920s)*

KEY DATES

1890 Arthur Stanley Jefferson (later known as Stan Laurel) is born on 16 June in Ulverston, Lancashire, England

1892 Norvell Hardy Jr (later known as Oliver Hardy) is born on 18 January near Atlanta, Georgia, USA

1900 Hardy runs away from home to join a travelling minstel show

1900s Jefferson performs as a member of impresario Fred Karno's touring vaudeville company, where he understudies Charlie Chaplin

1910 Jefferson first visits the USA, on tour with the Karno troupe

1913 Hardy makes his film debut, in the short *Outwitting Dad* (released 1914)

c.1918 Jefferson makes his screen debut

1918 Jefferson adopts the name Laurel, inspired by a picture of the Roman general Scipio Africanus wearing a laurel wreath

c.1920 Laurel and Hardy (L and H) appear on screen together for the first time, in *A Lucky Dog*

1925 Hardy plays the Tin Man in *The Wizard of Oz*

1926 L and H make *Forty-Five Minutes from Hollywood*, their first film together at the Hal Roach Studios

1927 L and H begin their ongoing partnership in earnest, making 14 shorts this year

1931 L and H make the feature film *Pardon Us*

1932 L and H make the feature film *Pack Up Your Troubles*, and win an Academy Award for the short *The Music Box*

1933 L and H make the feature film *Sons of the Desert* (a.k.a. *Fraternally Yours*)

1935 L and H make the feature film *Bonnie Scotland*

1936 L and H make the feature film *Our Relations*

1937 L and H make the feature film *Way Out West*

1938 L and H make the feature film *Blockheads*

1939 L and H make the feature film *A Chump at Oxford*

1940 L and H make the feature film *Saps at Sea*

1942 L and H make the feature film *A-Haunting We Will Go*

1943 L and H make the feature film *Jitterbugs*

1951 L and H make their last film together, *Atoll K*

1957 Hardy dies on 7 August in California, aged 65

1965 Laurel dies on 23 February in California, aged 74

Film-making brothers

Many adjectives have been applied to the Coen brothers' films, including eccentric, funny, intelligent, weird, beguiling, experimental, moving, grotesque and surprising. In fact, their films have such a characteristic style that this entire list can be summed up in one coinage: Coenical. One of the things that makes their films so distinctive is that, being a two-man production team, the brothers have almost total control of the outcome: they write the scripts together, elder brother Joel directs and Ethan produces. Additionally, they have a unified vision of what they are hoping to achieve, having made films together since childhood when they would shoot abridged versions of their favourite feature films on Super8.

One of the results of collaborating from such a young age is that the brothers' scriptwriting process is almost symbiotic. The archetypal screenwriter will smoke a lot, pace around the room, smoke some more and eventually start typing. The Coen brothers share these chores – in his article 'The Brothers from Another Planet', David Handelman describes how, while writing *Raising Arizona*, Joel would pace and smoke, leaving Ethan free to smoke and type. The outcome of all this pacing, smoking and typing was a brilliantly inventive comedy about which a reviewer for *Time Out* magazine wrote: 'Starting from a point of delirious excess, the film leaps into dark and virtually uncharted territory to soar like a comet.'

But the distinctive Coen brothers' style is not simply in the scriptwriting, it is also in the film-making. On many feature films the writer, director and producer will all have slightly (or drastically) different visions of what the film should be, but with Joel as director and Ethan as producer the shared vision that went into the script reaches the screen in its purest form. Despite this complete control over the style of their films, the brothers claim to be collaborative film-makers rather than *auteurs*. This may be true, but in the course of three decades of film-making the brothers have created a regularly used group of performers and technicians whose collaborative contributions come together to make the Coen brothers' films so … Coenical.

INSET TOP RIGHT *Oscar winner Frances McDormand in* Fargo **RIGHT** *Ethan (l) and Joel Coen arrive for the world premiere of their feature film* Ladykillers *(12 March 2004)*

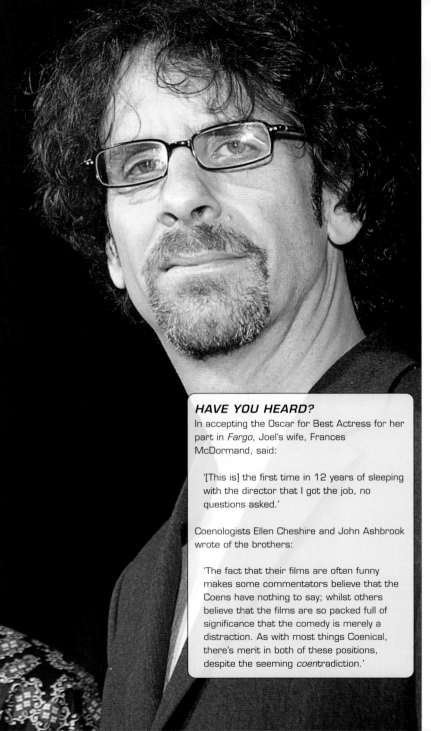

HAVE YOU HEARD?

In accepting the Oscar for Best Actress for her part in *Fargo*, Joel's wife, Frances McDormand, said:

'[This is] the first time in 12 years of sleeping with the director that I got the job, no questions asked.'

Coenologists Ellen Cheshire and John Ashbrook wrote of the brothers:

'The fact that their films are often funny makes some commentators believe that the Coens have nothing to say; whilst others believe that the films are so packed full of significance that the comedy is merely a distraction. As with most things Coenical, there's merit in both of these positions, despite the seeming *coen*tradiction.'

KEY DATES

1955 Joel Coen is born on 29 November in St Louis Park, Minnesota, USA

1958 Ethan Coen is born on 21 September in St Louis Park, Minnesota, USA

1960s The Coen brothers (J and EC) grow up remaking their favourite feature films on Super8

1970s Joel studies film at New York University and then at the University of Texas at Austin. Ethan studies philosophy at Princeton

1983 J and EC make their first feature film, *Blood Simple*

1985 The feature film *Crimewave* is released, written by J and EC with Sam Raimi and directed by Sam Raimi

1987 J and EC's feature film *Raising Arizona* is released

1990 J and EC's feature film *Miller's Crossing* is released

1991 J and EC's feature film *Barton Fink* is released

1994 J and EC's feature film *The Hudsucker Proxy* is released

1996 J and EC's feature film *Fargo* is released

1998 J and EC's feature film *The Big Lebowski* is released

2000 J and EC's feature film *O Brother, Where Art Thou?* is released

2001 J and EC's feature film *The Man Who Wasn't There* is released

ISMAIL MERCHANT JAMES IVORY

Co-founders of Merchant–Ivory films

The linked surnames of Ismail Merchant and James Ivory have come to represent a characteristic sub-genre of 'literary' films, which, the company proudly boasts, 'have been praised for their visual beauty, their mature and intelligent themes, and the shrewd casting and fine acting from which they derive their unique power'. As producer, director and production company, Merchant and Ivory are in a strong position to ensure that their artistic vision reaches the screen intact and their unusual combination of cultural influences makes theirs a particularly rich vision – the more so for their frequent and ongoing collaboration with novelist and screenwriter Ruth Prawer Jhabvala, who is tantamount to being a third member of the 'duo'.

James Ivory considered a career as a set designer before being seduced by the idea of directing films and, to that end, enrolling on a film course at the University of Southern California. Meanwhile, half a world away in India, Ismail Merchant was developing a love of film and a head for business, eventually moving to the West and graduating from New York University with a degree in Business Administration. Each had made a film in the other's country before they first met, en route to the 1961 Cannes Film Festival. Immediately recognizing that they had a lot of ideas in common and a good combination of skills to realize those ideas, they set up Merchant–Ivory Productions that same year with the stated aim of making English-language feature films in India for the international market.

Merchant–Ivory's first feature film was *The Householder* and the company's first international success was *Shakespeare Wallah*, both written by Ruth Prawer Jhabvala, who was born in Germany, educated in England and Indian by marriage. These and her subsequent collaborations with the Indian producer and American director added significantly to the cultural richness of the Merchant–Ivory oeuvre. In the 1970s Merchant and Ivory expanded their geographical horizons and began making films outside India – their roll call of locations now includes: Delhi, Bombay and Benares on the Indian subcontinent; London, Paris and Florence in Europe; and New York, New England and Texas in the USA, evoking periods ranging from the British Raj and 19th-century America to Edwardian England and 1920s' Paris.

KEY DATES

1928 James Ivory is born on 7 June in Berkeley, California, USA, and later raised in Oregon, USA, where he studies at the University of Oregon, after which he studies film at the University of Southern California

1936 Ismail Merchant is born on 25 December in Bombay, India, and is later educated at St Xavier's College, Bombay, and New York University, USA

1960 Merchant directs and co-produces his first short film, *The Creation of Woman*. Ivory is awarded a grant by the Asia Society of New York to make a documentary about India

1961 Merchant and Ivory meet en route to the Cannes Film Festival, France. They form Merchant-Ivory Productions (M-IP)

1963 M-IP produces its first feature film, *The Householder*, written by Ruth Prawer Jhabvala and based on her own novel

1965 M-IP produces its first international success, *Shakespeare Wallah*

1970 M-IP produces *Bombay Talkie*

1982 M-IP produces *Heat and Dust*

1985 M-IP produces *A Room With a View*

1991 M-IP produces *Howard's End*

1993 M-IP produces *The Remains of the Day*

2002 M-IP produces *The Mystic Masseur*

2003 M-IP produces *Le Divorce*

RIGHT *(l–r) Ivory, Prawer Jhabvala and Merchant receive a joint British Academy film fellowship (24 February 2002)* **OPPOSITE TOP** *Emma Thompson and Anthony Hopkins in Merchant–Ivory's* The Remains of the Day *(1993)*

HANNA & BARBERA

Award-winning animation duo

Millions of people worldwide know William Hanna and Joseph Barbera, if not by their names then through the cartoon characters they created together, which include Tom & Jerry *(see p72)*, the Flintstones *(see p76)*, Scooby-Doo, Yogi Bear and Huckleberry Hound, among many, many others. Born a year apart at opposite ends of the USA, Hanna and Barbera grew up on converging paths, both knowing that they wanted to be animators, both struggling to find employment during the Depression, both joining animation studios in the early 1930s and both moving to MGM's newly established animation studio in 1937, where they met for the first time.

After working on an unsuccessful series foisted on him by MGM, Hanna reached the conclusion that: 'I would have to obtain two things that were critically essential to my professional fulfilment. The first was a decent cartoon property that I could really get my teeth into. [The other was] a creatively inspired partner who was also a distinctively talented artist.' He found the latter in Barbera and together they created the former in Jasper and Jinx, a cat and mouse cartoon duo that became the prototype for the immensely successful Tom and Jerry. Hanna and Barbera happily produced Tom and Jerry cartoons for nearly two decades until, in 1957, MGM closed its animation studios, prompting Hanna and Barbera to set up Hanna–Barbera Productions. Barbera later remembered: 'Bill Hanna and I tossed a coin to decide which of our names should come first in the logo of our partnership. Bill won the toss, but I never minded a bit. As far as we were concerned, the partnership of Hanna–Barbera was a winning combination from either end.'

And so it proved, the duo reaching the millennium with seven Academy Awards, nine Emmys, an Annie, a Golden Globe and a star on the Hollywood Walk of Fame. But it was not just about awards. In his autobiography, Hanna describes 'the fundamental spirit of friendship cartoons communicate to those who love them', and concludes: 'Looking back over miles and years of countless frames of footage, I can see how that one quality of comradeship runs constant. From Tom and Jerry to Ruff and Reddy, Yogi and Boo Boo or Fred and Barney, or for that matter Bill and Joe or Hanna–Barbera and Company, we were always on the buddy system.'

RIGHT *Joe Barbera (l) and Bill Hanna doing what they did best (c.1960)*

HAVE YOU HEARD?
Summing up their partnership in the introduction to Hanna's autobiography, Barbera wrote:

'Shakespeare once asked: "What's in a name?" For Bill Hanna and myself, the name of Hanna–Barbera inaugurated a lifelong creative alliance that I will always cherish.'

KEY DATES

1910 William Denby Hanna is born on 14 July in Melrose, New Mexico, USA

1911 Joseph Roland Barbera is born on 24 March in New York City, USA

1930 Hanna joins Harmon-Ising Studios, creators of Looney Tunes and Merrie Melodies, as a lyricist and composer

1930s Barbera joins the Fleischer Studios, creators of Betty Boop and Popeye

1937 Hanna becomes one of the first directors of MGM's new animation studio. Barbera moves to the new MGM studio, where he teams up with Hanna

1939 Hanna and Barbera (H and B) make the animation *Puss Gets the Boot* (released February 1940), starring a cat and a mouse named Jasper and Jinx, the prototypes of Tom and Jerry

1941 H and B introduce Tom and Jerry to the world in *The Midnight Snack*

1957 MGM closes its animation studio and H and B form their own studio, Hanna-Barbera Productions (H-BP)

1958 H-BP launches *Huckleberry Hound and Friends*, which becomes the first animated series to win an Emmy, winning the award for outstanding achievement in children's programming

1960 H-BP introduces Stone-Age family the Flintstones to the world. Yogi Bear, a popular character originally from *Huckleberry Hound and Friends*, is given his own show

1962 H-BP introduces the Jetsons to the world as a futuristic parallel to the Flintstones

1969 H-BP introduces Scooby-Doo to the world in the series *Scooby-Doo, Where Are You*?

1976 H and B are honoured with stars in Hollywood's Walk of Fame

1993 H and B are inducted into America's Television Academy Hall of Fame

2001 Hanna dies on 22 March at home in Hollywood, USA, aged 90

GOSCINNY
UDERZO
Co-creators of cartoon duo Asterix and Obelix

René Goscinny

René Goscinny was the storyteller behind *Asterix*. Born in Paris, France, he was brought up in Argentina and lived briefly in the USA before returning to Paris at the age of 24 to work as a writer and illustrator. The job that had lured him back to Paris proved unsuccessful, but there was a happy outcome because it was in Paris that he met the man with whom he would collaborate for the rest of his life – Albert Uderzo.

Albert Uderzo

The illustrator of all the *Asterix* adventures, Uderzo began his career as an illustrator at the age of 13 when he was employed and trained by the Paris Publishing Society. The Second World War interrupted his fledgling career, but after the war he created several successful strip cartoons including one called *Arys Buck*, about an indomitable Gaul who can be seen, in spirit at least, as a precursor of *Asterix*. Uderzo was already a rising star in the world of illustrators when he met Goscinny in 1951 and began the professional partnership that would make them both world-famous.

KEY DATES

1926 René Goscinny is born on 14 August in Paris, France, and brought up in Argentina from the age of two

1927 Albert Uderzo is born on 25 April in France, the son of Italian immigrants

1940 Uderzo is employed by the Paris Publishing Society (SPE), where he learns design and picture editing. His first illustration, a parody of Aesop's fables, is published in the SPE magazine *Junior*

1945 Goscinny moves to New York, USA

1949 Goscinny works briefly as an illustrator for Davis, Elder and Wood, who later go on to found *MAD* magazine. Uderzo works for the magazines *France Dimanche* and *France-Soir*

1950 Goscinny returns to Paris, where he and Uderzo meet in 1951

1952 Goscinny and Uderzo (G and U) produce their first joint works, *Jehan Pistolet* and *Luc Junior*

1959 G and U and Jean-Michel Charlier launch the comic magazine *Pilote*, for which G and U create the new cartoon series *Asterix*

1967 The first album of *Asterix* cartoons is published as a book

1974 G and U form their own cartoon studio, Studio Idéfix

1977 Goscinny dies on 5 November, aged 51, and Uderzo continues writing *Asterix* stories alone, though fans agree that he never reaches the standard that the duo achieved together

2004 Uderzo is awarded a German special lifetime achievement award

ABOVE *Albert Uderzo, flanked by (l–r) Asterix, Getafix and Obelix, receives a special lifetime achievement award in Germany (12 June 2004)* **OPPOSITE** *René Goscinny with Asterix and Obelix (undated)*

Goscinny and Uderzo

Goscinny and Uderzo created their first joint cartoon characters, *Jehan Pistolet* and *Luc Junior*, in 1952. These characters ran until 1957, but in the meantime, wanting more artistic freedom, in 1955 Goscinny, Uderzo and two colleagues set up their own syndicate. Four years later three of the four partners launched their own comic magazine, *Pilote*, and on 29 October 1959 *Pilote* published the first episode of a cartoon that would ensure that the names of Goscinny and Uderzo were linked for evermore – *Asterix*.

The stories of Asterix, which run to 31 adventures and have been translated into 100 languages, are set in Gaul (now France) during the Roman occupation. Asterix is a diminutive but shrewd Gallic warrior who gets superhuman strength from a magic potion brewed for him by the druid Getafix (known as Panoramix in the original French) and shares his adventures with his faithful gargantuan sidekick, Obelix, who is willing to join Asterix on any adventure on two conditions: there must be plenty of wild boar to eat, and plenty of fighting.

BARNUM
BAILEY

Circus showmen who formed 'The Greatest Show on Earth'

P.T. Barnum

Phineas Taylor Barnum worked in a variety of jobs before moving to New York at the age of 24 to seek his fortune. He made his break as a showman in 1835 by buying the services of Joice Heth, a woman purporting to be 161 years old and the former nurse of US President George Washington, whose birth she claimed to have attended in 1732. After his success with Heth, Barnum established Barnum's American Museum and during the 1850s he set up a travelling museum and menagerie that was the precursor of his three-ring circus, 'P.T. Barnum's Greatest Show on Earth'.

James Bailey

James McGinnes ran away from home at the age of 13 to join the circus. He began by doing odd jobs for Frederick H. Bailey of the Robinson & Lake Circus and proved so able that Bailey not only took McGinnes on permanently but he also persuaded him to adopt his name. As James Bailey, the teenager soon gained the respect of experienced circus veterans and quickly rose to become the youngest general agent in the business. In 1873 he invested his savings in a quarter share of the Hemmings, Cooper and Whitby Circus and by the end of the decade he had turned the business, now known as Cooper & Bailey's Circus, into a serious rival to Barnum's Greatest Show on Earth.

Barnum and Bailey

In the winter of 1880 one of Bailey's circus elephants gave birth to the first elephant calf known to have been born in captivity. Barnum offered to buy mother and baby, but Bailey refused and made great publicity out of Barnum's offer. Barnum was so impressed by Bailey's one-upmanship that he decided he should join forces with his rival, and so originated one of the world's most famous circuses ever – the Barnum & Bailey Circus, later 'Barnum & Bailey's Greatest Show on Earth'.

Barnum was a great self-publicist, and thereby remained the more famous of the duo, but he openly credited the semi-reclusive Bailey as the innovator, businessman and manager behind the phenomenal success of

> **HAVE YOU HEARD?**
> Barnum once described the business principle behind his success as a showman:
>
> 'I knew the only way to make a million from my patrons was to give them abundant and wholesome attractions for a small sum of money … Year after year I bought genuine curiosities regardless of cost wherever I could find them in Europe or America.'

ABOVE *James Bailey (undated photograph)*

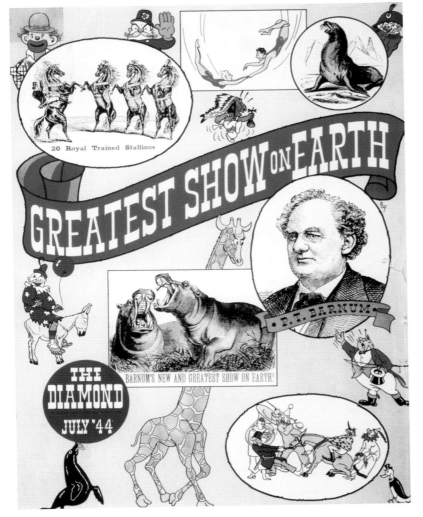

KEY DATES

1810 Phineas Taylor Barnum is born on 5 July in Bethel, Connecticut, USA

1835 Barnum begins his career as a showman by exhibiting Joice Heth

1841 Barnum establishes Barnum's American Museum in New York City, offering exhibits, lectures, plays and curiosities

1842–47 Barnum makes a fortune as the manager of the midget Charles Sherwood Stratton, whom he renames General Tom Thumb

1847 James Anthony McGinnes (also given as McGinness and McGinniss), later Bailey, is born on 4 July in Detroit, Michigan, USA

1851–56 Barnum tours the Great Asiatic Caravan, Museum and Menagerie

1860 McGinnes begins his circus career by doing odd jobs for Frederick H. Bailey, whose name he later adopts

1871–80 Barnum tours a two-ring circus that he bills 'The Great Travelling World's Fair', adding a third ring in 1874 and later billing it 'P.T. Barnum's Greatest Show on Earth'

1873 Bailey invests in the Hemmings, Cooper and Whitby Circus

1881 Barnum joins forces with Bailey and his partners to form the Barnum & Bailey Circus, later 'Barnum & Bailey's Greatest Show on Earth'

1891 Barnum dies on 7 April, aged 80, and Bailey takes over

1906 Bailey dies on 11 April, aged 58

1907 The Ringling Brothers buy the Barnum & Bailey Circus

their partnership. For most of the life of the Barnum & Bailey Circus the two partners worked separately: their character differences made it hard for them to work side by side and in 1888 Bailey went into semi-retirement, leaving Barnum in charge until Barnum persuaded him to return in 1890. After Barnum's death in 1891, Bailey took sole charge until his death in 1906, after which the Barnum & Bailey Circus was bought by the Ringling Brothers.

ABOVE *'The Greatest Show on Earth', poster advertising P.T. Barnum's circus (July 1944)*

MUSIC & DANCE

GILBERT & SULLIVAN

Composer and librettist of the 'Savoy operas'

W.S. Gilbert

W.S. Gilbert (who was always known by his initials rather than his Christian name) embarked on a career as a barrister, but when he failed to attract sufficiently lucrative briefs earned his living instead by submitting humorous contributions to magazines such as *Fun* and *Punch*. He then had some success as a playwright before beginning the partnership that would turn him into a national institution, when he collaborated with composer Arthur Sullivan on an operetta entitled *Thespis*.

Arthur Sullivan

Arthur Sullivan was establishing himself as the best known serious composer of his day when in 1867 he discovered his talent for comic opera. His first meeting with Gilbert was in 1869 when he was invited by a friend, composer Frederic Clay, to attend a rehearsal of the operetta *Ages Ago*, at which Clay introduced Sullivan to his librettist, W.S. Gilbert. Two years later Gilbert and Sullivan worked together for the first time, when impresario John Hollingshead commissioned Gilbert's script for *Thespis* and urged Gilbert to approach Sullivan to write the music.

Gilbert and Sullivan

Thespis ran for only 80 nights, but it made a sufficiently good impression on impresario Richard D'Oyly Carte for him to bring Gilbert and Sullivan together again four years later when he produced their first major success, *Trial by Jury*. When Gilbert first read the libretto to Sullivan, he decided that he was not happy with it and stopped reading before the end – Sullivan, however, was delighted and later wrote: 'I was screaming with laughter the whole time.'

 Trial by Jury was the beginning of a long and successful partnership, Sullivan's musical settings perfectly reflecting the rhythm and humour of Gilbert's lyrics. D'Oyly Carte formed a business partnership with the duo and built the Savoy Theatre in 1881 specifically to stage their shows, which later became known collectively as the 'Savoy operas'. But the relationship between Gilbert and Sullivan was argumentative as well as successful and a

RIGHT *Composer Sir Arthur Seymour Sullivan (c.1875)* TOP RIGHT *Poet, playwright and librettist Sir William Schwenck Gilbert (c.1895)*

quarrel over the costs of *The Gondoliers* temporarily ended their partnership after 11 successful shows in 14 years. They did not work together again until three years later and although they went on to create two more comic operas neither show had the wit and sparkle of their earlier work.

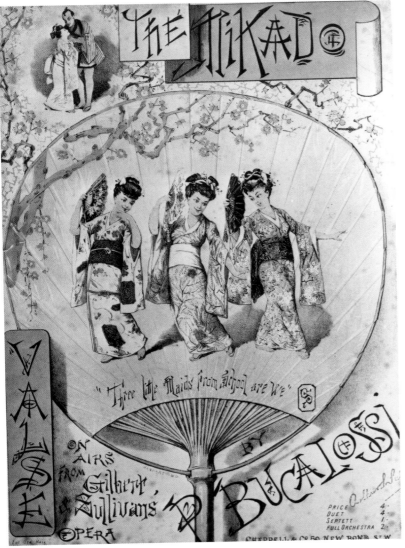

KEY DATES

▼ **1836** William Schwenck Gilbert is born on 18 November in London, England

▼ **1842** Arthur Seymour Sullivan is born on 13 May in London

▼ **1861–72** Sullivan is organist and choirmaster of St Michael's, London

▼ **1864** Gilbert becomes a barrister, but makes his living from contributions to magazines

▼ **1866–70** Gilbert writes a number of plays

▼ **1867** Sullivan begins his association with theatre by writing the music for *Box and Cox*

▼ **1869** Gilbert and Sullivan (G and S) meet for the first time, at a rehearsal of *Ages Ago*

▼ **1871** G and S collaborate for the first time, on a Christmas show entitled *Thespis* at the Gaiety Theatre, London. Sullivan becomes the first Principal of the National Training College (later the Royal College of Music)

▼ **1875** G and S have their first major success, with *Trial by Jury*

▼ **1877–89** *Trial by Jury* is followed by a run of successes including *HMS Pinafore*, *The Pirates of Penzance*, *Iolanthe*, *Princess Ida*, *The Mikado*, *Ruddigore*, *The Yeomen of the Guard* and *The Gondoliers*

▼ **1896** G and S collaborate for the last time, on *The Grand Duke*

▼ **1900** Sullivan dies on 22 November, aged 58, and is buried in St Paul's Cathedral

▼ **1911** Gilbert dies on 29 May in Harrow Weald, Middlesex, aged 74, when he drowns in his swimming pool after a suspected heart attack

ABOVE *Song-cover from Gilbert and Sullivan's operetta* The Mikado *(c.1870)*

RODGERS & HAMMERSTEIN

Pulitzer prize-winning writers of hit musicals

Rodgers and Hart

Richard Rodgers was in the rare position of being part of two highly acclaimed songwriting duos, composing dozens of hit Broadway musicals, first with Lorenz Hart and then with Oscar Hammerstein II. He began writing songs at the age of 11 and in 1916, when aged 14, was inspired by seeing Jerome Kern's musical *Very Good Eddie*, later saying: 'Life began for me at 2:30' (the starting time of the Saturday matinees). Rodgers met Lorenz Hart two years later and they worked together with little success until two of their songs were included in *The Garrick Gaieties* in 1925, which instantly brought them the critical and financial success they had been waiting for. They went on to collaborate on 28 musicals over the next 15 years, together writing some of Broadway's greatest-ever show songs, including: *The Most Beautiful Girl in the World*, *The Lady is a Tramp*, *My Funny Valentine*, *I Wish I Were in Love Again*, *Blue Moon* and *Bewitched, Bothered and Bewildered*.

Rodgers and Hammerstein

After working with Hart on the musical *Pal Joey* in 1940, Rodgers sought another collaborator because he could no longer cope with Hart's alcoholism. Hart died three years later in 1943, shortly after attending the premiere of Rodgers' first collaboration with lyricist and librettist Oscar Hammerstein II – the phenomenally successful *Oklahoma!*

Like Rodgers, Hammerstein was already a seasoned writer of Broadway

ABOVE *Rodgers and Hart (c.1930s)*

KEY DATES

1895 Lorenz Milton Hart is born on 2 May in New York City, USA. Oscar Hammerstein II is born on 12 July in New York City

1902 Richard Rodgers is born on 28 June in New York City

1918–40 Rodgers collaborates with Hart on 28 hit musicals, including *The Girl Friend*, *Babes in Arms*, *The Boys from Syracuse* and *Pal Joey*

1920s Hammerstein writes the book and lyrics for a number of Broadway musicals including *Showboat* with composer Jerome Kern

1943 Rodgers collaborates with Hammerstein for the first time, on *Oklahoma!*, which wins a Pulitzer prize. Hart dies of pneumonia on 22 November, aged 48

1945–59 Rodgers and Hammerstein collaborate on a string of hit musicals including *Carousel*, *South Pacific* (which wins a Pulitzer prize), *The King and I* and *The Sound of Music*

1960 Hammerstein dies of cancer on 23 August in Doylestown, Philadelphia, aged 65

1979 Rodgers dies on 30 December in New York City, aged 77

musicals, having collaborated with a number of composers including George Gershwin, Harold Arlen and Jerome Kern, with whom he wrote *Showboat* in 1927. *Oklahoma!* won a Pulitzer prize and proved to be one of the biggest ever Broadway hits, instantly placing Rodgers in a duo to rival the one that had just ended. While critics argue that the individual songs of Rodgers and Hart are greater than those of Rodgers and Hammerstein, there is no doubt that the complete shows of the latter duo were a great advance on those of the former, revolutionizing American musicals and transforming the entire genre from, in the words of one critic, 'flimsy melodramas with songs tacked on' into 'seamless and powerful dramatic works'. After continued critical acclaim with *Carousel*, *South Pacific* and *The King and I*, Rodgers and Hammerstein's success waned during the 1950s until it was revived with the success in 1959 of their last musical together, *The Sound of Music*.

ABOVE *Richard Rogers (l) and Oscar Hammerstein II prepare to help three actresses enact the showstopper 'I'm Gonna Wash That Man Right Out of My Hair': (l–r) Mary Martin, Janet Blair and Martha Wright all played Ensign Nellie Forbush during the Broadway run of* South Pacific *(17 January 1954)*

FRED ASTAIRE GINGER ROGERS

Hollywood's answer to Nureyev and Fonteyn

Fred and Adele

Fred Astaire's name will forever be associated with that of Ginger Rogers, but the groundwork for his phenomenally successful dancing career was laid in a partnership with his older sister, Adele. Fred and Adele began touring together as a vaudeville duo in 1916 and during the 1920s they starred together on Broadway and in London's West End in a number of stage musicals including the Gershwin shows *Lady Be Good* and *Funny Face*. Fred and Adele might well have become as famous a duo as Fred and Ginger later became, were it not for the fact that in 1932 Adele married English aristocrat Lord Charles Cavendish and gave up her stage career.

Fred and Ginger

After Adele married, Fred travelled to Hollywood to begin a career on the big screen. There he found a new dancing partner in Ginger Rogers, 12 years his junior, whose career had followed a similar path to his own: she had

started in vaudeville and then switched from Broadway to Hollywood after starring in the Gershwin musical *Girl Crazy*. Fred and Ginger co-starred in 10 film musicals including *Top Hat*, *Swing Time* and *Follow the Fleet*. Together they delighted audiences during the Depression of the 1930s, captured the hearts of film fans around the world, and revolutionized the genre with their elaborate, graceful, stylish and innovative dance routines. Famous for his sartorial elegance, Astaire admitted after his retirement that he did not actually enjoy wearing his trademark top hat, white tie and tails.

KEY DATES

1899 Frederick Austerlitz, who later uses the stage name Fred Astaire, is born on 10 May in Omaha, Nebraska, USA

1911 Virginia Katherine McMath, later better known as Ginger Rogers, is born on 16 July in Independence, Missouri, USA

1916 Astaire and his sister Adele begin touring as a vaudeville duo

1920s Astaire and Adele star together in a number of Broadway musicals. Rogers stars in a number of vaudeville shows and Broadway musicals

1933 Astaire and Rogers team up for the first time, eventually making 10 films together

1940 Rogers wins an Academy Award for her role in *Kitty Foyle*

1949 Astaire wins a special Academy Award for 'unique artistry and contributions to the technique of motion pictures'

1987 Astaire dies on 22 June in Los Angeles, aged 88

1995 Rogers dies on 25 April in Rancho Mirage, California, aged 83

HAVE YOU HEARD?

When Fred Astaire left his stage career for the film industry, his Broadway reputation counted for nothing in Hollywood. The report on his first screen test read:

'Can't act. Can't sing. Slightly bald. Can dance a little.'

Ballet dancers and choreographers Rudolf Nureyev and George Balanchine both described Fred Astaire as 'the best dancer in the world'.

ABOVE *Poster for the film version of Irving Berlin's* Follow the Fleet, *starring Fred Astaire and Ginger Rogers (1936)* **OPPOSITE** *Ginger Rogers as Penelope 'Penny' Carroll and Fred Astaire as John 'Lucky' Garnett in the film* Swing Time *(1936)*

NUREYEV & FONTEYN

The world's greatest balletic duo

Margot Fonteyn

Margot Fonteyn's real name was Margaret Hookham, which she always shortened to Peggy, and it was as Peggy Hookham that she made her professional debut as a snowflake in *The Nutcracker*. By then Peggy was already a seasoned ballerina, having first performed at the age of four as a 'Wind' in the annual show at her local ballet school in Ealing, West London. And her connection with Russian ballet predated her famous partnership with Rudolf Nureyev by 35 years – when she was eight her father took a job in Shanghai, China, where her mother employed two Russian ballet teachers, the second of them a former member of the Bolshoi.

After the family returned to England, Peggy joined the Vic-Wells Ballet at Sadler's Wells, London, which later moved to Covent Garden and became the Royal Ballet. Soon after joining she adopted the stage name Margot Fontes, later modulated to Fonteyn, and launched the career that was to bring her international acclaim as a 'ballerina among ballerinas'.

Rudolf Nureyev

In 1929 10-year-old Peggy Hookham and her mother travelled on the Trans-Siberian railway for a visit home from Shanghai. Nine years later, a pregnant woman named Farida Nureyev travelled on the same railway to join her husband who was working more than 2,000 miles away. En route she gave birth to a boy she named Rudolf, after her idol Rudolph Valentino.

On 31 December 1945, when Rudolf was seven, an event took place that was to shape the rest of his life: he saw his first ballet, *The Song of the Cranes*. Nureyev was captivated and often said that from that moment he felt that dance was his calling, writing in his autobiography: 'From the moment I entered that magic place [the theatre] I felt I had really left the world, borne far away from everything I knew by the dream staged for me alone. I was speechless.'

Nureyev then doggedly followed his calling, beginning classical training at the Kirov Ballet School at the advanced age (for ballet) of 17 and rising rapidly to become principal dancer of the Kirov Ballet. Six years later, on ▶

ABOVE *Rudolf Nureyev backstage at the London Palladium (13 November 1963)* **TOP** *Margot Fonteyn in Granada, Spain (c. 1953)* **OPPOSITE** *Nureyev and Fonteyn rehearsing* Marguerite and Armand, *at the Royal Opera House, Covent Garden, London (8 March 1963)*

HAVE YOU HEARD?

Nureyev once said of his most famous partnership:

'If I hadn't found Margot, I don't think I would be dancing now. It would have been two, three years, chasing everywhere. Big noise! Then phtt! Burnt out.'

17 June 1961, came another pivotal moment: while on tour in Paris, France, Nureyev defected from the Soviet Union and claimed political asylum in France.

Nureyev and Fonteyn

In October 1961 Nureyev visited London at the invitation of Fonteyn to perform in a charity gala that she organized annually in aid of the Royal Academy of Dancing. By then Fonteyn was firmly established as the world's greatest ballerina, and Nureyev was naturally keen to dance with her. Fonteyn, however, was reticent, not wanting to risk her reputation with someone she had never seen dance. On that visit Nureyev had to be satisifed with a solo and a duet with Rosella Hightower, but his elegant bow caught the eye of Ninette de Valois, artistic director of the Royal Ballet, who wrote in her memoirs: 'I could see him suddenly and clearly in one role – Albrecht in *Giselle*. Then and there I decided that when he first danced for us it must be with Fonteyn in that ballet.'

Fonteyn was still unsure: at the age of 43, she claimed that pairing her with Nureyev would be like billing 'mutton with lamb'. However, her husband Tito was convinced that Nureyev would be a big hit and advised her to make sure she was part of that success or risk being eclipsed by it, which would effectively end her career. On Tito's advice, Fonteyn accepted de Valois' suggestion that she and Nureyev perform together and so, on 21 February 1962, began the partnership that would secure Nureyev's place as an international star, extend Fonteyn's career by more than a decade and transform the very nature of Western ballet.

Expectations of this electrifying partnership were extremely high before it even began and they did not disappoint. Nureyev biographers write: 'Nureyev was applauded "within an inch of his life"'; 'That night there were 30 curtain calls, during the course of which a legend was being minted'; and 'The audience reacted as if Mafeking had been relieved'. The magic of their partnership was not confined to rehearsals and performances, and close friendship soon led to rumours of a romance, although the rumours ended when Fonteyn decided to stand by her philandering husband, Tito, when he was shot and paralysed by the jealous husband of one of his mistresses. Their artistic relationship, however, continued triumphantly for 14 years, until their last full performance together at Covent Garden, on 10 January 1976, when they danced *Romeo and Juliet*.

KEY DATES

1919 Margaret Hookham, later Margot Fonteyn de Arias, is born on 18 May in Reigate, England, and later studies ballet in Shanghai, China, and in London

1933 The Hookhams return to England

1934 Fonteyn makes her professional debut with the Vic-Wells Ballet (later the Sadler's Wells Ballet and finally the Royal Ballet), London, as a snowflake in *The Nutcracker*

1938 Rudolf Hametovich Nureyev is born, in Razdolnaya, north of Vladivostok, Siberia, probably on 17 March; there is evidence, but no documentation, that he was actually born on 14 March and the birth registered on 17 March

1939 Fonteyn makes her first solo appearance, in *The Haunted Ballroom*

1951 Fonteyn receives the CBE

1955 Nureyev begins training at the Kirov School, Russia

1956 Fonteyn is made a Dame

1961 While visiting Paris, France, with the Kirov Ballet, Nureyev defects, later joining Le Grand Ballet du Marquis de Cuevas

1962 Nureyev and Fonteyn perform together for the first time

1976 Nureyev and Fonteyn perform together for the last time

1983–89 Nureyev is artistic director of the Paris Opera

1991 Fonteyn dies on 21 February in Panama, aged 71

1993 Nureyev dies on 6 January in Paris, France, aged 54

OPPOSITE *Nureyev and Fonteyn on San Simon Beach near Beirut, Lebanon, between performances at the Baalbeck Festival (28 July 1964)*

HERB ALPERT
JERRY MOSS

Co-founders of A&M Records

A former editor of *Rolling Stone* magazine referred to Herb Alpert, Jerry Moss and the legendary record label they formed together as 'The Adroit Muse, the Artful Merchant, and the Appetite for Music' – a series of 'A's and 'M's that are an apt *multum* of how A&M came to be. Alpert, the adroit muse, first displayed his interest in music at the age of eight when he used his pocket money to rent a trumpet from his school, and later studied music at the University of Southern California before publishing his first song, 'Circle Rock', in 1958. That same year Moss, the artful merchant, took his first music industry appointment, as a promoter for Coed Records.

They discovered that they shared an appetite for music after Moss moved to Alpert's home town of Los Angeles in 1960. Both socialized in restaurants and bars used by the music industry crowd (Alpert was fast becoming a trumpet legend in his own right) and they soon struck up an acquaintance and working partnership. After they had had a false start with a novelty single they produced in 1961 for the Seattle World's Fair, Moss asked Alpert to play on a record he was producing, Alpert offered Moss an unreleased track he had written, and the collaboration began in earnest.

Moss suggested that since they were both investing their time and money they should form a partnership and so, with $100 each, they formed Carnival Records and on 25 July 1962 released their first single. They subsequently discovered that the name Carnival was already in use, and less than a month later they came up with an alternative that would become world-renowned as a symbol of quality for listeners and of integrity for the artists who recorded with them: A&M Records.

After several big hits, A&M developed into what Moss later described as 'a sort of semi-hip, jazz, Latin-sounding label'. The awards began rolling in annually and A&M soon branched out into folk, rock and pop, after which the label's roster of artists began to read like a who's who of the music industry. The awards and artists associated with A&M since 1962 are too many to list, but the remarkable achievements of Alpert and Moss were summarized in a single 1997 accolade: a special Grammy Trustees Award for 'inspiring music executives to artist-oriented philosophy'.

KEY DATES

1935 Herb Alpert is born on 31 March in Los Angeles, USA. Jerome Sheldon Moss is born on 8 May in West Bronx, New York, USA

1958 Moss takes his first job in the music industry, promoting singles for Coed Records. Alpert co-writes his first published song

1961 Alpert and Moss (A and M) collaborate for the first time: as the Diddley Oohs, they write and perform 'Hooray for the Big Slow Train' for the upcoming Seattle World's Fair

1962 A and M form Carnival Records (as a subsidiary of Moss's publishing company, Irving Music) and the Almo/Irving music publishing company (Almo being a contraction of Alpert and Moss). In August they change the name of Carnival Records to A&M Records

1965 A&M releases its first two No.1 albums

1966 A&M wins its first four Grammys

1967 A and M launch the international music publishing company Rondor, named for Moss's son Ron and Alpert's son Dore

1968 A&M opens its own recording studios

1989 A and M sell A&M to PolyGram for $500 million, signing a five-year agreement to remain as members of the board

1993 A and M leave A&M when it appears that PolyGram is going back on its agreement to allow them to continue to run the company autonomously

1997 A and M receive the Grammy Trustees Award

ABOVE Herb Alpert's Tijuana Brass, Whipped Cream and Other Delights, *A&M Records* (1965) **OPPOSITE** Herb Alpert (l) and Jerry Moss outside A&M's recently acquired premises, formerly Charlie Chaplin's film studio (15 July 1967)

LENNON & McCARTNEY

Lennon and McCartney

Popular music changed forever as a result of an event that took place on 6 July 1956 – 14-year-old Paul McCartney visited St Peter's church fête in Woolton, Liverpool, in search of pretty girls. History does not record whether he met any girls that day, but he did meet 15-year-old John Lennon, who was playing at the fête with the Quarrymen, a skiffle band inspired by Lonnie Donegan. Four months later McCartney saw Donegan play at the Liverpool Empire and he, too, was inspired. He bought a guitar and taught himself how to play so well that in 1957 Lennon invited him to join the Quarrymen.

Until then the Quarrymen had been playing cover versions of American hits, but when McCartney joined he and Lennon began writing their own songs. Thus, in the front room of a terraced house in Liverpool, began the most successful songwriting partnership of the 20th century. McCartney remembers: 'When John and I decided to try and write songs, the most convenient location to do this was my home in Forthlin Road. My father went out to work and this left the house empty all day, so I would take off school, sagging off, we called it, and John would take off from art college.' They would sit in the house for hours at a time working out chords and lyrics, honing the sound that would define a generation, and McCartney recalls: 'We had a rule: if we couldn't remember a song the next day, it was no good.' One of the songs that they did remember the next day was 'Love Me Do', which survived the metamorphosis of the Quarrymen into the Beatles and, in 1962, became the Beatles' first UK Top 20 hit.

The Beatles scored their first UK No.1 the following year with 'From Me to You' and then became the first band to knock itself off the top spot, with 'She Loves You', both written by Lennon and McCartney. In total the Beatles had no less than 17 UK No.1 singles, 13 of which also made it to the top of the US charts, and all of them written by Lennon and McCartney except 'Lady Madonna', which was written by McCartney alone. But despite this phenomenal success, or perhaps because of the pressures it brought about, the partnership ended acrimoniously in 1970. Any chance of a reunion was lost forever when John Lennon was murdered in 1980, but there was a ▶

HAVE YOU HEARD?

The Quarrymen, later Johnny and the Moondogs, changed their name to the Silver Beetles in homage to Buddy Holly's Crickets. Then, in 1960, they changed it again to the Beatles because, according to John Lennon, 'a man in a flaming pie appeared and said, "You shall be the Beatles with an 'a'".'

RIGHT *The Beatles (l–r: George Harrison, John Lennon, Paul McCartney and Pete Best) perform in Liverpool before signing their first recording contract (1962)*

KEY DATES

1940 John Winston Lennon is born on 9 October in Liverpool, England

1942 James Paul McCartney is born on 18 June in Liverpool, England

1956 Lennon forms skiffle group the Quarrymen. Lennon and McCartney (L and M) meet for the first time

1957 Lennon invites McCartney to join the Quarrymen, whose name later changes to Johnny and the Moondogs and then to the Silver Beetles

1960 The Silver Beetles change their name to the Beatles

1963 The Beatles have their first UK No.1 single, with L and M's 'From Me To You', and their first US No.1, with L and M's 'She Loves You'

1965 The Beatles are created MBE; in 1969 Lennon returns his insignia in protest at British involvement in the Nigerian Civil War and Britain's support of US involvement in Vietnam

1969 Lennon marries Yoko Ono

1970 The Beatles disband. John and Yoko form the Plastic Ono Band

1971 McCartney forms Wings with his wife, Linda, and others

1980 Lennon is shot dead, aged 40, on 8 December outside his home in New York, USA

1995 L and M are reunited on record as the surviving members of the Beatles record 'Free as a Bird'

1997 McCartney is knighted

coda to the story when, in 1997, McCartney and the late Lennon were reunited on record – the surviving members of the Beatles reunited to record 'Free as a Bird', adding their contributions to a previously unreleased demo tape sung by Lennon.

John and Paul launch Mick and Keith

Lennon and McCartney were generous with their talent, even providing a hit for the fledgling Rolling Stones before Mick Jagger and Keith Richards *(see p198)* began to write their own songs. The Stones' first single was a cover of Chuck Berry's 'Come On', but their manager, Andrew Loog Oldham (left), was not convinced that their existing repertoire would provide another hit. Loog Oldham became so frustrated during one rehearsal in a basement jazz club off Charing Cross Road, London, that he left the Stones to it and went out to walk and think. Then he saw two familiar faces getting out of a taxi near Leicester Square: John Lennon and Paul McCartney, whom he knew well, having worked for them as a publicist. He hurried over to the famous duo, perhaps hoping, but certainly not expecting, that this fortuitous meeting might be the answer to his problem.

LEFT *Andrew Loog Oldham, manager of the Rolling Stones* (see p198) *(July 1966)* **TOP** *(l–r) Yoko Ono, John Lennon and Paul McCartney subliminally advertising Apple Records at the premiere of the Beatles' film* Yellow Submarine *at the London Pavilion (1968)*

Lennon and McCartney asked the glum-looking Loog Oldham what was wrong and he explained that he couldn't find anything to record for the Stones' next single. Then, states Loog Oldham in his autobiography *Stoned*: 'They smiled at me and each other, told me not to worry and our three pairs of Cuban heels turned smartly back towards the basement rehearsal. Once downstairs, the boys quickly got to work teaching the Stones 'I Wanna Be Your Man'. Yeah, they gave us a hit, but more than that they gave us a tutorial in the reality they were forging for themselves; lesson of the day from John and Paul.'

ABOVE *Paul McCartney (l) and John Lennon posing on the set of* The Ed Sullivan Show *(9 February 1964)*

MICK JAGGER KEITH RICHARDS

Perennial rock'n'roll songwriting duo

Born within five months of each other in Dartford, Kent, Mick Jagger and Keith Richards attended the same primary school and later emerged as rock'n'roll's greatest songwriters, becoming the driving force behind what has regularly been described as 'The Greatest Rock'n'Roll Band in the World' – their satanic majesties, the Rolling Stones.

Jagger and Richards both attended Wentworth County Primary School, Dartford, where, according to Jagger: 'We weren't great friends, but we knew each other.' Three years later Jagger changed schools because his parents moved house, and he and Richards went their separate ways until they met up again years later, as teenagers, on the platform at Dartford railway station. Jagger was carrying a Chuck Berry album, which attracted the attention of his former friend, also now a Chuck Berry fan, and they discovered a shared passion for rhythm and blues. They also discovered that they had a mutual friend: Dick Taylor, one of Richards' friends at Sidcup Art College, played in a band with Jagger. Taylor remembers that after the meeting at the station: 'I told [Richards] to come along and hear us, which he did and next thing he was in the band. Simple as that.'

Calling themselves the Rollin' Stones, the fledgling R&B band was discovered in 1963 by publicist Andrew Loog Oldham who took over as manager and changed the band's name to the Rolling Stones, later explaining: 'They were not an abbreviation, they were not slang.' More importantly, Loog Oldham secured a record deal with Decca, whose executives were beginning to realize the enormity of their error in turning down the Beatles (for whom Loog Oldham had previously worked, *see p194*). The Stones proved hugely successful with cover versions of R&B songs, but this was not enough for Loog Oldham, who played midwife to a legendary songwriting partnership by persuading a reluctant Jagger and Richards to begin writing their own material. Richards later asserted in *The Rolling Stones in Their Own Words*: 'It had never crossed my mind to be a songwriter until Andrew came up to me and Mick and said, "Look, how many good records are you going to keep on making if you can't get new material? You can only cover as many songs as there are and I think you're capable ▶

HAVE YOU HEARD?

Rock journalist David Wild described Mick Jagger as 'simply the greatest frontman in rock history, a phenomenal showman with the offstage songwriting chops to back it all up', and Keith Richards as 'the unchallenged King of Cool, our aging youth culture's Lickmaster General. As rock guitar's foremost practitioner of the rhythm method and a songwriter of remarkable skill and staying power, he's long embodied the dogged, undying spirit of rock'n'roll.'

RIGHT *Mick 'n' Keef show how rock'n'roll should be done, on stage in Munich, Germany (18 June 2003)*

of more." He locked us in a room about the size of a kitchen and said, "You've got a day off, I want to hear a song when you come out." … in his own way Andrew was right. We walked out of there with a couple of songs.'

The first Jagger–Richards composition to be recorded was 'That Girl Belongs to Yesterday', recorded by American artist Gene Pitney in December 1964, but the first to be written was 'As Tears Go By', recorded in 1965 by Marianne Faithfull, who relates the story of the locked room in her autobiography *Faithfull*: 'This was the first song Mick and Keith had written. Andrew had locked them in a kitchen and told them, "Write a song, I'll be back in two hours." Andrew had given them the sense and feel of the type of thing he wanted them to write – "I want a song with brick walls all around it, high windows and no sex" – and they came up with a song called "As Time Goes By".'

The first Jagger–Richards composition to be recorded by the Rolling Stones was 'Tell Me (You're Coming Back)', of which Loog Oldham later said: 'It stood out with its echo-drenched sloppy blues puppy-in-love feel, and carried the space of a blues traveller resting his head in a commercial place. I loved it!' Four decades later 'Mick 'n' Keef' are still writing great songs, adding to an oeuvre so balanced that rock journalist David Wild was able to write of the Stones' 2002 compilation *Forty Licks*: 'Listen closely and you'll discover that it's all here – the yin and the yang, the old and the new, the rockers and the ballads, the Mick and the Keith.'

ABOVE *The Rolling Stones in 1964 with Jagger front left and Richards centre back* **RIGHT** *Mick Jagger (l) and Keith Richards shortly after being bailed on drug charges (7 January 1967)*

KEY DATES

1943 Michael Philip Jagger is born on 26 July in Dartford, Kent, England. Keith Richards is born on 18 December in Dartford, Kent. (With fame and a falling-out with his father, Richards will drop the 's' from his surname, later restoring it after a reconciliation with his father)

1951 Jagger and Richards (J and R) meet at Wentworth County Primary School

1961 Jagger begins studying at the London School of Economics. J and R meet on Dartford station and Richard joins Jagger's band

1962 On 12 July J and R, together with Brian Jones, Dick Taylor, Mick Avory and Ian Stewart, play their debut gig as the Rollin' Stones, at the Marquee Club, London, for a fee of £20

1963 Now named the Rolling Stones, the band secures a record deal and releases its first single, a cover of Chuck Berry's 'Come On'

1964 J and R begin writing songs together

1965 J and R write their first UK No.1, 'The Last Time', and their first two transatlantic No.1s, '(I Can't Get No) Satisfaction' and 'Get Off Of My Cloud', which all top the charts this year

2002 Jagger is knighted on 15 June

SIMON & GARFUNKEL

Folk–rock duo

Paul Simon and Art Garfunkel were a somewhat reluctant duo, performing together as children, achieving phenomenal joint success almost in spite of themselves (Garfunkel wanted to do something more serious and Simon had already begun a solo career) and then splitting up at the height of their joint fame. They first performed together in summer 1953, when both were 11 years old, as the White Rabbit and the Cheshire Cat in a school production of *Alice in*

Wonderland. The two young performers lived just three blocks apart in Queens, New York, and they became firm friends as they rehearsed the play together, walked home afterwards and, at weekends, recorded themselves singing together on a tape recorder at Garfunkel's house.

After the play was over they continued to sing together and began to look for outlets for their burgeoning talent, occasionally performing at private parties as Tom and Jerry *(see p72)*. In 1955 they made their first public performance as a vocal duo, singing the rock'n'roll hit 'Sh-Boom' at their junior high school, and that same year they co-wrote their first original song together, 'The Girl For Me'. Just two years later, still calling themselves Tom and Jerry, the two 15-year-olds recorded and released their first single, 'Hey Schoolgirl', which charted at No.49.

After this initial success, subsequent releases by Tom and Jerry flopped and the duo temporarily went their separate ways: Garfunkel enrolled to study mathematics at Columbia University, while Simon began a solo music

KEY DATES

1941 Paul Simon is born on 13 October in Newark, New Jersey, USA. Arthur Garfunkel is born on 5 November in Queens, New York, USA

1954 Simon receives his first guitar, as a birthday present from his parents

1955 Simon and Garfunkel (S and G) make their first public performance as a vocal duo, singing the rock'n'roll hit 'Sh-Boom' at their junior high school. S and G write their first song together and register the copyright at the US Library of Congress

1957 As Tom and Jerry (Garfunkel uses the name Tom Graph and Simon Jerry Landis), S and G record the hit 'Hey Schoolgirl'

1964 S and G record their first album, *Wednesday Morning 3am*

1965 S and G score their first US No.1 with the single 'The Sound of Silence'

1968 Simon's songs are used for the soundtrack of the film *The Graduate*, giving the duo a smash hit with 'Mrs Robinson'

1970 S and G release their most successful album, *Bridge Over Troubled Water*. Garfunkel makes his acting debut in *Catch-22*

1971 S and G split and pursue solo careers

1981 S and G temporarily reunite for a concert in Central Park, New York.

1982–83 The temporary reunification is extended to a world concert tour

1990 S and G are jointly inducted into the Rock and Roll Hall of Fame

1990s–2000s S and G mount a second short reunion tour and continue to appear together intermittently.

ABOVE *Simon and Garfunkel in concert (1960s)*

career, releasing singles under several pseudonyms. Then, in 1963, two things happened that were to ensure success, fame and fortune for Simon and Garfunkel. In September the duo reunited and started co-writing songs again (Simon providing lyrics and melodies, Garfunkel writing the harmonies), and on 22 November US President John F. Kennedy was assassinated, inspiring Simon to write what in 1965 would become their first No.1 hit, 'The Sound of Silence'.

From there the successes came thick and fast for six years, culminating in the 1970 album *Bridge Over Troubled Water*, which became the first album and single to simultaneously top the US and UK album and singles charts. To the dismay of Columbia Records and their millions of fans, it was the last studio album they would make as a duo (although they would later contribute to each other's solo albums). Paul Simon later said: 'Paradoxically, as *Bridge Over Troubled Water* was selling 10 million copies, our relationship was disintegrating.'

HAVE YOU HEARD?

Remembering his appearance on the television programme *American Bandstand* when he had just turned 16, Simon said:

'It was an incredible thing to have happen to you in your adolescence. I had picked up a guitar because I wanted to be like Elvis Presley and suddenly there I was!'

ABOVE *Simon and Garfunkel on stage in Cologne, Germany (20 July 2004)*

ELTON JOHN
BERNIE TAUPIN

Flamboyant singer and reclusive lyricist

Some great pop duos emerge together from similar backgrounds and others are brought together by a simple twist of fate, but there is little mystique in the way in which Elton John (then Reg Dwight) and Bernie Taupin met – in 1967 they both answered the same talent-spotting advertisement in the music paper *New Musical Express* (*NME*). By then 20-year-old Dwight was already a professional musician while Taupin, three years younger, was a labourer, a teenage poet and an avid reader of escapist literature. As a result of the *NME* advert, both were invited separately to meet Ray Williams at Liberty Records, who was not impressed enough to offer Dwight a recording contract, but did hand him Taupin's lyrics and ask if he could set them to music. Dwight found that his musical style suited the rhythm of Taupin's words, and he had set 20 of the songs to music before the two eventually met six months later.

In November 1967 music publisher Dick James offered them a joint publishing contract. This was soon followed by a separate recording contract for Dwight, who adopted the alias Elton John. At

KEY DATES

1947 Reginald Kenneth Dwight is born on 25 May in Pinner, Middlesex, England	later becomes the backing band for singer Long John Baldry	saxophonist Elton Dean, the carthorse Hercules from TV sitcom Steptoe & Son, and the singer Long John Baldry	**1997** Taupin rewrites the lyrics of 'Candle in the Wind' for John to perform at the funeral of Diana, Princess of Wales, on Saturday 6 September. A recording is made the same day, which becomes the world's biggest-selling single to date, the proceeds going to Diana's charities
1950 Bernie Taupin is born on 22 May in Lincolnshire, England	**1967** Dwight and Taupin meet after answering an ad in *NME*, and sign a joint publishing contract in November	**1969** John launches his career as a solo artist with the album *Empty Sky*	
1960s Dwight studies piano at the Royal Academy of Music, but decides that he prefers pop to classical music and forms the soul band Bluesology, which	**1968** Dwight signs a recording contract in January and adopts the alias Elton Hercules John, derived from the names of Bluesology	**1976** John becomes owner and chairman of Watford Football Club, of which he becomes life president in 1993	

ABOVE *Elton John (l) and Bernie Taupin after the former was inducted into the Rock and Roll Hall of Fame (1994)* **OPPOSITE** *Elton John at the piano (7 November 1970)*

first the new songwriting duo wrote 'English bubblegum pop' for other artists, until Steve Brown of Dick James Music (DJM) suggested that they write songs they would like to listen to instead of those they thought Dick James wanted to sell. The result was 'Skyline Pigeon', which was recorded by two other DJM artists before John's own version later appeared on his first album, *Empty Sky*. 'Skyline Pigeon' was the first song in true John–Taupin mould, a style that continued evolving as they worked together on more than a dozen albums before a temporary split in the late 1970s. Reunited in the early 1980s, their partnership has continued intermittently, through another 10 albums, into the 21st century.

In September 1997, almost exactly 30 years after he and Taupin had begun writing songs together, John was asked if he would sing at the funeral of his late friend Diana, Princess of Wales. The song 'Candle in the Wind', originally written about Marilyn Monroe, had been adopted as an anthem by those mourning the Princess, so John contacted Taupin at his ranch in California to discuss writing a new song with a similar feel to *Candle in the Wind*. In the end they decided to adapt the original and Taupin completely rewrote the lyrics, faxing them to John less than 24 hours later for him to perform at the funeral in Westminster Abbey.

HAVE YOU HEARD?

Taupin's rewritten version of 'Candle in the Wind', performed by Elton John at the funeral of Diana, Princess of Wales, began:

Goodbye England's rose; may you ever grow in our hearts.
You were the grace that placed itself where lives were torn apart.
You called out to your country, and you whispered to those in pain.
Now you belong to heaven; and the stars spell out your name.
And it seems to me you lived your life like a candle in the wind;
Never fading with the sunset when the rain set in.
And your footsteps will always fall here, along England's greenest hills;
Your candle's burned out long before your legend ever will.

TOM WAITS
KATHLEEN BRENNAN

Songwriters, record producers, husband and wife

Barfly troubador turned lunatic showman, Tom Waits has been co-writing and co-producing plays, songs, albums and film soundtracks with his wife, Kathleen Brennan, for more than 20 years and yet so little is known about their partnership that interviewer Richard Grant recently wrote: 'The biggest mystery about his life is the role of Brennan.' For if Waits plays his cards close to his chest regarding their relationship, professional and personal, Brennan doesn't play cards at all – she has never given an interview and very few photographs of her have ever been published.

Their paths crossed in 1980 when film director Francis Ford Coppola commissioned Waits to write the soundtrack for his musical *One From the Heart*. Brennan was a script editor at Coppola's studio – sparks flew, she and Waits married soon afterwards, and the rest is mystery.

Swordfishtrombones, Waits' first album after marrying Brennan, was a complete departure from his earlier work, introducing the surreality and atonal sound effects that would characterize his work from then on. This, he said, was because Brennan encouraged him to look at his music from a completely new angle, to handle it roughly and to take new risks with it. And the family influence on his music now extends to their three children, all of whom were involved in his 2004 album *Real Gone*, co-written and co-produced, like most of his recent work, by Brennan.

Asked how their collaboration works, Waits told Grant: 'Well, it's like setting off firecrackers. You get to hold the cracker and I get to light the fuse and you throw it.' Lowering his cards slightly, Waits conceded that Brennan occasionally offers critical appraisal: 'Do you have to put a one-eyed guy in every tune? Why do you have to put a midget in every song?' He then adapts the songs accordingly: 'OK, we'll give him back his eye. We'll make him a little taller. There, you feel better now?' Asked which of them comes up with the ideas in the first place, Waits reverted to evasion: 'The songs are out there, but you have to sneak up on them if you're gonna catch them alive. Other songs just come out of you, like you're talking in tongues.'

KEY DATES

1949 Thomas Alan Waits is born on 7 December in Pomona, California, USA

1950s Kathleen Brennan is born in Johnsburg, Illinois, USA

1960s Waits later claims to have slept through the 1960s; in fact, he has several dead-end jobs, including roadhouse cook and nightclub doorman

1969 Waits becomes a singer–pianist on the Los Angeles cabaret circuit

1972 Waits is signed to Asylum Records

1973 Waits releases his first album, *Closing Time*

1980 Waits and Brennan (W and B) meet for the first time and marry in August

1983 The album *Swordfishtrombones* marks a watershed between Waits' early music and the Brennan-influenced surrealism of his later work

1985 The album *Rain Dogs* contains the first composition to be credited jointly to W and B, 'Hang Down Your Head'

1986 Waits performs his first major film role, in Jim Jarmusch's *Down By Law*. W and B finish co-writing their first play, *Frank's Wild Years*, which premieres in Chicago (album released 1987)

1987 to present Brennan's credits on Waits' albums escalate from associate producer of the album and co-writer of some songs to co-producer and co-writer of the entire album

ABOVE Swordfishtrombones *(1983)* **OPPOSITE** *Kathleen Brennan and Tom Waits (1984)*

HAVE YOU HEARD?

Acknowledging the extent of Brennan's importance to his career, Waits said:

'If it wasn't for her I'd be playing in a steakhouse somewhere. No, I'd probably be cleaning the steakhouse.'

Describing what attracted him to marry her, he said:

'She can lie down on nails, stick a knitting needle through her lip and still drink coffee, so I knew she was the girl for me.'

MALCOLM McLAREN
VIVIENNE WESTWOOD

Co-creators of British punk

Together Malcolm McLaren and Vivienne Westwood defined a new fashion style and a new genre of rock music, embodied in their creation of British punk band the Sex Pistols. But McLaren's greatest creation was Westwood herself, transforming her from a one-time primary-school teacher into the woman who would become one of the world's most original and controversial fashion designers. As Westwood later put it: 'I was a coin and he showed me the other side.'

After separating from her husband, Derek Westwood, whom she later said was 'too kind for me', Vivienne returned to her parents' house. It was there that she first met Malcolm McLaren (then Malcolm Edwards), a dosser who was sleeping in her brother's car. McLaren's earliest memory of Westwood is of 'a shy Christian out of *Picture Post* dressed in home knits and kilt', but he soon began to change her style and her outlook, later claiming that 'the fashion industry was in *my* blood, not hers' and that he forced her into it. Forced or not, Westwood describes fashion as 'a baby I picked up and never put down'.

In 1971 McLaren and Westwood opened a 1950s, retro boutique at 430, King's Road, Chelsea, named Let it Rock. Two years later, bored with their success, they closed Let it Rock and reopened the boutique weeks later as Too Fast to Live Too Young to Die (TFTLTYTD). Later that year they were invited to take part in the

HAVE YOU HEARD?
In the script for his unfinished film *Oxford Street*, McLaren sums up the attitude that gave birth to British punk:

'Be childish, be irresponsible, be disrespectful, be everything this society hates.'

In 1987 Westwood made a comment that encapsulates her fashion design and her contribution to punk: 'I've never been happier than when I'm parodying the English.'

ABOVE *The Sex Pistols with Malcolm McLaren (third from right) signing for A&M Records (see p192) outside Buckingham Palace (March 1977)*

America's National Boutique Show in New York. The duo's subsequent creation of the Sex Pistols would be heavily influenced by their experiences in New York, which included meeting glam rock band the New York Dolls and seeing the Ramones, Patti Smith and Richard Hell play at the legendary music venue CBGBs.

McLaren and Westwood returned home to outrage British sensibilities by reinventing TFTLTYTD in 1974 as an S&M fetish boutique called SEX and by creating the Sex Pistols in 1975 in homage to Richard Hell's torn-T-shirt-and-safety-pinned-jeans look. The Sex Pistols heralded the arrival of British punk rock, and for a while Mecca for British punks was McLaren and Westwood's boutique on the King's Road. But the punk movement soon burned itself out, as did McLaren and Westwood's partnership, since when Westwood has grabbed far more international acclaim as a fashion designer than McLaren has as an impresario. She is accepted by the mainstream fashion industry while steadfastly refusing to conform to its expectations, in fulfilment of her own 1983 observation: 'I may be a rebel, but I'm not an outsider.'

KEY DATES

1941 Vivienne Isabelle Swire is born on 8 April in Glossop, Derbyshire, England, and later becomes a primary-school teacher

1946 Malcolm Robert Andrew Edwards is born on 22 January in Stoke Newington, London, England

1962 Swire marries Derek Westwood

1965 Vivienne Westwood meets Edwards

1971 Edwards changes his name to McLaren. He and Westwood open the boutique Let It Rock

1973 Let it Rock is reopened as the boutique Too Fast to Live Too Young to Die (TFTLTYTD)

1974 TFTLTYTD reopens as SEX. Westwood dresses American glam rock band New York Dolls

1975 McLaren and Westwood (M and W) create the Sex Pistols, initiating British punk

1980 SEX reopens as Worlds End

1981 McLaren leaves

Westwood, though their working relationship continues

1983 M and W's professional partnership is dissolved. Westwood goes on to become an internationally acclaimed fashion designer while McLaren continues as a music industry manager and producer

RIGHT *Malcolm McLaren and Vivienne Westwood (1981)*

Record-sleeve designers, co-founders of Hipgnosis

The names of graphic artists Storm Thorgerson and Aubrey 'Po' Powell may not be instantly recognizable, but the artwork they created together for the album covers of some of the world's biggest rock supergroups is familiar to more than one generation of music fans across the globe. It all began at Cambridge High School for Boys, where one of Thorgerson's classmates was Roger Waters, who went on to become bassist and vocalist of the rock band Pink Floyd. Thorgerson and Waters stayed in contact after leaving school and in 1968 Waters asked his old friend to design the cover for Pink Floyd's second album, *A Saucerful of Secrets*.

By then Thorgerson had teamed up with Powell, and Pink Floyd found themselves with the landmark first album cover to be produced by a partnership that was to dominate the industry for more than a decade with its flair for inventive, witty and visually striking imagery. Powell remembers: 'The first album cover that Storm or I ever did was the Pink Floyd's second album *A Saucerful of Secrets*, which we did under the name of the photo/design company we had started called Hipgnosis. Although it is not one of our better-known covers, the success of that cover led to our being offered work by many other rock stars, purely by chance. Subsequently we became well known as album cover artists, but it was unintentional – just right time right place.'

Their initial break may have been a question of right time right place, but continuing success relied on imagination, skill and hard work to create

MUSIC + DANCE

210 + 211

HAVE YOU HEARD?

Thorgerson and Powell describe record sleeves as:

'...the visual signposts, the flags, symbols, the awning, the camouflage, the 'skin' of these much loved records ... A cover design is the icon that identifies – and is invariably associated with – the music it represents. Your favourite record conjures to mind the accompanying cover, which gets to be cherished either by association or in its own right. People like music. People like album covers.'

ABOVE LEFT *Storm Thorgerson* **ABOVE RIGHT** *Aubrey 'Po' Powell*

scores of memorable album covers that still look good two decades later, despite being created without the use of computer graphics. Instead, Thorgerson and Powell relied on stuntmen, clever camerawork and the physical process of cutting, pasting, bleaching, painting and retouching to create sleeves for the biggest bands of their era. Powell's favourites are the covers for Pink Floyd's *Dark Side of the Moon* and Led Zeppelin's *Houses of the Holy*, which, he is proud to point out, 'have had more recognition and won more awards than just about any other album cover bar the Beatles' *Sgt. Pepper* ... I think in the context of Storm and my successful partnership in Hipgnosis as a duo they're worth noting'.

KEY DATES

1944 Storm Thorgerson is born in Middlesex, England, and later gains a BA in English from Leicester University and an MA in Film & Television from the Royal College of Art

1946 Aubrey Powell is born on 23 September in Sussex, England, and later studies at the London School of Film Technique

1968 Thorgerson and Powell (T and P) co-found Hipgnosis, whose first album cover is Pink Floyd's *A Saucerful of Secrets*

1970s T and P design sleeves for the biggest bands and solo artists of their era, including Pink Floyd, Led Zeppelin, Black Sabbath, Paul McCartney, the Rolling Stones, Peter Gabriel and 10CC

1983 Thorgerson, Powell and Peter Christopherson form Green Back Films, making music videos for Paul Young, Nik Kershaw, Robert Plant and Yes among others, as well as concert films for Pink Floyd and Paul McCartney's concert film *Live in the New World*

1994 Thorgerson directs six short films for Pink Floyd, to be screened at concerts during their world tour. Powell's book *Classic Album Covers of the 1970s* is published

1999 T and P's book *100 Best Album Covers* is published

21st century Thorgerson continues to design album covers, direct films and write and design books. Powell continues to write, direct and produce books, films and musicals

ABOVE Dark Side of the Moon, *Pink Floyd (1973), and* Houses of the Holy, *Led Zeppelin (1973)* **TOP** A Saucerful of Secrets, *Pink Floyd (1968)*

COMMERCE & INDUSTRY

FORTNUM & MASON

Grocers by royal appointment

The story of Fortnum & Mason, 'the royal grocer', begins with the Great Fire that destroyed London in 1666, after which tradesmen, including an Oxfordshire builder named William Fortnum, flocked to the capital to help rebuild it. Perhaps encouraged by Fortnum's success, his young cousin, also named William, arrived in London in 1705 and immediately made one of the chance encounters that resonate through history, renting a room above a small shop owned by Hugh Mason.

Two years later the younger Fortnum became a footman in the Royal Household of Queen Anne, establishing a royal connection that has continued without a break into the 21st century. One of Fortnum's jobs was to replenish the royal candelabra each night, and one of the perks was that he kept the used candles; these he sold to the Queen's Ladies-in-Waiting. Encouraged by his success as a used-candle salesman, William persuaded his landlord, Hugh Mason, to join him as co-partner in a grocery business, and in 1707 Fortnum & Mason came into being with a stall in St James's market, close to where the famous Piccadilly store stands today. With William's royal connections the

KEY DATES

1705 William Fortnum moves to London, England, and rents a room from Hugh Mason

1707 Fortnum becomes a footman in the Royal Household of Queen Anne and later forms a partnership with Mason in a small grocery business

1761 Charles Fortnum, grandson of William, enters the service of Queen Charlotte

1808 Charles Fortnum sells the business to his son Richard and to Mason's grandson, John

1886 Henry Heinz takes 'seven varieties of our finest and newest goods' to Fortnum & Mason's, which becomes the first shop in Britain to stock Heinz canned foods when the purchasing manager famously tells him: 'I think, Mr Heinz, we will take the lot'

1923–25 The famous shop on Piccadilly is rebuilt by Wimperis, Simpson, Guthrie & Fyffe

1933 Fortnum & Mason opens a store on the Isle of Wight, providing deliveries by

motorboat to yachts participating in Cowes Week

1953 Fortnum & Mason is asked to arrange the hire of coronets for titled persons attending the coronation of Queen Elizabeth II. The company also creates the 'Coronation' shoe, a design now exhibited in the Bata Shoe Museum, Toronto, Canada

1957 To celebrate the 250th anniversary of Fortnum & Mason, Mr H.J. Heinz II is driven in a hansom cab from

his hotel to the shop in Piccadilly, reliving his grandfather's journey of 71 years earlier, to present his congratulations

1964 Piccadilly acquires a new landmark when the famous Fortnum & Mason articulated clock is installed, featuring figures of Mr Fortnum and Mr Mason, who turn and bow to each other every hour on the hour. It is the biggest clock made in Britain since 'Big Ben' in 1861

ABOVE *Fortnum & Mason's famous store front on Piccadilly, London*

FORTNUM & MASON

business was an instant success, provisioning everyone from domestic servants to courtiers and the nobility.

Despite this initial success, it was two generations before Fortnum & Mason established the reputation upon which today's fame is built. In 1761 Charles Fortnum, grandson of the co-founder, entered the service of George III's wife, Queen Charlotte, and it was the trade generated by *his* royal connections that cemented the company's lasting success. Charles Fortnum retired from royal service in 1788 to devote himself full time to the store and 20 years later, when he was recalled to the Palace as Page of the Presence, he sold the business to another Fortnum and Mason: his son Richard and Hugh Mason's grandson, John. The company has remained a British icon ever since, provisioning British forces abroad from the Peninsular War to the Second World War, supplying attendants at the Queen's coronation in 1953, and launching on-line shopping in 1998.

HAVE YOU HEARD?

The following story is told in a 1950' Heinz advertisement:

'In June 1886, a hansom cab drew up outside Fortnum & Mason's famous shop in Piccadilly. From it alighted a man of forty-two. He had with him five cases of goods. Shortly afterwards he hailed another hansom – without the five cases. For Fortnum & Mason had decided to take them all.'

Thus, Mr H.J. Heinz himself first introduced his now famous products to England.

ABOVE *The Royal Coat of Arms proudly displayed on the store front above the names of Fortnum and Mason*

MARKS & SPENCER

From penny bazaar to global retailer

In 1881 Tsar Alexander II of Russia was assassinated in St Petersburg. The repercussions included widespread anti-Semitic pogroms that forced Michael Marks to flee from Russian Poland to the north of England where, soon after arriving, he happened to ask wholesaler Isaac Dewhirst for directions to Barrans, a company known to employ immigrant Russian Jews. Instead of giving Marks directions, Dewhirst lent him £5 to set himself up as a pedlar – Marks spent the money on goods from Dewhirst's warehouse and returned for another £5's worth of credit when he had sold them.

Marks thought of an ingenious way of getting round the fact that he spoke little English, attaching a sign to his pedlar's tray that read: 'Don't ask the price, it's a penny.' This ingenuity, together with determination and a charming personality, meant that he soon did well, progressing quickly from his pedlar's tray to a stall at Kirkgate open-air market and then to a covered stall at Leeds indoor market, where he changed his sign to 'M Marks: the original Penny Bazaar' and, later, 'Marks Penny Bazaar'.

Having graduated to some dozen market stalls, Marks had the foresight

HAVE YOU HEARD?

According to *The Times* newspaper, Queen Mary visited Marks & Spencer's Marble Arch store in 1932 and bought an Axminster rug, a leather handbag, a willow-pattern teapot and a 21-piece tea service. Writer Judi Bevan reports that the Queen said it was 'the most successful shopping she had ever done' and that afterwards the public flocked to M&S to buy Axminster rugs and willow-pattern teapots. Bevan also cites Queen Mary's visit as the moment that M&S was elevated 'from a simple chain of shops into a national institution'.

ABOVE LEFT *Michael Marks* **ABOVE CENTRE** *Tom Spencer* **ABOVE RIGHT** *Michael Marks' Original Penny Bazaar in Leeds indoor market*

to recognize that in order to expand further he needed a business partner. He approached Dewhirst, who declined, and then realized that he had been doing business almost daily with the ideal partner: Dewhirst's cashier, Tom Spencer. Spencer was the perfect foil for Marks' imaginative abilities and people skills: a thorough accountant, with good administrative and business knowledge. In September 1894 Spencer bought a half share of Marks's penny bazaars and, the same month, Marks moved to Cheetham Hill Road, Manchester, where his family lived above a shop named 'Marks & Spencer Penny Bazaar' – the first M&S store.

The partnership proved to be hugely prosperous, but surprisingly short-lived. In 1905, just 11 years later, Tom Spencer retired. Two years after that both partners died, Spencer at 53, reportedly from over-indulging in drink, and Marks at 47, reportedly from overwork and cheap cigars. It may have been a short-lived partnership, but its impact on the high street was to resonate into the next century. In the words of author Judi Bevan: 'The Jew and the Gentile formed a partnership from which grew the most successful retailing dynasty in British history.'

KEY DATES

1854 Tom Spencer is born in Yorkshire, England

1859 According to his British naturalization papers, Michael Marks is born this year in Russian Poland, the youngest of five children. However, his son Simon later states 1863, and his wedding certificate implies 1864

1882 Marks arrives in Britain; wholesaler Isaac Dewhirst lends him £5 to establish himself as a pedlar

1884 Marks sets up his first market stall, at Kirkgate open-air market, Leeds

1894 Marks forms a partnership with Tom Spencer and they open the first Marks & Spencer store, in Cheetham Hill Road, Manchester

1903 Marks & Spencer (M&S) is established as a limited company, with 36 bazaars and shops

1905 Spencer retires

1907 Spencer dies. Marks dies

1926 M&S is floated on the stock market

1930 M&S opens its first Oxford Street, London, store, close to Marble Arch

1938 M&S opens its second Oxford Street store, on the site of an 18th-century entertainment venue known as the Pantheon

1939–45 Sixteen M&S stores are destroyed and 100 damaged by German bombing raids

1974 M&S acquires 55% of Peoples' Department Stores, Canada

1975 M&S opens its first European store, on Boulevard Haussmann in Paris, France

1988 M&S buys the Brooks Brothers menswear chain in the USA

1990 M&S opens its first Southeast Asian store, in Hong Kong

ABOVE *Advertisement for clothes by St Michael, the brand name of Marks & Spencer first registered in 1928 (undated, c.1970s)*

MOËT & CHANDON

Champagne manufacturer *par excellence*

During the 18th century French vintner Claude Moët dazzled the court of King Louis XV with his champagnes. More than 250 years later the company Moët founded is dazzling commoners as well as royalty and Moët & Chandon is able to boast: 'Today, we are proud to say that a bottle of Moët & Chandon is enjoyed by someone every second of every hour, somewhere in the world.'

Claude Moët was born in 1683 in Soissons, a small market town in northern France. His elder brother was a wine merchant in Paris and advised Claude to set up business in the Champagne region, which was just becoming famous for the sparkling wines created there. Claude followed his brother's advice and settled in Epernay, where he became a wine trader and broker and went on to found the champagne house known as La Maison Moët, which is now one of the oldest companies in France. However, it was to be another two generations before the name Chandon was linked with that of Moët to create the brand name that is so famous today.

Moët was 60 when he founded La Maison Moët and soon involved his son Claude Louis-Nicolas in the business, which proved to be a great success with father and son shipping most of their champagne to Paris to supply the court of Louis XV. When the founder's grandson Jean-Rémy Moët inherited the company in 1792 he began to build the export market, eventually making Moët the official supplier to the Vatican and to the royal houses of England, Spain, Belgium, Sweden and Denmark.

In 1816 Jean-Rémy's daughter Adélaïde married Pierre-Gabriel Chandon de Briailles, linking the names of Moët and Chandon for evermore. Since then the company has continued to grow and is now the largest wine grower as well as the largest grape buyer in the Champagne region. In 2000 Moët & Chandon celebrated the new millennium, and more than 250 years of excellence, by creating a historic cuvée named *Esprit du Siècle*, an *assemblage* (blend) of the 11 most significant vintages of the 20th century. Just 323 magnums were produced, making it one of the rarest champagnes ever made.

HAVE YOU HEARD?

Rock supergroup Queen made Moët & Chandon the drink of choice for the subject of their song 'Killer Queen':

She keeps Moët et Chandon
In her pretty cabinet
'Let them eat cake,' she says
Just like Marie Antoinette
A built-in remedy
For Khrushchev and Kennedy
At anytime an invitation
You can't decline
Caviar and cigarettes
Well versed in etiquette
Extraordinarily nice
She's a Killer Queen...

The chronicles of Louis XV's court record that the King's favourite, Madame de Pompadour, said of Moët's champagne that it was 'the only wine that leaves a woman beautiful after drinking'.

OPPOSITE *Á votre santé!* ABOVE LEFT *Claude Moët* ABOVE RIGHT *Pierre-Gabriel Chandon de Briailles*

BEN & JERRY

'Legendairy' ice-cream makers

Ice-cream manufacturer Ben & Jerry's is best known for its punning flavours, such as Cherry Garcia, Peace of Cake and Phish Food. Others, including Honey I'm Home and One Sweet Whirled, have sadly been consigned to the Ben & Jerry's Flavour Graveyard to make way for new taste sensations, the most recent being Karamel Sutra. The wackiness is all part of the image of a company that describes itself as 'an antidote to seriousness', reflecting the character of its founders, 'hippie ice-cream gurus' Ben Cohen and Jerry Greenfield.

Born four days apart in Brooklyn, New York, Ben and Jerry first met at junior high school. They then both attended Calhoun High School in Merrick, Long Island, where Jerry remembers that he and Ben were 'two of the wildest students in their school' and got to know each other while struggling to run round the athletics track; he also remembers that they double-dated in Ben's convertible Camaro.

For a while Ben worked as a craft teacher at a community school and Jerry as a lab technician, but then, in 1977, they resolved to pursue their dream of starting a food business together. They decided to make ice cream because the machinery required to make bagels was too expensive, and enrolled on a $5 Pennsylvania State correspondence course in ice-cream making. Then, within months of both graduating with 'A' grades, they set up Ben & Jerry's Ice-Cream Parlour in a renovated petrol station on a busy street corner in Burlington, Vermont. Ben & Jerry's soon gained a reputation for its rich, unusual flavours

HAVE YOU HEARD?

Ben's biography states that as the business grew, his jobs included:

'Scooper and taste-tester, truck driver, marketing director, salesperson, president, CEO, not-CEO, and Chairperson of the Board. He's also had to learn all sorts of new and critically needed skills on demand over the years, like plumbing, roof-repair, belly-bouncing, dangerous carnival acts, and the art of samurai pint-slicing.'

Jerry's biography states that:

'His favourite course [at college] was 'Carnival Techniques', where he picked up several useful skills, including fire-swallowing. It was the sledgehammer-and-brick trick, though, that was to become a very important component at various Ben & Jerry's special events. It involved suspending Ben, a.k.a. "Habeeni-Ben-Coheeni", between two chairs and placing a cinder block [breeze block] on his ever-rounding bare belly, whereupon a serious, pith-helmeted Jerry would raise a sledgehammer and subsequently smash the cinder block, without harming Habeeni.'

ABOVE *Phish Food* **RIGHT** *Ben (l) and Jerry with the two things they love best – ice cream and a cow (June 1990)*

and its community approach to business, something for which the company is now world-famous. This fame is partly the result of 'home-fangled' marketing initiatives such as the 'cross-country marketing drive' of 1986 when Ben and Jerry travelled across the United States together in their 'Cowmobile', giving out free samples of their ice cream. The Cowmobile caught fire and burned to the ground outside Cleveland, but luckily neither Ben nor Jerry was hurt, and Ben made the best of the situation by providing news agencies with the perfect soundbite, claiming that the burning Cowmobile 'looked like a giant Baked Alaska'.

KEY DATES

1951 Jerry Greenfield is born in Brooklyn, New York, USA. Bennett Cohen is born four days later in Brooklyn, New York, USA. Cohen and Greenfield (C and G) subsequently meet at junior high school

1960s C and G both attend Calhoun High School in Merrick, Long Island, USA. Cohen works as an ice-cream man during his last year of high school. Greenfield works as an ice-cream scooper in his college cafeteria

1974–77 Cohen teaches at the Highland Community School for emotionally disturbed adolescents, where with the students he experiments with ice-cream making

1978 C and G found Ben & Jerry's Ice-Cream Parlour in Burlington, Vermont, USA

1988 America's Council on Economic Priorities awards Ben & Jerry's the Corporate Giving Award for donating 7.5% of their pre-tax profits to non-profit organizations through the Ben & Jerry's Foundation. The US Small Business Administration names C and G US Small Business Persons of the Year

1994 Ben & Jerry's is launched in Britain

2003 Ben & Jerry's celebrates its Silver Jubilee

TATE
LYLE

Rival sugar refiners who eventually joined forces

Henry Tate

There is no record that Henry Tate and Abram Lyle ever met, but their joint legacy created one of the world's leading sugar refining conglomerates, and Tate's individual legacy endowed one of the world's most famous art galleries. Tate, the elder of the two by a year, was born in northern England and Lyle in Scotland, and their careers followed converging paths until, within five years of each other, they opened rival sugar refineries less than two miles apart in Silvertown, London.

After being apprenticed to his brother Caleb, Henry Tate spent 20 years as a successful grocer, a career that made him well aware of the value of sugar as a commodity, and in 1859 he went into partnership with Liverpool sugar refiner John Wright. Ten years later he bought out Wright and renamed the business Henry Tate & Sons, opening a new Liverpool refinery in 1872 and then expanding operations into London with the Thames Refinery in Silvertown, which opened in 1878 and specialized in the production of cube sugar.

Five years before Tate died, he endowed the National Gallery of British Art (later Tate Gallery, now Tate Britain) on Millbank, London, and bequeathed his collection of paintings and sculptures to the nation – appropriately, nearly a century later, the gallery opened an outpost in Liverpool, where Tate's business began.

Abram Lyle

Meanwhile, Abram Lyle, after serving as a lawyer's apprentice, had built up a successful shipping business with his friend John Kerr. Having handled sugar and molasses in his shipping business, Lyle entered the sugar refining industry in 1865, forming a partnership and buying the Glebe Refinery in his home town of Greenock. Like Tate, he later struck out on his own, forming Abram Lyle & Sons in 1881 and opening the Plaistow Wharf Refinery two years later in West Silvertown, London, where he specialized in producing golden syrup.

RIGHT TOP *The Tate & Lyle sugar refinery, London, England (1908)* **CENTRE** *Henry Tate*
BOTTOM *Abram Lyle*

Tate & Lyle

Rivalry between the two family companies was intense and continued after the deaths of their founders, Lyle in 1891 and Tate in 1899.

After the First World War the rival companies between them were refining more than half of Britain's sugar and good business sense dictated that rivalry should become partnership. In 1921 they merged to become Tate & Lyle, a move that would no doubt have surprised both founders, but one that has brought greater success than either could have imagined, resulting in a global organization with large-scale operations in 28 countries.

KEY DATES

1819 Henry Tate is born on 11 March in Chorley, Lancashire, England, the son of a clergyman

1820 Abram Lyle is born in Greenock, Scotland, the son of a cooper

1832 Henry Tate moves to Liverpool to enter the grocery trade as an apprentice to his older brother, Caleb Ashworth Tate

1839 Tate establishes his own grocery business

1859 Tate forms a sugar refining partnership in Liverpool

1865 Abram Lyle forms a partnership and buys the Glebe Refinery in Greenock

1869 Tate buys out his partner and renames the company Henry Tate & Sons

1872 Tate opens a refinery in Love Lane, Liverpool

1875 Tate buys the British rights to Eugen Langen's patented method for cutting sugar cubes

1878 Tate opens a new refinery at Silvertown, London

1881 Lyle moves to London where he establishes Abram Lyle & Sons and opens the Plaistow Wharf Refinery in 1883

1891 Abram Lyle dies

1894 By deed of gift, Tate offers his art collection to the British nation and endows a gallery to house it

1897 The National Gallery of British Art (later Tate Gallery) opens in London

1898 Tate is created a baronet

1899 Tate dies on 5 December, aged 80

1921 The rival companies of Henry Tate & Sons and Abram Lyle & Sons are amalgamated on 27 February

1949 Tate & Lyle launches the trademark 'Mr Cube' to publicize the fight against government plans to nationalize the company

1976 Tate & Lyle invests in starch production, marking the beginning of a diversification from purely sugar-related operations

1990s Tate & Lyle acquires numerous overseas operations and develops into a global sugar, cereal sweetener and starch processing group

21st century Today Tate & Lyle produces a diverse range of ingredients made from renewable resources such as maize, wheat and sugar. These include cereal sweeteners and starches, sugar and sucralose, and fermented products such as citric acid, biogums and ethanol

ABOVE *Mr Cube, the trademark character conceived to champion Tate & Lyle's fight against nationalization (see Key Dates 1949)*

ALBERT ROUX
MICHEL ROUX

Michelin-starred chefs and restaurateurs

For more than a quarter of a century the Roux brothers have been recognized as two of the world's greatest chefs, a reputation achieved by another quarter of a century of hard work: apprenticeships in French pâtisseries, a decade working in private aristocratic households (where they might be asked to prepare anything from a simple meal such as shepherd's pie to a huge banquet for distinguished guests) and then the realization of a long-held ambition to establish their own restaurant.

Born six years apart in the region of Saône et Loire, France, the brothers decided, when they were 14 and 20, that they wanted to open a restaurant together and make it one of the finest in the world. Albert later wrote: 'If ever anybody's profession was decided at an early age, it was that

KEY DATES

1935 Albert Henri Roux is born on 8 October in Semur, France

1941 Michel André Roux is born on 19 April in Charolles, France

1949–51 Albert serves as an apprentice at the Pâtisserie Leclerc in St Mande, France

1952 Albert works as *commis de pâtisserie* at the Pâtisserie Bras République in Paris, France

1953 Albert works at the French Embassy in London, England

1954 Albert works as *commis de cuisine* for Lady Astor and her family and for Sir Charles Clore

1955–58 Michel serves as an apprentice at the Pâtisserie Loyal in Paris

1958–60 Albert works as sous chef and Michel as *commis pâtissier cuisinier*, both at the British Embassy in Paris

1960s Albert works as chef to Major P.V.C. Cazelet. Michel works as chef to Miss Cecile de Rothschild

1967 The Roux brothers open their first restaurant, Le Gavroche, in London, England

1969 The Roux brothers open their second restaurant, Le Poulbot, in London

1971 The Roux brothers open their third restaurant, Le Gamin, in London

1972 The Roux brothers open their fourth restaurant, The Waterside Inn, at Bray, England

1975 The Roux brothers are awarded the Chevalier du Mérite Agricole by the French government

1979 The Roux brothers win the Krug Award of Excellence

1981 The Roux brothers open their fifth restaurant, Gavvers, in London

1982 The Roux brothers are awarded a Wedgwood Plate of Excellence for Le Gavroche and the Waterside Inn

1988 The Roux brothers appear in the television programme *At Home With the Roux Brothers*

1993 Le Gavroche and the Waterside Inn are the first two restaurants in Britain to achieve three Michelin stars

ABOVE *Albert (l) and Michel Roux after receiving honorary OBEs for their services to cooking (31 October 2002)*

of my brother … During my apprenticeship in our local pastry shop, I remember him calling in to say hello on his way home from school and I could see even then that he was eager to enter the profession.' Michel duly followed in his elder brother's footsteps with an apprenticeship in a pâtisserie, after which Albert extended his effect on Michel's career from inspiration to practical influence: 'I am proud to say that I directed his first steps in the kitchen, for he came to work for me as commis chef at the British Embassy in Paris. Then, as now, he was rarely satisfied with his own results, or the results of others. He was always striving for perfection.'

The Roux brothers often mention 'perfection' as a goal, but never as something they considered themselves to have achieved. They describe cooking as 'a living art', but they go on to say: 'Cooking is not like painting – you cannot stand back, think, make alterations. Everything is in the timing…' This shared passion for cooking as an art form led to the opening, in 1967, of their first restaurant, Le Gavroche, in Mayfair, London. Since then, they write: 'We believe we have worked with perseverance and determination to gain the respect of the public, the press and, especially, our peers across Europe.'

ABOVE *Albert (l) and Michel Roux*

DOLCE GABBANA

Italian fashion designers

Domenico Dolce and Stefano Gabbana were born four years apart, Dolce on the Mediterranean island of Sicily and Gabbana in Milan, Italy, where the duo's world-famous fashion house now has its headquarters. Each brought very different aspects of design to their partnership – Dolce studied fashion design in Sicily and worked in his father's clothing business, while Gabbana had no formal fashion training and initially specialized in graphic design. They first met in 1980 when they were both working as assistants in a fashion design studio in Milan, where they immediately realized that they shared a creative vision. Two years later, displaying what they call 'a total lack of prudence combined with a wealth of enthusiasm', they started a business together.

At first, Dolce and Gabbana continued their freelance design work for others, but in 1985 they launched the Dolce & Gabbana trademark when they were chosen for the New Talents show at the Milano Collenzioni, since when they have devoted themselves to their own label. Initially designing women's fashion, Dolce and Gabbana soon expanded their range to include knitwear, lingerie and beachwear. They launched their first men's collection in 1990 and quickly gained global recognition with their first New York fashion show and their first New York showroom that same year. Two years later they added scarves, ties, beachwear, perfume and accessories to their extensive range, and in 1994 they launched the hugely successful young 'D&G Dolce & Gabbana' line. The designers describe the original Dolce & Gabbana line as being 'dream-like with a strong Mediterranean influence' and the younger, less traditional D&G line as 'a modern and ironic take' on fashion.

By the turn of the millennium Dolce and Gabbana had become the darlings of the music and film industries, designing clothes and accessories for tours by singers such as Whitney Houston, Madonna and Kylie Minogue and publishing the books *Hollywood* and *Music* in 2003 and 2004 respectively, featuring more than 250 portraits of Hollywood stars and music business icons wearing Dolce & Gabbana designs.

> ### HAVE YOU HEARD?
> A press profile of Dolce and Gabbana describes them as:
>
> 'Two designers who have made a flag out of their Italian character. Two designers who have made their sensual and unique style recognized around the world. Two young designers who address themselves to young people and draw inspiration from them. Two designers adored by the Hollywood stars who have made the duo their favourites. Two designers who dress all the rock stars of the moment and who have elected them as their unquestionable leaders.'

ABOVE *Madonna on stage in Paris during her world tour* The Girlie Show, *wearing a costume designed by Dolce & Gabbana (September 1993, see Key Dates 1993)* **OPPOSITE** *Domenico Dolce (r) and Stefano Gabbana*

KEY DATES

1958 Domenico Dolce is born on 13 August in Polizzi Generosa, Palermo, Sicily

1962 Stefano Gabbana is born on 14 November in Milan, Italy

1970s Dolce studies fashion design in Sicily and then works in his family's clothing factory. Gabbana studies graphic design

1980 Dolce and Gabbana (D and G) meet for the first time

1982–85 D and G work together as freelance designers

1985 The Dolce & Gabbana trademark is first launched at the Milano Collezioni New Talents fashion show

1987 D and G open a showroom in Milan

1990 D and G stage their first show in New York, USA, and open their first New York showroom

1992 Dolce & Gabbana introduces scarves, ties, beachwear and accessories to its range, as well as the first of many successful perfumes

1993 Dolce & Gabbana exclusively designs 1500

costumes for Madonna's World Tour *The Girlie Show*

1994 Dolce & Gabbana launches the young line 'D&G Dolce & Gabbana'

1995 Dolce & Gabbana launches a men's and women's eyewear and sunglasses collection

1999 Dolce & Gabbana exclusivey designs clothes and accessories Whitney Houston's world tour

2000 Dolce & Gabbana designs clothes, accessories and scenery to celebrate Madonna's album *Music*

2002 Dolce & Gabbana exclusively designs clothes and accessories for Kylie Minogue's European tour

2003 The book *Hollywood* is published, featuring portraits of Hollywood stars who have worn Dolce & Gabbana designs during the previous decade

2004 The book *Music* is published, featuring 150 portraits of some of the music industry's most influential icons wearing Dolce & Gabbana, including Jennifer Lopez, Madonna, Beyoncé, Alicia Keys, Kylie, Lenny Kravitz and Mary J. Blige

BANG OLUFSEN

Global icon of quality and design in audio and video

Peter Bang and Svend Olufsen grew up in very different backgrounds, but combined their common interests and talents to create what would become one of the world's best-respected manufacturers of audio, television and video equipment. Svend, born in 1897, was the son of a politician and provincial landowner, a shy but inquisitive boy whom family and friends described as 'slightly odd' and 'a bit eccentric'. He spent a lot of time experimenting with electricity and chemistry and, being dyslexic, was far more interested in making ideas work than in writing them down. Peter Bang was born three years later, the son of a successful city businessman, and grew up in and around Copenhagen where, like Svend, he would conduct experiments, his interests being 'technology in general and radio in particular'.

These two young men first met at Århus Electrotechnical School, from where they graduated in 1924. Afterwards Svend returned to the family

HAVE YOU HEARD?

Knud Davidsen, who worked for B&O for 41 years, remembers meeting Peter Bang while working overtime late one night during the 1950s:

'For someone as young as I was, it was remarkable to meet the director in person, and in the middle of the night at that! When we had talked a little [about what I was testing], he went on his way in the dark and said: "It's good to see there are some Vikings left!"'

Omringet af musik med B&O Stereofoni

KEY DATES

1897 Svend Andreas Grøn Olufsen is born in Quistrup, Denmark

1900 Peter Boas Bang is born on 14 March in Copenhagen, Denmark

1924 Bang and Olufsen both graduate from the Electrotechnical School in Århus, Denmark

1925 The public limited company of Bang & Olufsen (B&O) is established on 17 November near Struer, Denmark, where B&O's main factory remains to this day

1926 B&O launches the 'Eliminator', a device enabling battery-powered radios to be connected to mains electricity, bringing immediate success to the company

1929 B&O sells its first sound system to cinemas and launches its landmark 'five-lamp' radio

1930 B&O launches its first radio-gramophone

1945 The B&O factory is blown up on the orders of the Gestapo because B&O employees have been active in

the Danish resistance, including Duus Hansen, who established radio connections with the free world. Production recommences 11 months later

1949 Olufsen dies

1950 B&O launches its first television

1957 Bang dies. B&O launches the world's first stereo pick-up

1960 Danish pirate radio station Mercur (Mercury) begins broadcasting stereo

radio programmes with the cooperation of B&O

1967 B&O launches its first colour television

1972 New York's Museum of Modern Art includes seven B&O products in its permanent collection, later describing their design as being 'typified by a quiet elegance'

1977 B&O is floated on the Copenhagen Stock Exchange

2002 B&O launches its first plasma screen home cinema system

TOP *Svend Olufsen (l) and Peter Bang (1932)* **ABOVE** *'Surrounded by music with B&O Stereo', record sleeve for Bang & Olufsen's first stereo record (1960)*

estate of Quistrup, where he continued experimenting with radio technology, and Peter went to America, where he worked in a radio factory and, after six months, wrote to his father: 'I've been giving a great deal of thought to when it would be possible to start my own business... In order to gain a respected name within the radio industry, it's essential to be in at the start.'

In 1925, shortly after Peter returned from America, Svend invited him to Quistrup, hoping to establish a partnership. Soon they had set up a working laboratory at the estate, described by their friend, novelist Johannes Bucholtz, as '[looking like] an altarpiece, perhaps not surprisingly since it was the new great god of radio that was being worshipped here'. Although Peter's mother expressed her doubts (she did not think Peter's 'radio foibles would result in anything lasting'), his father, Camillo, saw the potential of what he and Svend were doing and, a businessman himself, helped them to establish the limited company of Bang & Olufsen on 17 November 1925, with Camillo as its first chairman.

Camillo built various safeguards into the structure and running of the company in case business went badly, but none of them was needed – business started well and went from strength to strength. During a century of previously unimaginable technological advance, Bang & Olufsen branched out into cinema sound systems, home sound systems, television, video and home cinema, always keeping abreast of advancing technology and building an envious global reputation for quality and design.

RIGHT *Image from the 1960 brochure*

CHARLES ROLLS & HENRY ROYCE

The Rolls-Royce of duos

Henry Royce

As a synonym for excellence and quality the names of Charles Rolls and Henry Royce are now inseparable, but these men's backgrounds were so different that, given the social mores of Edwardian England, it is remarkable they should ever have met. Royce was born near Peterborough into a family so impoverished that his father, a failed miller, died in the workhouse when Henry was just nine. Royce's aunt later paid for him to be apprenticed to the Great Northern Railway, where he discovered an aptitude for engineering before having to curtail the apprenticeship because the money ran out. He then studied electrical engineering at night school and by 1884 he was able to start his own business, establishing the electrical engineering firm of F.H. Royce & Co. (later Royce Ltd) with his friend Ernest Claremont.

In 1903, at the age of 40, Royce bought himself what was then still a very new form of transport: a car. Dissatisfied with the engineering of his French-built Decauville, he set about building an engine and chassis of his own design. By the end of the year he had built a far superior car and the following year Royce Ltd expanded the scope of its business from electrical engineering into car manufacture.

Charles Rolls

Meanwhile, Charles Rolls had been growing up in the very different world of the landed gentry. Born the third son of John Allan Rolls (later 1st Baron Llangattock) in Mayfair, one of London's most affluent districts, he was educated at Eton, one of Britain's most exclusive schools. He then studied Mechanisms and Applied Science at Cambridge University, where he was known by his Eton nickname 'Dirty Rolls', acquired because of the number of times he was found with his sleeves rolled up tinkering with engineering projects.

After graduating, Rolls dedicated himself to promoting the car as a viable means of transport, becoming a founder-member of what would become the Royal Automobile Club, taking part in various motoring events including the famous 1,000-Mile Trial of 1900, and establishing the car sales

ABOVE *Henry Royce attending the Schneider Cup at Calshot (28 August 1929)* **OPPOSITE** *The famous Rolls-Royce radiator grille and Spirit of Ecstasy mascot*

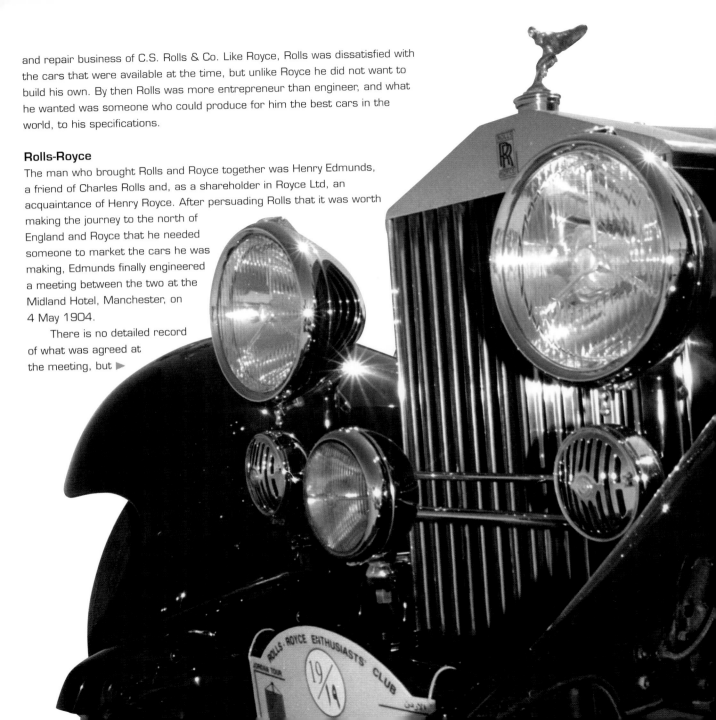

and repair business of C.S. Rolls & Co. Like Royce, Rolls was dissatisfied with the cars that were available at the time, but unlike Royce he did not want to build his own. By then Rolls was more entrepreneur than engineer, and what he wanted was someone who could produce for him the best cars in the world, to his specifications.

Rolls-Royce

The man who brought Rolls and Royce together was Henry Edmunds, a friend of Charles Rolls and, as a shareholder in Royce Ltd, an acquaintance of Henry Royce. After persuading Rolls that it was worth making the journey to the north of England and Royce that he needed someone to market the cars he was making, Edmunds finally engineered a meeting between the two at the Midland Hotel, Manchester, on 4 May 1904.

There is no detailed record of what was agreed at the meeting, but ▶

evidently the self-made man and the aristocrat got on well, and Rolls must have been suitably impressed with Royce's engineering because he immediately agreed to take all the cars that Royce could produce and market them under both men's names. There is an apocryphal story, featured in the BBC television series *The Edwardians*, that when Rolls suggested this Royce replied: 'I like that. Royce-Rolls! Yes, it has a certain ring to it.'

Whether or not there was really any such rivalry over precedence, it was a fruitful partnership. In 1904 Rolls was selling four makes of car, including the new Rolls-Royce; by the end of 1905 he was selling only Rolls-Royces; in 1906 his confidence was such that Rolls-Royce was incorporated as a limited company, and in 1907 Rolls-Royce Silver Ghost earned the

HAVE YOU HEARD?

Charles Rolls' ambition was that his name should be attached to a car 'so that in the future it might be a household word just as much as Broadwood or Steinway in connection with pianos'. His wish has been more than fulfilled – today a Steinway is more likely to be described as the Rolls-Royce of pianos than a Roll-Royce the Steinway of cars.

Rolls' obituary in the *Morning Post* newspaper the day after his death stated:

'He remarked, not long ago, that for him motoring was no longer pleasurable because being such a reliable mode of transport it had become positively monotonous. If it had not been for the excitements in connection with [aviation], he would, he declared, have longed for the old days when, undertaking a road journey, it was the regular experience to spend most of the time under the car.'

ABOVE *Charles Rolls (13 January 1908)*

accolade 'best car in the world'. The 1906 Memorandum of Association stated that the company was established 'to provide motor vehicles for use on land, water or in the air' and, nearly a century later, Rolls-Royce continues to produce motor vehicles for use on land as well as world-class maritime and aeronautical engines.

However, although the company has lasted more than a century, the partnership itself was short-lived, surviving a mere five years from the founders' first meeting: as well as being a motoring pioneer Rolls was also a pioneer of aviation, and in 1909 he resigned as Technical Director of Rolls-Royce in order to concentrate on flying. In June the following year he made the first-ever nonstop double crossing of the English Channel by aeroplane, but then, on 12 July, disaster struck – Charles Rolls became the first Briton to be killed in an aeroplane crash when the Wright biplane he was piloting crashed during a flying competition at Bournemouth.

KEY DATES

1863 Frederick Henry Royce is born on 27 March in Alwalton, near Peterborough, England

1877 Charles Stewart Rolls is born on 27 August in Mayfair, London, England

1884 Royce sets up F.H. Royce & Co. (later Royce Ltd) with Ernest Claremont

1892 At the age of 15, Rolls installs a dynamo at the family's country estate near Monmouth, Wales, and converts part of the house to electricity

1895–97 Rolls studies at Trinity College, Cambridge University

1896 Rolls buys his first car, a Peugeot, in Paris, France, and brings it back to England. This makes him the first

Cambridge undergraduate to own a car

1902 Rolls establishes C.S. Rolls & Co.

1903 Royce buys his first car, a Decauville, then immediately improves it and the following year diversifies Royce Ltd into car manufacture

1904 Rolls and Royce meet for the first time on 4 May

1906 Rolls-Royce (RR) is established as a limited company. The Silver Ghost chassis appears at the London Motor Show. Rolls crosses the English Channel by balloon

1907 The engine of a RR Silver Ghost is stripped down after an unprecedented nonstop trial of 15,000 miles and passed as new, with only minor wear to one or two

parts, earning RR a reputation for producing 'the best car in the world'

1908 Rolls becomes only the second Englishman to fly in a powered heavier-than-air craft when he takes a flight with Wilbur Wright in France

1910 Rolls makes the first-ever nonstop double crossing of the English Channel by aeroplane. On 12 July Rolls is killed, aged 32, in a plane crash during a flying competition at Bournemouth

1911 Royce survives a near-fatal illness, during which he is told he has only three weeks to live

1914 RR begins developing its first aircraft engine, the Eagle

1919 The RR Eagle engine powers Alcock and Brown's

Vickers Vimy aircraft on the world's first nonstop transatlantic flight

1930 Royce is made a baronet

1933 Royce dies on 22 April, aged 70

1940 RR Merlin engines power the Hawker *Hurricane* and the Supermarine *Spitfire* in the Battle of Britain

1953 RR engines power HMS *Grey Goose* in the world's first sea voyage to be powered by gas turbine

1976 Concorde, powered by RR Olympus engines, becomes the first and (to date) only supersonic airliner to enter passenger service

2004 RR celebrates the centenary of its founders' first meeting

ABOVE *Unattributed painting of Rolls' first meeting with Royce, at the Midland Hotel, Manchester, England, in 1904*

SMITH WESSON

Makers of 'the most powerful handgun in the world'

Horace Smith

Silas Smith's decision to accept a job as a carpenter at the US National Armory in Springfield, Massachusetts, was to have profound repercussions on the history of firearms. Smith's son Horace was just four when the family moved to Springfield, but in time he followed his father into the gun-making trade, gaining 18 years' experience at the National Armory (during which time he invented and patented several types of gun-making machinery) before going on to work for several other major arms manufacturers.

Daniel B. Wesson

Wesson's interest in guns began when his elder brother Edwin established himself as a gunsmith and riflemaker. In October 1842, when Wesson was 17, another of his many brothers wrote to Edwin: 'Daniel likes to hunt, but he had rather be at work in the shop on gun locks, springs or something of that kind.' Three months later his parents, who had hoped that Wesson would help on their farm, reluctantly allowed him to become an apprentice to Edwin. Wesson quickly rose to become manager, developing his business expertise as well as his gun-making skills, but found himself out of a job in 1849 when Edwin died suddenly and creditors took over the company – Wesson even had to file a law suit to retrieve his own tools.

Smith and Wesson

It is almost certain that Smith and Wesson first met in the summer of 1851, although the details are not recorded. The following year they established their first partnership, with the aim of realizing their shared

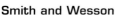

ABOVE *Daniel Baird Wesson (c. 1875)* **TOP** *Horace Smith (c. 1875)*
RIGHT *Clint Eastwood in Dirty Harry, brandishing the Smith & Wesson .44 Magnum*

dream of developing a new type of firearm that could be fired repeatedly without the need to reload with loose powder, ball and primer.

The partnership brought together Smith's expertise in the design of machines and tooling with Wesson's enthusiastic inventiveness and his organizational and sales skills. Unfortunately, the business was not a success and in 1855 they were forced to sell the company, but Wesson, knowing from past experience the value of patents, insisted they retain the rights to their patent for a metallic cartridge. Less than a year later they formed their second partnership, the Smith & Wesson Revolver Company, to exploit that patent by producing the first practicable revolver to fire a fully self-contained cartridge.

This time they made no mistake, and over the next century and a half the company founded by Smith and Wesson has created innovation after innovation to maintain its position as a world leader in the manufacture of handguns. Its ongoing success is a reflection of the comment with which Wesson closed the order book of Wesson Rifle Co. after his brother's death in 1849: 'No thing of importance will come without effort.'

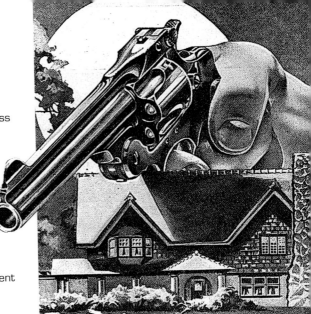

KEY DATES

1808 Horace Smith is born on 28 October in Cheshire, Massachusetts, USA

1812 The Smith family moves to Springfield, Massachusetts, the home of the National Armory (now the Springfield Armory)

1824–42 Smith works at the National Armory

1825 Daniel Baird Wesson is born on 18 May in Worcester, Massachusetts, USA, one of 10 children

1835 Edwin, one of Wesson's elder brothers, establishes what will become the Wesson Rifle Co., sparking Wesson's interest in guns

1843 Wesson is apprenticed to his brother Edwin

1849 Edwin Wesson dies and the Wesson Rifle Co. is taken over by creditors

c.1851 Smith and Wesson (S and W) meet for the first time

1852 S and W form their first partnership, the Smith & Wesson Arms Co., later known as the Volcanic Repeating Arms Co., in Norwich, Connecticut, USA

1855 Shirt manufacturer Oliver Winchester buys the failing Volcanic Repeating Arms Co. and later renames it the Winchester Repeating Arms Co., beginning another American legend

1856 Smith and Wesson form their second partnership, the Smith & Wesson Revolver Co. (S&W), on 17 November

1870 S&W begins marketing the Model 3 American, the first large-calibre cartridge revolver, which establishes the company as a world leader in handguns

1874 Smith retires, selling his share of the company to Wesson

1893 Smith dies on 15 January, aged 84

1899 S&W introduces its most famous revolver, the .38 Military & Police, the precursor of the modern Model 10

1906 Wesson dies on 4 August, aged 81

1935 S&W introduces the first Magnum revolver, the .357 Magnum

1954 S&W introduces its first double-action (automatic) pistol, the Model 39

1956 S&W introduces the Model 29 chambered .44 Magnum, made famous by Clint Eastwood in the film *Dirty Harry*

1965 S&W introduces the world's first stainless steel revolver, the Model 60

1980s S&W introduces its most popular revolver to date, the L-Frame .357 Magnums

ABOVE *'Security! Protect your home with the best revolver'*: advertisement for Smith & Wesson revolvers

CHARLES SAATCHI
MAURICE SAATCHI

Charles and Maurice

'Everyone with a television set in the Free World has seen their advertisements; everyone in advertising knows the legend. Few know the real story,'
writes biographer Ivan Fallon of the Saatchi brothers. Often described as the
Italian ice-cream men who gave Margaret Thatcher's image a make-over, they
are not, in fact, Italians but second-generation Iraqi-Jewish immigrants, and
their contribution to the presentation of Britain's Conservative party was just
a small part of their influence on global advertising culture.

Charles and his younger brother Maurice are the middle two of four
children, and grew up behaving very differently from each other. Charles took
little interest in schoolwork and, instead of going into further education, took
a series of jobs before getting his break in advertising as a copywriter at
London agency Benton & Bowles. By contrast, Maurice gained a first-class
honours degree from the London School of Economics and quickly became
an executive at the first firm he worked for, Haymarket Publishing. It was not
until 1970, at the ages of 27 and 24 respectively, that they worked together
for the first time, joining forces to create what was destined to become the
world's biggest and best-known advertising agency.

Saatchi and Saatchi

In 1967 Charles co-founded the advertising consultancy Cramer Saatchi with
his friend Ross Cramer, a colleague from Benton & Bowles. Three years
later, tired of acting as a consultant and therefore not being able to take the
credit for his own ideas, Charles was keen to establish his own agency.
Cramer decided he was more interested in a film career, so Charles wasted
no time in recruiting his brother Maurice and making play of their unusual
surname: 'It's a bloody good name for a new advertising agency. Saatchi &
Saatchi – it's so bizarre noone will forget it in a hurry.' And no-one did.

Despite having grown up with such different outlooks, Charles and
Maurice made a formidable team, so much so that Fallon points out: 'Over
the years people would find it impossible to imagine one without the other.'
Both had the drive and the ambition to succeed, but each brought ▶

HAVE YOU HEARD?
In a 1987 letter to *The Guardian* newspaper
one company chairman acknowledged the
effect that the Saatchis were having on the
advertising world:

'Before the Saatchi phenomenon, those of us
in the surprisingly small industry were
accustomed to obscurity. No agency was a
household name, very few people knew what
agencies did.'

RIGHT *Maurice (l) and Charles Saatchi (c. 1975)*

different skills to the partnership. Charles provided the creative writing spark and advertising nous, while Maurice brought an innovative business mind, ignoring what was considered standard practice – by doing things his own way, rather than following the norm, he was to revolutionize the entire industry.

As well as setting the advertising world alight with their creative, witty and often shocking advertisements, the Saatchis also began to climb the company rankings in size, profits and profile. By 1981, through a series of mergers and takeovers, theirs was the biggest agency in Britain. A year later they gained a foothold in New York by buying a company twice the size of their own. Five years after that, in May 1986, the Saatchis achieved their ultimate goal – by buying Bates Advertising agency, Saatchi & Saatchi became the world's biggest advertising agency.

Meanwhile, the Saatchi brothers were also making their mark on British politics and the world art scene. While it is not true that they engineered a makeover of soon-to-be Prime Minister Margaret Thatcher's personal appearance, it is true that in 1978 Saatchi & Saatchi became the first advertising agency to be employed full-time by any

KEY DATES

1943 Charles Saatchi is born on 9 June in Baghdad, Iraq

1946 Maurice Saatchi is born on 21 June in Baghdad, Iraq

1947 Due to increasing persecution of Iraqi Jews, the Saatchi family leaves Iraq for England

1960 Charles travels round the USA, taking particular interest in American television culture and advertisements. On his return he briefly joins an advertising agency

1964–67 Maurice studies at the London School of Economics, graduating with first-class honours in Economics

1965 Charles becomes a copywriter at advertising agency Benton & Bowles (B&B), where he meets Ross Cramer

1966 Charles and Cramer both leave B&B to join Collett Dickinson Pearce (CDP), and together win an industry award for their Selfridges campaign

1967 Charles and Cramer both leave CDP to join John Collings & Partners, but it does not work out and six months later they co-found their own advertising consultancy, Cramer Saatchi. Maurice begins working for Haymarket Publishing as assistant to the owners, Michael Heseltine MP

and Lindsay Masters, and later becomes Business Development Manager

1970 Charles and Maurice (C and M) co-found the advertising agency Saatchi & Saatchi (S&S)

1981 S&S buys Garrott Dorland Crawford to become the biggest advertising agency in Britain

1982 S&S buys the Compton Group to gain a foothold in New York

1986 S&S buys Bates Advertising to become the biggest advertising agency in the world

1994 C and M are ousted from S&S following a boardroom coup

1995 C and M set up a new agency, M&C Saatchi

1996 Maurice is made a peer

1999–2000 Maurice serves in the House of Lords as Conservative Spokesman on the Treasury and the Cabinet Office

2003 Maurice becomes Co-Chairman of the Conservative Party

ABOVE *Saatchi & Saatchi made a big breakthrough by winning an account with the British Health Education Council, for whom agency creative Jeremy Sinclair devised this poster of a pregnant man (1970s)*

British political party, playing a vital and often controversial role in the Conservative election victories of 1979, 1983 and 1987. And while the brothers' political leanings were Conservative, Charles' artistic preferences were far from conservative. Charles began collecting minimalist modern art in the late 1960s, a passion fanned in the 1970s by his then-wife, Doris, who was an even more avid collector than Charles. Together they built up the now-famous and continuously evolving Saatchi Collection, elements of which have featured in numerous exhibitions around the world – like everything else associated with the Saatchi brothers, the art collection is characterful, uncompromising and controversial.

ABOVE Away from the Flock, *by British artist Damien Hirst, on display in the Saatchi Gallery, London*

OBJECTS & IDEAS

KNIFE
FORK

Dining partners *extraordinaire*

The knife

The knife was used as a tool or/and weapon long before it came to be employed as an eating utensil. The first step towards its domestication was its use as an implement to hack pieces off joints of meat – the resulting morsels would then be eaten with the fingers. This idea later developed into skewering the offcut with the point of the knife to transfer it to the mouth. By the Middle Ages etiquette had advanced to the use of two knives – one for holding the food steady and the other for cutting, skewering and transferring meat to the mouth.

The fork

Like the knife, the fork existed as a tool (for agriculture) and a weapon (the trident) before it was used as an eating utensil but, unlike the knife, eating forks evolved not from these tools and weapons but from the knife. The idea of *manufacturing* forks for eating (leaving aside the probability that ancient humans used forked sticks for the purpose) emerged from the use of two knives for eating – the food would often twist around the blade of the knife that was being used to hold the food, and the solution was to create a tool with a forked blade for the purpose.

The knife and fork

Once the knife and fork came to be used in tandem, each affected the development of the other. Two tines were ideal for holding meat while it was carved, but three and then four proved more useful for skewering the food to transfer it to the mouth (five proved too many). As the fork took over the function of skewering as well as holding the food, the pointed tips of knives became redundant and knives with bulbous tips evolved and were used for scooping up food. But then forks with curved tines developed, which were not only easier to eat with than straight tines but were also more efficient than bulbous knife blades for scooping up food. With bulbous blades thus obsolete, straight blades became the norm and by the 19th century the knife and fork had evolved to their modern form.

KNIFE & FORK FAQS

What was America's first fork?
A single fork was introduced to America in 1630 by Governor Winthrop of the Massachusetts Bay Colony. Prior to that it was, according to one historian, a case of 'knives, spoons and fingers'.

What does 'spic and span' have to do with forks?
Nothing. But some etymologists consider that the phrase may derive from the pre-fork use of a pointed knife and spoon instead of fingers for eating, although this interpretation is disputed – the theory is that the spike and spoon, or spik and spon, ensured that the fingers stayed clean.

Why is it polite to put the fork over the knife during a break in eating?
Legend has it that this derives from the time when weapons doubled as table knives – putting the fork over the knife signals peaceful intent. For the same reason, it is polite in Italy to leave the unemployed hand in view of the table when eating with a fork and no knife.

When is a fork not a fork?
When it's a spork. There are conflicting theories as to the origins of the spork, which combines the bowl of a spoon with the tines of a fork. Some cutlery experts contend that it is a direct descendant of the runcible spoon, a name coined by Edward Lear in *The Owl and the Pussycat* (see p54) and since used to describe a type of pickle fork, while others say that it was invented in the 1940s by the American military in Japan, and still others that it evolved in the 1960s with the introduction of fast food.

OPPOSITE *Knife and fork in action*

OIL & VINEGAR

The original salad dressing

Oil

The oil most often referred to in the context of oil and vinegar is olive oil, something that has been of prime importance in Mediterranean countries since before the time of Christ – archaeologists have found evidence of olive mills, presses and oil storage jars from all across the region dating back several thousand years. Olives grown for oil must be harvested ripe, crushed carefully so that the stones are not broken, spread on fibrous mats and then pressed – the resulting fluid separates into two parts: a thin, bitter liquid and the all-important oil. This process is often done by hand, although mills have been used for at least 2,000 years – the Romans designed a mill called a *trapeti* that was accurate enough to crush the flesh of the olives without breaking the stones.

Vinegar

The history of vinegar is at least as old as that of olive oil – the ancient Greek physician Hippocrates wrote of the medicinal powers of vinegar as long ago as the 5th century BC, by which time vinegar was also being used as a flavouring, a seasoning and a preservative. The name comes from the French *vin aigre*, meaning 'sour wine', which indicates how mankind first discovered it. However, sour wine is no substitute for fine vinegar, which is carefully fermented and matured by various processes to produce variations such as balsamic, malt, cider, rice, sorghum and various fruit vinegars.

Vinaigrette

The idea of using oil and vinegar together as a salad dressing also dates back to prehistory, and it is still used today as the basis of vinaigrette, or French dressing. The combination of textures and flavours is exquisite, but oil and vinegar are not a true duo because they do not actually mix, separating almost immediately after they have been shaken together. In most vinaigrettes the proportion of oil to vinegar is 3:1 varying up to 4:1, and these basic ingredients are often seasoned with lemon juice, salt and pepper. Shallots, herbs, mustard, honey or other ingredients are sometimes added.

HAVE YOU HEARD?

The poet Lord Byron was obviously a long way from domestic bliss when he likened marriage to vinegar, writing:

'Tis melancholy, and a fearful sign
Of human frailty, folly, also crime
That love and marriage rarely can combine,
Although they are born in the same clime;
Marriage from love, like vinegar from wine –
A sad, sour, sober beverage – by time is
sharpened from its high celestial flavour,
Down to a very homely household savour.

OIL & VINEGAR FAQS

What does vinaigrette have to do with women fainting?

In the days when women wore corsets and therefore fainted a lot, a vinaigrette (or vinaigret) was a vital piece of handbag equipment. A small bottle, often intricately ornamented, contained aromatic vinegar or smelling salts to revive anyone who fainted.

Are olives really as marvellous as people try to make out?

Probably. The Bible, the Classics, literature and fine art all celebrate the olive, perhaps most famously in the form of an olive branch as a symbol of peace – conversely, destroying an enemy's olive trees, as Samson did to the Philistines (see p16), was considered a ruthless, sacriligeous act. Renoir, Matisse, Cézanne, Bonnard and Derain all painted olive trees, and Van Gogh made no less than 19 paintings of them (but then he was a bit obsessive). The Hellenophile author Lawrence Durrell memorably wrote that the Mediterranean 'seems to rise in the sour, pungent taste of these black olives between the teeth. A taste older than meat, older than wine.'

ABOVE Van Gogh's The Olive Orchard (1889)

SALT
PEPPER

The world's two most widely used condiments

Salt

The importance of salt throughout history can be judged from the fact that as long ago as biblical times a covenant of salt was considered perpetually incorruptible (God gave the kingdom of Israel to David by such a covenant) and as recently as the 20th century the downfall of British rule in India was brought about in part by Gandhi's salt march *(see Salt & Pepper FAQs, opposite)*. Salt is one of the four basic tastes that can be detected by taste receptors in the mouth and is therefore of prime importance as a seasoning. But historically, before refrigeration was available, it was even more important for preserving food by 'salting', a process now perpetuated in the developed world as a matter of taste rather than necessity.

There are two main types of salt: rock salt, which is mined from underground, and sea salt, which is evaporated from sea water. So-called 'table salt' is rock or sea salt refined into very small grains that are usually treated so that they pour easily even if slightly damp.

Pepper

In the sense that they are often used separately, and each has no effect on the other, salt and pepper are not really a duo, but they are often considered as such because they invariably appear side by side on the table. After salt, pepper is the world's second most popular seasoning and, like salt, it has been important throughout history – the historian Edward Gibbon records that in 410AD, after capturing Rome, the warrior Alaric the Goth demanded 1,360kg/3,000lb of pepper as part of his ransom demands for the city.

Both black and white pepper are the dried fruit of the spice plant *Piper nigrum*. Black pepper is produced by fermenting and then drying the fruit before it fully ripens, and white pepper by harvesting the berries slightly later and soaking them to remove the skin and the pulp, leaving just the white seeds. The reason for the popularity of pepper as a spice is that it stimulates the flow of saliva and gastric juices, improving both appetite and digestion.

> ### HAVE YOU HEARD?
> The Russian word for hospitality is *khleb-sol*, which literally means 'bread-salt'.
>
> The Jewish book of civil and canonical law known as the Talmud cautions:
>
> 'Three things are good in little measure and evil in large: yeast, salt and hesitation.'

ABOVE *'Pure, fine, dry': French advertisement for Cerebos Table Salt (1914)* **OPPOSITE** *Trade card depicting a pepper plant (c.1895)*

Fig.1

3

4

What was Gandhi's salt march all about?

In 1930 Indian nationalist leader Mahatma Gandhi led a 300-mile march to the coast at Dandi as part of his ongoing campaign of civil disobedience in protest at British rule. This march was in protest at the Salt Law, by which the British imposed taxes on the production of salt, and by picking up a single piece of sea salt when he reached the coast, Gandhi symbolically broke the law. He was later arrested for illegally selling salt, which sparked riots and ultimately forced a Round Table Conference on constitutional reform.

Where does the phrase 'salt of the earth' come from?

In St Matthew's account of the Sermon on the Mount, Christ says to his disciples: 'Ye are the salt of the earth.'

Weren't Roman soldiers paid in salt?

Not quite. They were given rations of salt and other necessities that all went by the general name of 'salt'. Later, instead of actual rations they were given a subsistence allowance to buy their rations. Named after the commodity it was intended to pay for, the allowance was called a *salarium*, from which we derive the word salary.

What is a peppercorn rent?

A token rent that does not reflect the value of the property being rented, so-called because a single peppercorn is of no appreciable value.

Who are Salt 'n' Pepa?

Hugely successful New York rap duo Cheryl 'Salt' James and Sandra 'Pepa' Denton, who had big hits with 'Push It', 'Shake Your Thang', 'Let's Talk About Sex' and 'Do You Want Me', among others.

GIN & TONIC

Spirit and mixer

Gin

Gin is an alcoholic spirit distilled from grain or malt and flavoured primarily with juniper berries, from which it gets its name as well as its taste. First made in Holland during the 16th century, this spirit was named by the Dutch as *genever* from the Old French word for juniper: *genèvre* (since modernized to *genièvre*). When travellers brought *genever* from the Low Countries to England the name was corrupted to the more familiar-sounding Geneva, although the drink had nothing to do with Switzerland. It soon became very popular in England and by the early 18th century the name had been shortened from Geneva to gin; the first record of the shortened name in print dates from 1714. In Australia gin is still known colloquially as juniper juice.

Tonic

Tonic literally means something that increases energy and vitality, originally in the form of a medicine. One such medicine, or tonic, was the alkaloid quinine, which reduces fever and pain and was once widely used for treating malaria. Shortly after the First World War the term 'tonic' or 'tonic water' came to be used for a carbonated soft drink flavoured with quinine.

Gin and Tonic

Apart from their complementary tastes, gin and tonic, or G&T, make an excellent duo for several other reasons. As with any mixer, adding tonic turns the spirit from a short drink into a long one, and the carbonation of the tonic carries the alcohol from the gin more quickly into the bloodstream. It is also said that the particularly mellow feeling induced by gin and tonic comes from the fact that the quinine in the tonic prevents the body from processing the alcohol as quickly as it would otherwise do. Although gin and tonic seem made for each other, there is no record of anyone drinking them together before the 1930s.

RIGHT *A skating waiter brings gin and tonic to Lady Scarsdale (right) and her children at St Moritz, Switzerland (8 January 1938)*

GIN & TONIC FAQS

What is a gin and it?
Gin and Italian vermouth (also known as a martini, which is now a generic term derived from the trademark of Italian winemakers Martini & Rossi).

What is a pink gin?
Gin mixed with angostura bitters, taking its name from the colour that the bitters give to the drink. And before you ask, angostura bitters are a blend of gentian and herbs, used as flavouring and named after a town in Venezuela now known as Cuidad Bolivar.

What is London gin?
After gin had been introduced to Britain, the English began distilling gin in their own style. London gin is drier and more subtly flavoured than the original Dutch *genever*, while Plymouth gin has a strength of flavour somewhere between the two.

Is gin rummy a particularly potent mix of two spirits?
No, it's a card game in which each player tries to collect sets or sequences of three or more cards.

Is a gin trap a way of catching alcoholics?
No, it's a wire noose used for catching game birds. The word derives from the medieval French *engin*, meaning an ingenious device.

What is a cotton gin?
A machine for separating cotton fibres from the seeds, again from the French *engin*.

HAVE YOU HEARD?

In the film *Casablanca*, Humphrey Bogart says:

'Of all the gin joints in all the towns in all the world, she walks into mine.'

Lady Elisabeth Clapham once said:

'I never drink gin. It makes me, by turns, bellicose, lachrymose and comatose.'

BRIMSTONE TREACLE

Medicine and sweetener

OBJECTS + IDEAS

Brimstone

Brimstone literally means 'burning stone' and is the archaic name for sulphur. Sulphur's foul smell, together with the fact that it is associated with volcanoes, means that traditionally it has been readily associated with the devil, death, destruction and the infernal regions.

Treacle

Originally, the name treacle had nothing to do with the sweet syrups for which it is now used. The word comes from the Greek *theriake antidotos*, meaning 'antidote to [the bite of] a wild beast' – the 'l' was added when the word *theriake* passed into Old French as *theriakle*. This sense of treacle as a medicine was so common during the 17th and 18th centuries that the phrase 'treacle carrier' was a disparaging term for a quack doctor.

Brimstone and Treacle

Often the medicine tasted so bitter that it would be sweetened with honey or sugar syrup, and by the mid-19th century the word treacle was being used for the sweetener rather than for the medicine itself. One such combination of bitter medicine and sweetener was sulphur and sugar syrup, known together as brimstone and treacle, which was such a common remedy during the 19th century that it was said to have been given 'to anyone with the least symptom of anything'.

Certainly the combination was well-enough known by 1838–39 for Charles Dickens to mention it in his novel *Nicholas Nickleby*, in which Mr Wackford Squeers says of the inmates of Dotheboys Hall: 'They have the brimstone and treacle, partly because if they hadn't something or other in the way of medicine they'd always be ailing and giving a world of trouble, and partly because it spoils their appetites and comes cheaper than breakfast or dinner.'

BRIMSTONE & TREACLE FAQS

Wasn't there a film about brimstone and treacle?
There was a 1982 film called *Brimstone & Treacle*, but it wasn't about brimstone and treacle, it was (supposedly) about the ambiguous qualities of good and evil. Denholm Elliott and Joan Plowright played a suburban couple with a recently brain-damaged daughter. Posing as the child's friend, an incubus character named Martin Taylor, played by the rock star Sting, arrives in the household. Taylor then proceeds to alternate between charming the parents with the angelic side of his character and performing singularly un-angelic acts with their daughter on the living room couch.

Brimstone is mentioned in the Bible, but what about treacle?
Not in most versions, but the Bishops' Bible of 1568 is popularly known as the Treacle Bible because three times this version substitutes 'tryacle' (treacle) for 'balm', so that the Book of Jeremiah chapter 8 verse 22 reads: 'Is there no tryacle in Gilead, is there no phisition [physician] there? Why then is not the health of the daughter of my people recovered?'

Isn't there a Sting Bible as well?
Yes, but it has nothing to do with the star of *Brimstone & Treacle* – it is so-called because the Book of Mark chapter 7 verse 35 reads: '… and the sting of his tongue was loosed, and he spake plain', instead of '…and the string of his tongue…'

HAVE YOU HEARD?

An 1804 edition of the *Medical Journal* referred to an 'anti-venereal treacle, well-known for curing the venereal disease, rheumatism, scurvey [*sic*] [and] old-standing sores…'

ABOVE *The Charles Dickens' character Wackford Squeers (1880s)* OPPOSITE *(l–r) Suzanna Hamilton, Sting and Joan Plowright in Dennis Potter's* Brimstone & Treacle *(1982)*

ROCK & ROLL

Rhythm and Blues

Rhythm and blues (R&B) emerged during the 1940s, bringing together traditional black music forms such as jazz, country blues and folk blues and adding strong rhythms through catchy bass lines and more prominent drumming. Pop music historian Donald Clarke describes rhythm and blues as 'magpie music; anything that was fun was thrown in' – saxophones from the swing era, drumbeats from the Caribbean, bass riffs from Cuba, vocal harmonies from the barbershop tradition. As Clarke puts it: 'country blues had come to town', and the result was that the jazz elements took a back seat and the electric guitar and bass came to the fore in a combination perfect for noisy taverns – the blues had been urbanized as rhythm and blues, a.k.a. R&B.

Rock'n'Roll

In simplistic terms, rock'n'roll was born in the 1950s when white people began playing R&B, which had previously been known as 'race music'. To avoid the racial overtones associated with the term R&B, American disc jockey Alan Freed coined the name rock'n'roll to describe a new phenomenon that saw white artists successfully rerecording black R&B songs and black R&B artists topping the national pop charts, which they had previously been unable to do because of what Clarke describes as 'institutionalized racism in broadcasting, publishing and everywhere else'.

But rock'n'roll is not a duo in the same sense as rhythm and blues; whereas rhythm and blues are two separate things that were brought together into one phrase, rocking and rolling are both part of the same sexual activity: Freed named his radio programme *Moondog's Rock and Roll Party*, borrowing a term that was well-established black slang for sexual intercourse, as in Trixie Smith's 1924 hit 'My Man Rocks Me With One Steady Roll'.

ABOVE Alan Freed (c.1954) **RIGHT** *Rockin'n'rollin' in New York's Paramount Theater while recording Alan Freed's* Don't Knock The Rock *(1957)* **INSET FAR RIGHT** *The Platters (1956)*

HAVE YOU HEARD?

John Lennon *(see p194)* had a pretty high opinion of both the Beatles and of rock'n'roll, telling journalists in 1966:

'We're more popular than Jesus now; I don't know which will go first – rock'n'roll or Christianity.'

Mick Jagger *(see p198)* had a better sense of proportion when he sang:

It's only rock'n'roll but I like it.

ROCK'N'ROLL FAQS

What was the first rock'n'roll record?

Because the transition from R&B is so blurred, it's hard to say. The Boswell Sisters performed a song called 'Rock and Roll' in the 1934 film *Transatlantic Merry-Go-Round*, but despite the title it wasn't a rock'n'roll song. The first No.1 rock'n'roll hit was 'Sh-Boom' in 1954, by white Canadian band The Crew Cuts, covering an R&B song originally recorded by black duo The Chords. The first R&B band to top the national pop chart was The Platters in 1955 with 'The Great Pretender'.

What's the difference between 'rock'n'roll' and plain 'rock music'?

All popular music with a strong beat and electrified instruments came to be called 'rock' during the 1960s in a sort of music industry re-branding exercise. 'Rock', of course, went on to spawn prog rock, pomp rock, art rock, classical rock, psychedelic rock, acid rock, jazz rock, country rock, folk rock, glam rock, punk rock, stadium rock, adult-oriented rock and, er, disco.

SKULL CROSSBONES

Traditional insignia of pirates

Pirate flags

The skull and crossbones, or 'Jolly Roger', is the archetypal pirate flag, but its history is unclear and various theories have been put forward as to its origins. One theory is that the first pirate flags took the form of a red banner known as the Bloody Flag, and that the name 'Jolly Roger' derives from the French *joli rouge*, or 'pretty red'. Another is that pirate flags developed from a plain black flag flown by those scorning a national identity.

From plain red or black flags it would be a natural progression for individual pirate captains to embellish their flag with symbols that would bolster their fearsome reputations and strike terror in the hearts of their victims. Many such flags are known, common symbols being skeletons, daggers, cutlasses and hourglasses (the hourglass being a signal to victims that their time was running out). By far the most common symbol was the skull, almost invariably accompanied by a pair of crossed bones – usually thighbones, the longest bones in the human body.

The skull and crossbones

The first known use of the skull and crossbones was c.1700, when the French pirate captain Emanuel Wynne raised his flag in that hotbed of piracy, the Caribbean. Wynne's flag featured a frontal view of a skull with the thighbones crossed behind it and an hourglass beneath, and other variations soon followed. His contemporary Richard Worley copied the arrangement of skull and bones, but omitted the hourglass, while other captains arranged the crossed bones beneath the skull rather than behind it. These included Edward England, whose flag featured a single skull and crossbones, Christopher Condent, who flew a long black pennant featuring three skulls and three sets of crossed bones, and Henry Every, a.k.a. John Avery, whose square flag featured crossed bones beneath the profile of a skull wearing a bandanna and an earring.

SKULL & CROSSBONES FAQS

You say that 'Jolly Roger' might mean 'pretty red', but aren't all pirate flags black?
No. Captain Christopher Moody sailed under a red banner adorned with a winged yellow hourglass, a white raised arm brandishing a dagger, and a yellow skull with crossed bones behind it.

What was Blackbeard's flag like?
Blackbeard's flag was quite elaborate, but it was not a skull and crossbones. It featured a horned skeleton holding an hourglass in one hand and a spear in the other, with the spear pointing at a red heart shedding three drops of blood.

We know about the bones, but did any flesh feature on any of these flags?
Yes. Several flags featured a muscular arm holding a cutlass or dagger, and Captain Bartholomew Roberts flew two flags, both featuring himself. In one he and a skeleton are holding up an hourglass and in the other he is depicted, sword in hand, standing on two skulls labelled 'ABH' and 'AMH' – a Bajan's head and a Martinician's head, commemorating his particular vendetta against inhabitants of the islands of Barbados and Martinique.

ABOVE *Blackbeard fights Abdullah the Prince (unattributed)* **OPPOSITE** *Maureen O'Hara as Spitfire Stevens in* Against All Flags *(1952)*

HAVE YOU HEARD?
In his infamous *The Devil's Dictionary*, Ambrose Bierce defined piracy as 'commerce without its folly-swaddles – just as God made it'.

STARS
STRIPES

The flag of the United States of America

The Stripes

The first US flag, which had stripes but no stars, was raised by George Washington on 2 June 1776, a month before the Declaration of Independence from Britain. It had 13 alternate red and white stripes representing the 13 states that were to ratify the declaration and, strangely for a young nation declaring its independence, incorporated the British Union Flag (a.k.a. Union Jack) in the top left corner, which at that time comprised the crosses of St George and St Andrew, patron saints of England and Scotland.

The Stars

The stars followed just a year after the stripes, when Congress declared that the Union Flag in the top left corner should be replaced by 13 white stars and the number '76', the year of Independence, on a blue background – and so, in 1777, the first Stars and Stripes was born.

The Star-Spangled Banner

The stars and stripes have appeared in no less than 27 variations since they first came together in 1777. The first change came in 1794, after the admission of Vermont (1791) and Kentucky (1792) to the Union, when the number of stars and stripes were both increased to 15. In 1818, after the admission of 6 more states, it was decided that the original 13 stripes would be restored, signifying the original 13 states, and that stars only would be added as more states joined the Union. The current flag, with 13 stripes and 50 stars, came into being in 1959 after the admission of Alaska in January and Hawaii, the 50th and last state to date, in August of that year.

OBJECTS + IDEAS

256 + 257

HAVE YOU HEARD?
The first US national anthem, used long before the adoption of 'The Star-Spangled Banner', was sung to the tune of the current British national anthem, but with the words: 'God save George Washington.'

ABOVE *The first Stars and Stripes was reputedly made in 1777 by seamstress Betsy Ross in Philadelphia* **RIGHT** *Astronaut Pete Conrad places the Stars and Stripes on the lunar surface*

STARS & STRIPES FAQS

What came before the stars and stripes?

Before 1776 the flag of the territories that would become the United States showed a rattlesnake with 13 rattles and the motto: 'Don't tread on me.' This was a deliberate homage to Scotland's Order of the Thistle, whose motto is: *Nemo me impune lacessit*, meaning 'No one assails [attacks] me with impunity'.

What are the stars and bars?

Choosing rhyme instead of alliteration, the 11 Confederate States that seceded from the Union in 1860 at the start of the Civil War adopted the Stars and Bars, a flag comprising two broad red bars and one narrow white one, with 11 white stars arranged in a circle on a blue background in the top left. After the admission of Missouri and Kentucky to the Confederacy in 1861, the number of stars was increased to 13.

Who coined the name 'Star-Spangled Banner'?

A lawyer named Francis Scott Key wrote 'The Star-Spangled Banner' during the War of 1812, the last war between the USA and Britain. It was officially adopted as the national anthem in 1931:

'Tis the star-spangled banner; O long may it wave
O'er the land of the free and the home of the brave!

SQUARE COMPASSES

Insignia of Freemasonry

The square

The square is an L-shaped or T-shaped tool used by carpenters and stonemasons to construct right angles. A geometric square is only a true square if its corners form four exact right angles, so by extension any right angle is said to be 'square' despite the fact that it does not have four sides; the tool takes its name from this usage.

The compasses

Although the name is plural, the compasses, more correctly known as a pair of compasses, is a single tool made up of two hinged legs, one leg having a spike at the end and the other either a pencil lead or a clamp to hold a pencil. A pair of compasses is used for drawing circles by using the spike as a pivot around which the pencil can be rotated, the distance between the legs of the compasses being the radius of the circle.

The square and compasses

In medieval times skilled workers (freemen, as opposed to tied apprentices) would travel from place to place to find work, and they often formed guilds of free masons, free carpenters, etc. to help and support fellow craftsmen. Later, particularly after the decline in cathedral building, skilled workers did not travel as often, membership of the guilds diminished and many guilds accepted honorary members; by this process the emphasis of the guilds moved from craft association to fraternal societies.

While many former guilds simply became defunct, Freemasonry was revived in Britain after the reign of James II and prospered as a national organization, soon spreading to Europe and the USA. In some ways the organization echoed the medieval guilds, with members helping each other as brothers in times of difficulty, but also dedicating themselves to the ideals of charity, equality and morality. The Craft, as Freemasonry is often known, also revived many of the ranks and rituals of the medieval freemasons, including the use of the masons' tools, the square and compasses, as its insignia.

SQUARE & COMPASSES FAQS

Do Freemasons have undue political influence?
Because Freemasonry is a secretive (but not secret) society, and has a stated aim that Masons will assist other Masons, it has attracted suspicion and criticism over the centuries. However, there is no evidence that people in positions of influence are any more or less likely to be corrupt because they are Masons than if they went to the same school, supported the same football team or had any other common interest.

And what about the funny handshake?
The medieval guilds would have had private signs and passwords to identify themselves as members and modern Freemasonry continues this as well as many other rituals and traditions. Whether or not this includes a secret handshake – well, that's secret, isn't it?

Do Freemasons believe in God?
It is a requirement of membership to profess a belief in a higher being, whom Masons refer to as the 'Great Architect of the Universe'. However, this higher being is not denominational, and Masonry accepts members of any religion that professes a belief in a single god.

ABOVE *Freemason's Annual General Meeting, London, England (1992)* **OPPOSITE** *Insignia of the Masonic Grand Lodge of France*

HAVE YOU HEARD?

In modern times, Freemasonry has come to mean an instinctive understanding between like-minded people. It is in this sense that English writer Sir Max Beerbohm used the word when he wrote:

'Women who love the same man have a kind of bitter freemasonry.'

YIN YANG

Complementary principles of Eastern culture

Yin and yang are the two opposite and complementary principles underlying ancient Chinese philosophy, religion, medicine and cultural thinking. The interaction between the two energies provides balance and harmony in the universe and from their intermingling arise the five elements from which all things are created.

Although yin literally means 'dark' and yang 'bright or light', this does not really define what is meant by the concept of yin and yang. The familiar symbol of the intertwined yin and yang gives a better idea of the relationship between these two separate but interdependent elements or forces, each containing the seed of the other and each merging into and out of the other to create a balanced whole. This symbol is the symbol of life, and is said to represent the resolution of all opposites and the reconciliation of all paradoxes.

According to Taoism, the universe began with a single primordial breath that divided into an opaque, heavy energy known as yin and a pure, light energy known as yang. Everything in the universe evolves from the transformations of that breath and can be classified as yin or yang, each with its balancing force: woman is yin, man is yang; earth is yin, heaven is yang; the moon is yin, the sun is yang; night is yin, day is yang; cool and cold energies are yin, warm and hot energies are yang. This thinking even extends to food, where sour, bitter and salty flavours are yin, pungent and sweet flavours yang.

YIN & YANG FAQS

I thought Chinese philosophy was all about oneness, but isn't this all about division and separateness?
No, this is about oneness. Yin and yang are aspects of the same thing, and one cannot exist without the other. Where one is present the other is in a state of potentiality, limiting and defining the other.

So which is dominant?
Neither. Each plays a greater role at different times and in different places, this changing relationship providing balance and harmony in a universe whose equilibrium is constantly in flux.

Aren't there four elements, not five?
In Western thinking there are four elements: earth, air, fire and water. But in Chinese thinking there are five: wood, fire, earth, metal (or minerals) and water. Of these, metal and water are allied to yin, wood and fire to yang. Earth controls the transitions between the yin and the yang elements, both separating and joining them.

HAVE YOU HEARD?

Refuting the common Western interpretation of yin and yang as material opposites, author Isabel Robinet wrote:

'Rather, Yin and Yang are lines of force, directions whose nature is to cross and mingle, to play against and with each other, both self-generating and self-propelling, disappearing and alternating; and their function is to define a double syntax of polarity and ambiguity. Neither can exist at its extreme; at that point it reverses into its opposite.'

ABOVE *Stone carving of the Chinese zodiac signs surrounding the symbol of yin and yang, from a temple in Chengdu, Sichuan Province, China* **OPPOSITE** *The legendary Emperor Fu Hsi holding a* ba guadiagram, *with yin and yang surrounded by the eight trigrams of the I Ching*

INDEX

SELECT BIBLIOGRAPHY

Alcántara, Isabel & Sandra Egnolff. *Frida Kahlo and Diego Rivera*. Prestel, 1999.

Alvarez, A. *Beckett*. Fontana, 1973.

Bang, Jens. *Bang & Olufsen, From Vision to Legend*. Vidsyn 2. edition, 2000.

Bevan, Judi. *The Rise and Fall of Marks & Spencer*. Profile Books Ltd, 2001.

Brewis, Kathy. 'The Playwright and the Showgirl' in *The Sunday Times Magazine*, 2004.

Bright, Spencer. *Essential Elton*. Chameleon Books, 1988.

Campbell, Lady Colin. *Diana in Private: The Princess Nobody Knows*. Smith Gryphon Publishers, 1992.

Cannon, John (ed.). *The Oxford Companion to British History*. OUP, 1997.

Chernow, Burt. *Christo and Jeanne-Claude A Biography*. St Martin's Press, 2002.

Cheshire, Ellen & John Ashbrook. *Joel and Ethan Coen*. Pocket Essentials, 2002.

Clarke, Donald (ed.). *The Penguin Encyclopedia of Popular Music*. Penguin, 1998.

Daniels, Les. *Batman, The Complete History*. Chronicle Books, 2004.

Davidson, Alan. *The Penguin Companion to Food*. Penguin, 2002.

Edwards, I.E.S. *The Pyramids of Egypt*. Viking, 1986.

Fallon, Ivan. *The Brothers, The Rise & Rise of Saatchi & Saatchi*. Hutchinson, 1988.

Feinstein, Elaine. T*ed Hughes The Life of a Poet*. Weidenfeld & Nicholson, 2001.

Fox, Mike & Steve Smith. *Rolls-Royce The Complete Works*. Faber & Faber, 1984.

Garraty, John A. & Mark C. Carnes (gen. eds). *American National Biography*. OUP under auspices of American Council of Learned Societies, 1999.

Gold, Jeffrey (ed.). *A&M Records The First 25 Years*. Jeffrey Gold/A&M Records, 1987.

Grant, Richard. 'Trailer-Park Troubador' in *The Telegraph Magazine*, 2004.

Grisewood, John (ed.). *The Book of the Bible*. Macdonald & Co. (Publishers) Ltd, 1972.

Hanna, Bill with Tom Ito. *A Cast of Friends*. De Capo Press, 1996.

Hardin, Terri. *Frida Kahlo A Modern Master*. Smithmark, 1997.

Jackson, Laura. *Paul Simon The Definitive Biography*. Piatkus, 2002.

Jaggard, Geoffrey. *Wooster's World*. Macdonald & Co. (Publishers) Ltd, 1967.

Jinks, Roy G. *History of Smith & Wesson*. Beinfeld Publishing Inc., 1977.

Junor, Penny. *Burton – The Man Behind the Myth*. Sidgwick & Jackson, 1985.

Kelly, Fred C. *The Wright Brothers: A Biography Authorized by Orville Wright*. George G. Harrap & Co. Ltd, 1944.

Leaming, Barbara. *Marilyn Monroe*. Weidenfeld & Nicholson, 1998.

Lewis, Jon E. & Penny Stempel. *Cult TV: The Essential Critical Guide*. Pavilion Books Ltd, 1993.

Loog Oldham, Andrew. *Stoned*. Vintage, 2001.

March, Jenny. *Cassell's Dictionary of Classical Mythology*. Cassell, 2001.

Miller, Arthur. *Timebends – A Life*. Methuen, 1988.

Mitchell, Glenn. *The Laurel & Hardy Encyclopedia*. B.T. Batsford Ltd, 1995.

Moore, Pete. *E=mc²: The Great Ideas that Shaped Our World*. Friedman/Fairfax, 2002.

Mulvagh, Jane. *Vivienne Westwood, An Unfashionable Life*. HarperCollinsPublishers, 1998.

Parry, Melanie (ed.). *Chambers Biographical Dictionary*. Chambers, 1999.

Petroski, Henry. *The Evolution of Useful Things*. Vintage Books, 1994.

Plutarch. *Life of Marcus Antonius*, as extracted in Shakespeare's *Antony & Cleopatra*. Longman, 1971.

Pym, John (ed.). *Time Out Film Guide*. Penguin Books, 2003.

Ravn, Thomas Bloch. *The radio cult in retrospect – the fairy tale of Bang & Olufsen*. Struer Museums Venner, 1992.

Roux, Albert & Michel. *New Classic Cuisine*. Macdonald & Co. (Publishers) Ltd, 1983.

Ruffles, Philip. *1st Hon C S Rolls Lecture to the Institution of Mechanical Engineers*, 2002.

Smith, Sean. *Kylie Confidential*. Pocket Books, 2003.

Speaight, George. *Punch & Judy A History*. Studio Vista, 1970.

Spoto, Donald. *Elizabeth Taylor*. Little, Brown & Company, 1995.

Sturken, Marita. *Thelma & Louise*. British Film Institute, 2000.

Taliaferro, John. *Tarzan Forever, The Life of Edgar Rice Burroughs, Creator of Tarzan*. Scribner, 1999.

Tracy, Jack. *The Ultimate Sherlock Holmes Encyclopedia*. Gramercy Books, 1977.

Watson, Peter. *Nureyev A Biography*. Hodder & Stoughton, 1994.

Dictionary of National Biography. Smith, Elder & Co./OUP.

Dedicated to three generations of duos: to Mum & Dad, the duo without whom this book would not have an author; to Caroline, the perfect partner in my own duo; and to our duo of daughters, Megan and Edie.

ACKNOWLEDGEMENTS

With special thanks to Caroline Allen for conceiving the idea of this book and to Victoria Alers-Hankey for her support in getting it commissioned. Thanks, as ever, to the editor, Barbara Dixon, for ensuring that what I have written makes sense; to the designer, Thomas Keenes, for making it look so good; to Anna Cheifetz for being such a good chief. Thanks also to the following people and organizations for their help in the realizing of *The Book of Duos*: Philippa Adams (PA to Charles Saatchi), John & Maureen Allen, Dave Alpert (Almo Properties/A&M Records), Charlotte Baxendale (PA to Lord Saatchi), Jean Berchon (Moët & Chandon), Sue Bosanko, Gillian Bouzy (Moët & Chandon), Marion Cros (Fortnum & Mason), Richard Crowest, Rebecca Dallaway, Michael Grier (Tate & Lyle), Phil & Mary Harrison, Camilla Heiberg (Bang & Olufsen a/s), Roy G. Jinks (Official Historian, Smith & Wesson), Paola Locati (Dolce & Gabbana), Le Gavroche (Roux brothers), Frank McAweaney, Marks & Spencer, Richard Penfold, Aubrey 'Po' Powell, Clare Ridley (Revolver Communications [Ben & Jerry's]), Simon Rogers, Lord Saatchi, Charles Saatchi, Vickie Walters, Roseann Ward (Rolls-Royce plc).

PICTURE CREDITS